The French Enigma

Survival and Development in Canada's Francophone Societies

Robert A. Stebbins

Detselig Enterprises Ltd.

Calgary, Alberta, Canada

The French Enigma

© 2000 Robert A. Stebbins

Canadian Cataloguing in Publication Data

Stebbins, Robert A.

   The French enigma

Includes bibliographical references and index.
ISBN 1-55059-201-7

   1. Canadians, French-speaking--Social conditions.   I. Title.
FC136.S73   2000   971'.004114   C00-910334-1
F1027.S73   2000

Detselig Enterprises Ltd.

210-1220 Kensington Rd. N.W.

Calgary, AB T2N 3P5

Telephone: (403) 283-0900

Fax: (403) 283-6947

E-mail: temeron@telusplanet.net

Website: www.temerondetselig.com

We acknowledge the financial support of the Government of Canada through the Book Publishing Industry Development Program (BPIDP) for our publishing activities.

ISBN 1-55059-201-7

SAN 115-0324

Printed in Canada

Whatever the future of mankind in North America, I feel pretty confident that these French-speaking Canadians, at any rate, will be there at the end of the day.

Arnold Toynbee, *Civilisation on Trial* (1948), p. 161

Table of Contents

Foreword . . . . *vii*

Preface and Acknowledgements . . . .*xiii*

Part I: Present and Past

Chapter 1: Canada's Francophones 19

Chapter 2: A Short History of Francophone
Canada 37

Part II: Majority Societies

Chapter 3: Québec Society 59

Chapter 4: Contemporary Issues in Québec Society . . . 79

Chapter 5: Acadian Society 95

Chapter 6: Contemporary Issues in Acadian Society . .113

Part III: Minority Societies

Chapter 7: Francophone Societies: Newfoundland
and Ontario 131

Chapter 8: Contemporary Issues in Newfoundland
and Ontario 151

Chapter 9: Francophone Societies in Western
Canada 165

Chapter 10: Contemporary Issues in the Western
Francophone Societies 183

Part IV: The Future

Chapter 11: Canada's Francophones in Global
Perspective 197

Chapter 12: Survival and Development of
Francophone Canada 211

Notes 223

References 229

Index 243

Foreword
The Changing Canadian Francophonie

Robert Stebbins offers in this book an ambitious and original synthesis of the francophone fact in Canada, the result of many years of field observation. The author has often stayed in Québec and has visited Canada from coast to coast, stopping off in a good number of francophone communities. Here, then, is a synthetic work built on secondary analysis of previously conducted studies, but especially on first-hand observations by an experienced sociologist and specialist in qualitative methods, which he has used earlier in other notable studies.

The originality of the present book – *The French Enigma: Survival and Development of Canada's Francophone Societies* – is to bring a new perspective on the social organization of the Canadian *francophonie* in its broadest sense, an aspect less well analyzed and understood than the demographic and political situation of the francophone communities. Robert Stebbins has studied the organizational life, the routine social relations, the structure of the small isolated francophone communities, the educational system, and the visibility and public face of French. The francophone societies are examined comparatively, which helps him bring out the originality of the situations studied. Finally, it is necessary to highlight the originality of this book's organization: to determine first the characteristic traits of each society, then identify the existing issues within it.

In addition to these empirical observations, the author brings an important theoretical contribution to the study of the French fact in Canada. This he does by questioning the relevance of the concept of ethnicity. If the concept of ethnicity seems appropriate for the study of diverse minorities, it is not for one of the two great founding groups of the country (to which the native peoples should be added, of course, as they have been rediscovered in the present). Stebbins uses Raymond Breton's concept of institutional completeness and that of *l'espace francophone*, advanced by geographers who have studied the francophone diaspora across North America. To these two ideas, Stebbins adds another: parity societies. This last concept relates to the bilingual communities; they have in the minority language a rather complete institutional network, critical mass of speakers of both languages, and access to some public services (in stores, government, health, and voluntary associations). There is no doubt that this will be an outstanding contribution to the sociology and history of French Canada.

What stands out in the proposed analysis?

The author does not hide the difficulties faced by the French fact in Canada. He is aware that assimilation – despite problems in measuring it – is very real, and he reminds us of the role that exogamous marriage is known to play in this process. Robert Stebbins, for several reasons, remains optimistic nevertheless about the future of the French presence in Canada. First of all, the institutional and ideological context have changed considerably. The French fact is now well accepted, notwithstanding opposition from fringe groups like the Association for the Preservation of English in Canada. Immersion courses in French are popular (a trend that is still little understood and should be the object of several field studies), not to mention the constitutional protection which the French language now enjoys, protection that has given francophone communities outside Québec better control of their educational institutions. Stebbins embraces the thesis of Michael O'Keefe, who underscores the vitality of the francophone communities outside Québec, not just the difficulties they encounter.[1] Stebbins does not share the pessimism of many demographers and analysts, and he has painted the present and future of Canada's francophone societies "in the rosy colors of optimism," to use his own words. "Today it is evident that these francophone societies will not only survive but also develop, even if the kind and amount of development will vary significantly between them" (p. 159).

Stebbins also justifies his optimism by situating the Canadian *francophonie* in global perspective. Here is an external aspect that has not often been noted, since the majority of studies concentrate on the internal problems of French Canada. For him four new factors militate in favor of affirming the French fact: internationalization of francophone identity, internationalization of economic ties, increasing involvement in international francophone culture, and increasing involvement with francophone immigrants and refugees (chap. 11). This chapter, it should be noted, contains an original contribution: the study of the future of the Canadian *francophonie*.

Permit me here to signal a disagreement with the author – authors of forewords are not always in accord with all elements of the books they introduce – who states that globalization may undermine to some extent, perhaps eventually even to a considerable extent, both the Québec nationalist and French-Canadian foundations of their identities (p. 88). Stebbins argues that internationally-oriented francophones will come to value their linguistic identity more than their national identity. I think, on the contrary, that the opening up of the world is going to reinforce the break that has marked French Canada and that it is going to give a second wind to the affirmation of a distinct Québec identity. The historical break of French Canada is, without doubt, here to stay.

This question warrants further explanation, for it is central to the analysis of the Canadian *francophonie*. French Canada has changed considerably since its orgin in the middle of the 19th century (it should be noted, in passing, that Anglo-British Canada of the 19th century has also changed considerably). French Canada has defined itself as a nation, a nation having its own history, ideologies, vision of the world, and literature. *"Ton histoire est une épopée"* (your history is an epic), proclaims the French version of Canada's national anthem. It had its own network of institutions – parishes, schools, colleges, hospitals – which frame the francophone diaspora. During the 1930s, did the Lieutenant-Governor of Québec not give school prizes to francophone students in Manitoba? (Thus Gabrielle Roy, a young franco-Manitoban student, received several medals from Québec of which she was most proud.) To counteract the misfortunes that struck Ontario and Manitoba at the turn of the last century and to mark clearly the contribution of francophones to the symbolic foundation of Canada, the French Canadian elites invented the Utopian idea of the pact of the two nations, an idea the rest of English Canada preferred not to share and certain historians even fiercely challenged.[2]

Fernand Dumont analyzed the rise and decline of this nation in the sociological sense, and in a fine synthetic work, Yves Frenette has recalled its tortuous history.[3] Over the years, French Canadians have had to kiss their imaginary country goodby, to invoke the title of a book by Marcel Martel, and they have in a way become *"orphelins d'une nation"* (orphans of a nation) according to the poignant expression of Joseph-Yvon Thériault.[4]

An important question thus arises at the beginning of the year 2000: what is and what will be the normative unity of this new Canadian *francophonie*, the social organization of which Stebbins describes so well? This question, as such, has not been tackled in this book, although the author is most aware of the difficulties it poses. He stresses that "the linguistic identity of contemporary Canadian francophones is now more complicated than ever" (p. 31). The Fédération des communautés francophones et acadienne (FCFA), by its very title, stresses its division into scattered communities and poses the French language as a common identity reference. French Canada, real and imagined (in the sense given this term by Anderson) has lost its Utopian and national character, and has been replaced by linguistic communities, Acadia and Québec. The francophone linguistic communities do not define themselves as "*communautés hors Québec*" (communities outside Québec), but rather as a Canadian *francophonie*, which even goes so far as to include anglophones who speak French. There is here a new effort in identity construction, which is underway at the dawn of a new century. Stebbins shares this vision of things, which at the time of writing these lines raises, however, many questions within the Canadian *francophonie*, for it marks the passage from a national French Canadian identity to a linguistic identity, but a very different linguistic identity marked by plurality and diversity. The Canadian *francophonie* welcomes new speakers who do not identify themselves as French Canadians in the traditional sense of the term, even if this francophone demographic contribution is still marginal outside Québec. The statistics on the *francophonie* of Toronto cited by Stebbins speak for themselves on this point.

For its part, Québec is asserting its own new national identity, illustrated by the present debate over the Québec nation, which is current at the beginning of the 21st century: a nation open to integrating immigrants and cognizant within itself of a national anglophone minority as well as of some communities of native peoples.[5] This new nationalist affirmation of Quebeckers, it should be noted in passing, is not without some analogies to the nation building underway in Canada. If this vision of things is accurate, we are presently undergoing a major change, passing from a national linguistic duality (French and English Canada of the 19th century), to a new Canadian societal duality. This is the new multicultural Canada shaped by immigration and a new post-Quiet Revolution Québec, itself also more and more multicultural; two societies in the process of redefining themselves, each having within a linguistic minority belonging to the other language group.[6] Therefore, not only has the Canadian *francophonie* become more complex since 1982, Canada has also undergone a similar transformation.

Robert Stebbins's book constitutes an important contribution to the analysis of the social organization of francophone Canada. In the coming years, the actors themselves will be able to tell which new definition harmonizes with the contours of this new social organization that is emerging and changing rapidly.

Simon Langlois, Professor of Sociology and Chair of *La Chaire pour le développement de la recherche sur la culture d'expression française en Amérique du Nord* (CEFAN), Université Laval (Québec)

Endnotes

[1] O'Keefe, Michael. 1998. *Francophone Minorities: Assimilation and Community Vitality*. Ottawa, ON: Government of Canada, Canadian Heritage.

[2] See the work of Stéphan Paquin. *L'invention d'un mythe*. Montréal, QC: VLB éditeur, 1999.

[3] Fernand Dumont. Essor et déclin du Canada français. *Recherches sociographiques, 38* (1997), 419-467; Yves Frenette. *Brève histoire du Canada français* (in collaboration with Martin Pâquet). Montréal, QC: Boréal, 1998.

[4] Marcel Martel. *Le deuil d'un pays imaginé. Rêves, luttes et déroute du Canada.* Ottawa, ON: Presses de l'Université d'Ottawa (Amérique française series), 1999; Joseph Yvon Thériault (Ed.). *Francophonies minoritaires au Canada. L'état des lieux*. Moncton, NB: Éditions d'Acadie, 1999.

[5] See, among others, Gérard Bouchard. *La nation québécoise au future et au passé.* Montréal, QC: VLB éditeur, 1999 or Michel Seymour. *La nation en question*. Montréal, QC: l'Hexagone, 1999.

[6] We developed this hypothesis earlier in Simon Langlois. Le choc de deux sociétés globales. In Louis Balthazar, Guy Laforest, and Vincent Liemieux (Eds.), *Le Québec et la restructuration du Canada 1980-1992* (pp. 95-108). Sillery, QC: Septentrion, 1991.

Preface and Acknowledgements

Although I have gained immense satisfaction from years teaching and doing research on Canada's francophones, this reward has been blunted by my awareness that far too many of their anglophone compatriots know and care little about them. True, thanks to some extent to the hubbub surrounding the Québec separatist issue, some of the latter are now reasonably conscious of certain fundamental differences distinguishing that province, and a few in this informed group are even aware of differences distinguishing Acadian New Brunswick. But when it comes to francophones residing elsewhere in the country, anglophone awareness of and knowledge about them generally plunges dramatically. My experience of living in and travelling through various parts of Canada has revealed that anglophones are often surprised to learn that their city contains a viable francophone community. They typically opine that such people are found in only Québec, or in the case of the xenophobic minority, that such people **should** be found only in Québec.

This lack of knowledge about and interest in the country's francophones, whether it be all of them or only those living outside Québec, has created a most unfortunate cultural void. The 1996 Census shows that this lack concerns 23.7 percent of the population of our officially bilingual country, the ancestors of these mother-tongue francophones having helped found Canada as a nation and establish many of the communities presently thriving within it. This figure jumps to 31.5 percent when second-language francophones, of which I am one, are added to the picture. Furthermore, this lack of knowledge and concern is not only about the people who speak French, but also of the French language itself, one of the three truly world languages (along with English and Spanish) whose importance in the spheres of commerce, science, and tourism, for example, has been greatly inflated by the gusty winds of globalization.

Given these conditions – and this is but a sample of them – this ignorance is hardly blissful; it is ignorance that anglophone Canadians can ill afford. For fired by such an orientation toward the francophones in their midst, the country's anglophones might just brush aside as irrelevant them and their claims, when relevancy is a much more appropriate attitude, given the present situation. This is not the time in history to let wither a major commercial and scientific advantage we have gained over many of our First-World competitors: easy access to learning and using two main international languages in a rapidly globalizing world. Yet exactly that could happen in ignorance of the people in our communities who routinely use French and struggle to establish the social arrangements leading to its survival and development.

This book, then, is for people concerned about this ignorance, their own or someone else's. In it, using theory and data found primarily in the fields of history, linguistics, and education as well as sociology, geography, and political science, I shed light in the dark corner of francophone Canada, its language, culture, social worlds, and patterns of everyday life. As the Table of Contents indicates, Québec society is a central part of this exposition, even if it is by no means the only part. Six of the twelve chapters bear on francophone societies in Acadia, Newfoundland, Ontario, and the West. In writing about these different societies, I draw on a number of census-based, federal government publications as well as a vast, scattered, multidisciplinary, social science literature. I estimate that 90 percent of the social science literature is in French, a situation suggesting that part of the problem is the linguistic inaccessibility of writings that could help eliminate this cultural void.

The following pages, however, contain much more than a mere summary and review of the social science literature on francophone Canada. In fact, another reason for the cultural void is that no one has yet tried in either French or English to put it all together, to take the expansive multidisciplinary literature that has accumulated over the years on Canada's francophones and work it into a coherent statement. This is another goal of this book, although given certain space and market limitations, this literature can only be selectively reviewed and integrated here. But reasonable integration has nonetheless been achieved using a variety of social science concepts, the most prominent being: society, community, social world, linguistic lifestyle, ethnolinguistic vitality, and institutional completeness. Two geographic metaphors also frame discussion from time to time: the centre-periphery model, portraying francophone Canada as mountain, foothills, and prairie; and the sea metaphor of Canada as archipelago dotted with islands and clusters of islands of French communities. Further, the questions of personal and communal survival and development run through the text as leitmotifs, always set in the historical context in which they unfold.

Finally, before turning to chapter 1 and a broad introduction to Canada's francophones, certain conventions used in this book need explanation. First, all translations from French to English, which are always marked as such, are mine. Second, I occasionally use French phrases and wherever possible French place names expressly to add a pinch of cultural seasoning to this confection on francophone Canada. Some of these places also have English names (e.g., Church Point/Pointe de l'Église in Nova Scotia), but I favor the French version to underscore the presence there of an ongoing francophone community. Third, I have tried at various points to personalize this book by offering some anecdotes and comments from my experiences in Canada's francophone societies, many of which I visited as part of a personal automobile tour that took me from Newfoundland's Port-au-Port Peninsula to Calgary. This trip and others much shorter enabled me to augment what I learned during my ten-month stay in Québec, with some direct observations of the other societies, and to assess the ethnolinguistic vitality of a sample of the francophone communities that comprise them.

Turning to the acknowledgements, I wish to express my deep gratitude for the financial support given to this book by La Chaire pour le développement de la recherche sur la culture d'expression française en Amérique du Nord (CEFAN), based at Université Laval. Further, it should be noted that the provincial maps reprinted in chapters 5 through 10 were originally produced by the Department of Canadian Heritage and subsequently reproduced in this book with the permission of the Minister of Public Works and Government Services Canada, 2000. Last, but not least, I was most fortunate to have again the expert editorial help of Linda Berry, which was at least equal to the assistance she gave me in an earlier publication, *After Work: The Search for an Optimal Leisure Lifestyle*.

Part I
Present and Past

Chapter 1
Canada's Francophones

French-speaking Canada, with considerably more accuracy than English-speaking Canada, can be separated into regions, each distinguished from the other by a great number and variety of special social, cultural, historical, and geographic qualities. By all accounts, whether anglophone or francophone, Québec is the most obvious and celebrated exemplar of such distinctiveness. Yet it is by no means the only one, even though many an anglophone Canadian might be surprised by this assertion. For, from the typical English Canadian point of view, Acadia – Francophone New Brunswick, Nova Scotia, and Prince Edward Island – constitutes a much less obvious culturo-linguistic region, while Newfoundland, Ontario, the prairies, and British Columbia, according to that perspective, are merely slightly discernible variations on a theme of anglo-British culture.

Nevertheless, every francophone region has evolved far enough to justify calling it a society, or more accurately, a subsociety, where each is an enduring component of the larger Canadian society. Again, Québec is the most evolved, by far the most institutionally complete of the five francophone societies discussed in this book. "Institutional completeness" refers to a level of social and cultural organization of a community or society that, in terms of language use, is sufficiently developed to enable the typical person to sustain a full-scale linguistic lifestyle over the course of a normal year (modified from Breton, 1961). Certainly Québec, at the dawn of the twenty-first century, can be described from the point of view of the French language as institutionally complete. In terms of everyday requirements, there are few, if any, localities in that society where a person could not meet in French his or her routine needs, as these arise on a daily, weekly, monthly, or yearly basis.

By contrast, significant linguistic incompleteness **does** exist in parts of Ontario and Acadia and still greater incompleteness marks francophone life in Newfoundland and the West (Cardinal et al., 1994; Stebbins, 1994). Thus, in the eyes of Canadians (and Americans too), Québec is the benchmark for comparing all other North

American francophone societies. It will be the reference point for this book as well, although only Canada's provincial and regional francophone societies are examined here, space limitations obviating consideration of the francophone societies in the United States, the most developed of which are found in Florida, New England, and Louisiana. Moreover, although institutionally incomplete in many respects, a francophone lifestyle of sorts appears to exist in the Yukon and the Northwest Territories. Nevertheless, because of a severe lack of social scientific data, only sporadic reference will be made to it in the following chapters.

Francophone, Anglophone, Allophone

This book is primarily about Canadians who speak French and not about those whose origins are French, but who never knew or no longer speak that language. People who routinely speak French or English are known in linguistics as francophones or anglophones. In practice these terms mean they speak and aurally understand well enough in one of these two languages to conduct a significant proportion of their usual affairs in it. Thus, a person who has a reading knowledge of a language but is unable to converse at length in it (conversational knowledge is a typical operational measure of linguistic competence) lacks the capacity to use it routinely in daily life. Consonant with this definition, moreover, is the condition that being francophone, for instance, does not necessarily require that French be the person's mother tongue or even that he or she speak it at home. The only requirement is that it be routinely used in a main sphere of everyday life, whether inside or outside the home, a sphere such as work or leisure that consumes large portions of time in the typical Canadian week. In fact, francophones who use French at work or in their leisure could well have learned it in adulthood as a second language. All this amounts to a theoretical definition, however. In many places in this book there is no choice but to work with the practical definitions employed by the Census of Canada, which even when considered together, are much more restrictive than this theoretical definition.

It is necessary to be as precise as possible about the ideas of francophone and anglophone, because the two are subject these days to a good deal of confusion. First, some Canadian francophones limit application of the term francophone to those for whom French is their mother tongue, a language they learned at home as children. The chief drawback with this conception is that no French dictionary, whether published in Canada, France, or elsewhere, defines francophone in so restrictive a way, suggesting that, in circles where standard French guides good usage, this one is marginal. Second, some Canadian francophones are wont to identify second-language francophones as "francophiles," an idea that all dictionaries also define quite differently as people who like France and the French. To avoid the confusion generated by this convention, I will, when the discussion calls for such a distinction, use terms like first-language and second-language francophone.

Furthermore, the problem of who is francophone has much broader implications than how people linguistically identify each other. For example, it has of late been haunting the Census of Canada, as in 1996 when Statistics Canada enumerated people who speak the country's two official languages according to three criteria:

1) Question concerning knowledge of a language: "Can this person speak English or French well enough to conduct a conversation?" Reported only if the respondent can carry on a conversation of some length on various topics in that language.

2) Question on language spoken at home: "What language does this person speak **most often** at home?" Reported two languages only if the respondent uses them equally often.

3) Question on mother-tongue language: "What is the language that this person **first learned** at home in childhood and **still understands**?" As in (2), two languages are reported only if the respondent used them equally often in early childhood.

Even though Statistics Canada does not actually publish a definition of francophone, the results of its censuses using these three criteria, which suffer all the drawbacks set out in the preceding paragraph, have policy implications for every francophone society in the country, a matter taken up in the chapters dealing with the main issues facing each one.

Among the nations of the world, Canada is unusual in that a number of its francophones and anglophones can be classified as both. When used in Canada this is what is usually meant by the term "bilingual"; bilinguals routinely use both languages in everyday life. Some were raised doing this, others acquired the other language during adulthood as a second language. Working with the 1996 census data, Churchill (1998: 9) reports that 16.3 percent of the total population of Canada is bilingual, a figure that has been slowly increasing since at least 1961 (Joy, 1992: 12). Note, however, that some people routinely speak another language or two in addition to French or English and, in principle, they, too, are bilingual (or trilingual). Nonetheless, except for the chapters on Québec, these speakers are largely ignored in this book, since outside that society, they are small in number and lack significant influence.

But in Québec, bilinguals whose first language is a foreign, or nonofficial, language and whose second language is French or English, cut a big figure. They are the "allophones": Canadian citizens or Landed Immigrants who are neither mother-tongue francophone nor mother-tongue-anglophone. These Quebeckers have another language as their first language, while at this time in history it is highly probable that their second language is French. It will become evident that, as much as anything, being allophone is a political question, for such people have been shown to be mainly anti-separatist, helping through their considerable numbers to sway the vote in this direction in recent Québec referendums (Pinard, Bernier, and Lemieux, 1997: 307). Allophones in Québec have as their mother tongue such languages as Greek, Italian, and Portuguese.

Majority, Parity, and Minority Societies

People living in a **majority society**, from the point of view of language use, live in institutional completeness. They carry out their daily, weekly, and yearly rounds in the dominant language of that society, the language of the majority of its people. Although Québec is Canada's only majority francophone society, certain regions and communities within the other francophone societies in the country can also be described as "majority." These include the city of Caraquet and the Acadian Peninsula in New Brunswick, as well as the cities of Hearst and Kapuskasing in Ontario. Here, too, francophones dominate numerically and linguistically.

Outside Québec at the societal level, then, francophones live in either parity or minority circumstances, even if some live in majority regions or communities within those societies. **Parity societies** are of necessity bilingual, reasonably institutionally complete for both languages, and composed of sufficient numbers of anglophones and francophones to force the speakers of the other language to recognize their linguistic counterparts in all public areas of community life. In fact, Canada has no parity societies, though it has many parity communities and New Brunswick constitutes a parity region. In practice, parity refers to the existence of, at minimum, a significant minority of francophones in the region or community. To my knowledge, no one has defined "significant minority," but I should imagine that a three-to-one, English-French ratio in the population is the lower limit of parity (1 to 3 should then be its upper limit). Additionally, saying that a parity society is bilingual is not to suggest, however, that everyone in it is bilingual as defined earlier. Rather it suggests only that sufficient numbers of bilinguals fill the public roles (e.g., shop keepers, politicians, civil servants, health care providers) to enable the individual to operate more or less entirely in French or English. Pointe de l'Église (Church Point), Nova Scotia; Sudbury, Ontario; and Saint-Boniface in Manitoba are three of the several parity communities in Canada.

Francophones are numerically inferior in the **minority societies**. Thus most of them live in linguistic institutional incompleteness; in Canada they normally carry out in English a substantial proportion of their routine daily, weekly, and yearly activities. In general, this occurs in the spheres of commerce, health care, politics, government, and the work place. Depending on a variety of conditions and circumstances, French in these societies is much more often used, sometimes even exclusively so, in the areas of leisure, education, religion, and the family. The inhabitants of a francophone majority or parity society are obviously francophone according to the preceding definition. But so, too, are the francophones who live in minority circumstances, since they also routinely use French, even if they can do so only in certain segments of life. Not surprisingly, then, maintaining one's Frenchness, including especially the capacity to communicate in that language, is one of the main issues facing the francophones of Canada who live as a minority.

The concepts of majority, parity, and minority, used as both nouns and adjectives, have been carefully chosen by researchers specializing in the study of French-speaking Canadians. Their preference for these ideas simultaneously signals their rejection of two standard sociological concepts – "ethnicity" and "powerless minority" – concepts that fail to describe as effectively the situation of Canada's francophones. In fact, in this instance, these standard concepts mislead more than they edify. An ethnic group is composed of immigrants or native peoples distinguished by such criteria as race, religion, language, or nationality, who are not regarded as having established the country they now reside in. In Canada, francophones cannot be qualified as ethnic, because they from France and anglophones from Britain make up the two charter groups who founded this nation. Moreover, French and English are Canada's two official languages and this fact, as will be explained shortly, gives franco-phones and anglophones special legal rights throughout the country. Furthermore, that they have such rights is proof that anglo-phones and francophones living in minority circumstances are not so much a powerless as a numerical minority. This having been said, it is not inconsistent with what has just been observed to refer to as "ethnic" those attributes that delineate ethnicity: race, religion, language, and the like.

Types of Francophone Communities

The linguistic lifestyles of Canadian francophones are heavily influenced by whether they live in rural areas, villages, or small cities, on the one extreme, or in medium- or large-sized cities, on the other. First, outside Québec, the most institutionally complete majority communities are invariably small, which include, among many others, Caraquet, New Brunswick; Hearst, Ontario; Saint-Isidore, Alberta. By contrast, the francophone communities in the larger cities are always minority formations; they are much less complete and are dominated by anglophones to such an extent that their inhabitants are forced to live linguistically segmented lifestyles (Savas, 1990; Stebbins, 1994). Second, it is also true that, vis-à-vis big-city francophones, a significantly higher proportion of the rural-small city francophones have never moved from the locality of their birth. This creates in these communities a kind of stability unknown in their urban counterparts, where new arrivals and departures are commonplace.

In comparison with the villages and small towns outside Québec, whether partially or entirely francophone, the proportion of mother-tongue francophones in the cities is generally much lower, ranging in 1996 from 1.5 to 4.9 percent in the large cities, except in the Ontario portion of the Ottawa-Hull metropolitan area, where they make up 19 percent of the population and where they are presently militating for its official bilingual status. At the same time, in the large cities, francophones are far more multidimensional. For example, they are more fragmented; considerable variation is evident according to age, occupation, religion, country of origin, leisure preferences, and possibly other dimensions along which groups and categories of people make their own claims and follow their own interests. Finally, urban francophones, as compared with their rural and small town cousins, conduct their activities in an atmosphere of greater anonymity, impersonality, and tolerance of social differ-ences.

All this does not exhaust, however, the dimensions along which Canada's minority francophone communities can be classified. Thus to the rural-urban dimension just discussed, Louder and Dupont (1997) add the dimension of religion, labelled "Catholic-Laic," and that of multiculturalism, labelled "rural-urban-metropolitan." Table 1.1 contains a typology built from all three dimensions illustrated with selected Canadian francophone communities.

Table 1.1 Types of Francophone Communities in Canada

Dimensions	British Columbia	Prairies	Ontario	Acadia
Rural/Catholic	None	Debden, SK	Lafontaine, ON	Chéticamp, NS
Urban/Catholic	None	Edmonton, AB	Vanier, ON	Caraquet, NB
Urban/laic	None	Calgary, AB	Ottawa, ON	Moncton, NB
Metropolitan/ multicultural	Vancouver, BC	None	Toronto, ON	None

Source: Translated with adaptations from Louder and Dupont (1997: 54, figure 1).

Still, apart from the anglophone majority, francophones (as measured by mother tongue) constitute by far the largest linguistic group in Canada: 23.7 percent of the population in 1996. Moreover, according to the 1996 census (Statistics Canada, 1998a), again using mother tongue as the measure, 1 002 295 of Canada's 6 789 675 francophones live outside Québec, and 352 817 or just over 35 percent of the non-Québécois live in the 10 Census Metropolitan Areas (CMAs) with at least 300 000 population containing 8000 or more francophones. Of these areas, Ottawa (Ontario part) is home for the largest number of francophones (143 675), whereas the next largest concentrations are found in Toronto (62 850), Winnipeg (32 380), Vancouver (27 250), and Edmonton (21 221). Calgary with its 14 241 francophones has more in common with such cities as Hamilton (10 590) and Halifax (9960). These figures describe the distribution of francophones for whom French is their only mother tongue as well as francophones having multiple mother tongues, notably English, English and a third language, and French and a language other than English. When the 2 225 194 (7.8% of the national population)

French-speaking mother-tongue anglophones are added to this group, the proportion of Canadians having a knowledge of French rises to 31.5 percent.

Community and l'Espace Francophone

I spoke glibly in the preceding section about francophone communities. But anyone half familiar with francophone life in Canada outside Québec would quickly note that I just glossed a major theoretical and practical consideration. In Canada and other parts of the world where French-speaking people form a linguistic minority, local first-language francophones and a smaller number of second-language francophones coalesce into community-like structures, which francophone researchers have recently begun to refer to as *les espaces francophones*, or, literally translated, francophone spaces. This term has a number of advantages over its time-worn cousin, "community" (*la communauté*). As a scientific term the latter remains controversial, weakened by a professional dispute over whether a geographical or territorial basis is an essential quality of a true community (Almgren, 1992). In addition, debate continues about the degree of self-sufficiency, or completeness, a group of people must achieve before they can be said to meet one of the many sociological definitions of community.[1] The term *l'espace francophone* has enabled francophone researchers to escape such notional wrangling, while retaining their capacity to speak of an "ethnic formation" of some sort (Breton et al., 1990: 4-9) based on at least a moderate degree of completeness as rooted in certain spaces, or situations in which a person can express and experience his or her linguistic identity in the larger community. These spaces, in turn, are more inclusively structured, often without clear geographic locus, according to a set of organizations and networks of interpersonal relationships (Goldenberg and Haines, 1992).

L'espace francophone translates most accurately as "francophone situation," as experienced at home, in school, at work, or in the neighborhood, among various other places (see Orientation Committee, 1992: 8-9). This translation will be used from time to time in this book to refer to the ways francophones enact their linguistic lifestyles in the local francophone community. Thus, despite its many problems, I use the idea of community throughout, on the grounds that it is an idea sociologists can neither live with nor without. Much of the time, however, I use Anthony Cohen's (1985) important distinction of symbolic community, the essence of which is contained in the proposition that "the reality of [symbolic] community lies in its members' perception of the vitality of its culture. People construct community symbolically, making it a resource and repository of meaning, and a referent of their identity" (Cohen, 1985: 118). My use of community in these pages conforms not only to Cohen's conception but also to the descriptor *francophonie invisible*, which is current among French-speaking Canadians living in the minority societies.

This discussion about symbolic communities, many of which are aurally and visibly imperceptible, is of utmost importance, especially for cities like Calgary, Toronto, Hamilton, Vancouver, and Halifax. These cities never have had, or in the cases of Vancouver and Calgary, have not had for many years, active, geographically-identifiable francophone communities.[2] They are **migrant** communities; historically, the vast majority of their francophones migrated to them. Compare them with Ottawa, Winnipeg, and Edmonton, where such formations have existed from the birth of each city. These formations have been major rallying points over the years both as geographic communities – Vanier in Ottawa, Saint-Boniface in Winnipeg, Bonnie Doon in Edmonton – and as symbolic communities. They are **indigenous** communities, where a substantial number of native-born francophones are joined but not overwhelmed by a number of migrant francophones. In the indigenous type, members of the community have effected a notable degree of institutional continuity over the course of this century, particularly in the areas of work, leisure, family, religion, and education.

Before leaving this explication of community, it is important to deal with the related idea of *francophonie*, which will also be encountered from time to time throughout this book. *L'Année Francophone Internationale* (1997: 6) presents two definitions of this concept. When spelled with a capital F, it refers to the ensemble of governments, countries, and official instances having in common the use of the French language in their work and their exchanges with one another. When spelled with a small f, *francophonie* denotes the ensemble of people or groups of speakers – francophones – who, in whole or in part, use the French language in their everyday lives and communications. The first definition, in effect, advises against examining in isolation the Canadian francophone societies treated in this book. Rather they should be understood as part of an international community of francophone countries (see chapter 11). The second definition, which is a good deal vaguer, refers in more concrete terms to francophone formations of different levels of inclusivity, running from local, through provincial, regional, national, and even international, all of which, Breton (1994) observes, can be considered communities depending on the dimensions used to analyze them.

At its organizational level the Canadian *francophonie*, at first glance, has what might seem to be a curious structure. Since the Quiet Revolution of the 1960s, it has tended to function without Québec, where the opinion still prevails that Canadian francophones living outside the province are doomed to assimilation to English and anglophone culture. Therefore, until very recently, it has been seen as pointless to become involved with them in any official or formal way (see chapter 12). So Québec speaks mainly for itself by means of such organs as its National Assembly (equivalent of a provincial legislature), while the Fédération des Communautés Francophones et Acadiennes du Canada (FCFAC) speaks for the other nine provinces and the territories as a group. In addition, every province and territory has its own association (e.g., Association canadienne française de l'Ontario, Fédération des francophones de Terre-Neuve et du Labrador), each being a member of the FCFAC. The Association de la presse francophone (APF) gathers national news of interest to Canadian francophones and disseminates it through 23 local and provincial francophone newspapers. Finally, the Conseil de la vie française en Amérique (CVFA) occupies a role of its own in North America. Martel (1997: 22), in a rare scientific study of this organization, says that for Canada it

> has become a place for the discussion of vital issues about French Canada. It is also a forum where the spokespersons for the small worlds of the French-Canadian minority can express the many needs of francophones across the country, as perceived, imagined, and understood. . . . [The] Conseil acts publicly. It constitutes the tangible manifestation of solidarity between French-Canadian institutions. (translation)

Besides these three organizations, scores of groups have been founded to promote and facilitate the special interests of Canadian francophones living outside Québec. These groups centre on, for example, sport, aging, education, communication, and the arts (see Conseil de la vie française en Amérique, 1998). One of them – the Association canadienne d'éducation de langue française (ACELF) – organizes the *Semaine nationale de la francophonie*/National Francophone Week, the purpose of which is to enhance francophone togetherness through participation in a wide variety of community events. It is celebrated annually in March across the country.

A Demographic Portrait

Using 1996 Census data, Churchill (1998: 9) reports that 67.1 percent of Canadians are unilingual mother-tongue anglophones, 15.2 percent unilingual mother-tongue francophones, and 1.4 percent unilingual in a mother tongue other than the two official languages (as already mentioned 16.3 % of Canadians are bilingual). The proportion of mother-tongue francophones in Canada has been declining for many decades, while the number of mother-tongue anglophones has been rising. Often overlooked, however, is the fact that the absolute number of francophones is also rising, aided by natural increase and immigration, even though their rate of increase is lower than the rate of English speakers (Churchill, 1998: 12).

At the provincial level, Québec leads in the concentration of first-language francophones; for 81 percent of its population French is their mother tongue, a figure that includes bilinguals and trilinguals. Another 8.1 percent are mother-tongue anglophones, most of whom reside in the Montréal area, and far more than half of whom have a knowledge of French. New Brunswick is composed of one-third francophones and two-thirds anglophones. The remainder of the provinces range from 0.38 and 1.6 percent francophone in Newfoundland and British Columbia to 4.5 and 4.8 percent francophone in Manitoba and Ontario (Statistics Canada, 1998a).

Notwithstanding their lack of a geographically-identifiable francophone community – theirs are migrant communities – Calgary, Toronto, Hamilton, and similar cities, like the nation as a whole, have all shown increases between the census years of 1981 and 1996 in absolute numbers of francophones.[3] Evidence from the author's study (Stebbins, 1994) suggests that those in Calgary are not only multiplying numerically in some measure, but even thriving culturally. Yet Calgary's indigenous francophone community died approximately 95 years ago. A cardinal research question, then, is how do the migrant urban francophone communities survive and, if Calgary is typical, flourish even though they lack the native-born, geographically-delineated base of the indigenous communities.

As if to complicate matters, all these figures vary widely, depending on how the concept of francophone is operationalized. On the one hand, when measured by home language, the proportion of francophones drops everywhere outside Québec and New

Brunswick by as much as 40 percent. On the other, when knowledge of French is the measure (i.e., French as first or second language), their proportion jumps dramatically. Employing the second definition, Newfoundland and British Columbia can report 3.9 and 6.8 percent and Manitoba and Ontario 9.5 percent and 12.0 percent (Statistics Canada, 1998a). The proportion of Canadians outside Québec who know French has been slowly rising between 1961 and 1996, moving from 8.7 to 10.7 percent of that part of the national population (O'Keefe, 1998: 38). The growth of bilingualism among anglophones is the primary force driving this trend.

This brief statistical portrait contains a couple of important lessons. One is that Canadian francophones are by no means equally distributed across the country, suggesting that linguistic lifestyles should be different where they live in a minority situation compared with where they live as part of the majority. The second lesson is that linguistic lifestyles in medium and large cities differ in many important ways from those in towns and small cities. Approximately 28 percent of Canada's francophones living outside Québec presently reside in large cities. Their distinctive existence has prompted Réjean Beaudoin (1988: 266-69) to describe them as the "*nouveaux francophones.*" Sociologically speaking, we know much less about them and their lifestyles than about the other 72 percent and the lifestyles they lead.

The Charter of Rights and Freedoms

Adopted in 1982, the Canadian Charter of Rights and Freedoms, among other things, decrees that English and French are the two official languages of the land, and as such, have in all institutions of the Parliament and the government of Canada equal status, rights, and privileges. This also refers to the language of parliamentary debates, statutes, records, and journals and to that used in every court of law established by Parliament, including pleas. Moreover, any member of the public in Canada has the right to communicate with, and to receive available services from, any head or central office of an institution of the Parliament or the Government of Canada in the official language of their choice. This last right, however, can be claimed only where "significant demand for communications with and services" exists in the official language in question. The Charter was written into the Constitution Act of 1982.

Minority language educational rights were also made part of the Charter of Rights and Freedoms, with implementation according to the following rules:

(1) Citizens of Canada (a) whose first language learned and still understood is that of the English or French linguistic minority population of the province in which they reside, or b) who have received their primary school instruction in Canada in English or French and reside in a province where the language in which they received that instruction is the language of the English or French linguistic minority population of the province, have the right to have their children receive primary and secondary school instruction in that language in that province. (2) Citizens of Canada of whom any child has received or is receiving primary or secondary school instruction in English or French in Canada, have the right to have all their children receive primary and secondary school instruction in the same language (taken from Section 23, Constitution Act, 1982).

These rights must be honored where sufficient numbers of children exist to justify spending public funds to instruct them in the minority language.

The Official Languages Acts

Even though the first Official Languages Act predates the Constitution Act of 1982, the two languages acts in many ways fulfill the linguistic principles of the Charter of Rights and Freedoms. In this regard, the year 1969 is a turning point in the history of French and English in Canada. That year the federal policy of official bilingualism came into effect; its two main goals were to help anglophones and francophones living in minority circumstances maintain and transmit their languages and associated cultures. The goals were to be reached in part by institutionalizing both French and English as working languages in Parliament, the federal civil service, the Canadian Broadcasting Corporation/La Société Radio-Canada, and the various government departments and administrative agencies. The bulk of the responsibility for implementing the policy was lodged with the Department of the Secretary of State, whereas the responsibility for monitoring the progress of bilingualism across the country was given to the occupant of the new post of Commissioner of Official Languages, a post attached to the two chambers of Parliament.

In 1988, a second federal law on official languages gave the Department of the Secretary of State two additional goals to pursue: "enhancing the vitality of the English and French linguistic minority communities in Canada and supporting and assisting their development and fostering the full recognition and use of both English and French in Canadian society" (Commissioner of Official Languages, 1989: 63). In other words, the Secretary of State gained several new functions, including the promotion, extension, and improvement of teaching English and French in minority circumstances and the encouragement of "the business community, labour organizations, voluntary organizations and other organizations or institutions to provide services in both English and French and to foster the recognition and use of those languages" (Commissioner of Official Languages, 1989: 66). In practice this has meant stimulating the development of various French and English cultural institutions operating in minority circumstances, including community clubs, radio, and newspapers as well as networks, events, and festivals.

The passage and implementation of the second official languages act left no doubt that the federal government and Canada's francophones living in parity and minority circumstances are in effect pursuing the same four goals. The goals are the maintenance and transmission of the French language and its associated cultures and the growth and development of individual francophones and the francophone communities in which they live (Stebbins, 1994). In this manner implementation of the policy of official bilingualism and its revisions has substantially aided the linguistically-related interests of first- and second-language francophones living in Canada's parity and minority francophone societies (c.f., Savas, 1991: 68).[4]

French Canadian?

This book is about Canada's francophones and its francophone societies, but the francophones do not always think of themselves as "French-Canadian." Indeed, it may be evident by now that I have been avoiding use of this term. Why is that?

To be a French-Canadian, in the typical case, is to be a mother-tongue francophone (as defined earlier) and a citizen or landed immigrant of Canada. Many Canadians, if asked, would identify themselves this way, but they would not always make it their highest ranking linguistic identity. For instance, a substantial number Franco-Quebeckers would admit to being French-Canadians, given they are francophones and citizens of Canada, but would prefer nonetheless to refer to themselves as *Québécois*, a term that stresses membership in the francophone part of Québec society. Thériault (1994: 26) holds that a similar ranking of identity pertains among the Acadians of New Brunswick; they see themselves first as *Acadien*. He argues further that elsewhere in Canada many francophones identify more with their province or region than with the whole of Canada. For example, Franco-Manitobans and Franco-Albertans are more inclined to present themselves by these terms than by the label of French-Canadian, however legally correct the latter. The term French Canadian is occasionally used in this book, but only in its demographic sense as a convenient label for the French-speaking people living in Canada. When it comes to their identity, I employ other terms.

Taking a different perspective, Thériault (1994) and Denis (1996) hold that francophones living in minority circumstances in Canada are best understood as an ethnic group or nation. It is plausible that the concept of nation validly describes the francophones in northern and eastern New Brunswick and northern and eastern Ontario, but that, for reasons given earlier, the concept of ethnic group is of questionable utility in this regard. Moreover, if Calgary is representative (Stebbins, 1994), it is doubtful that metropolitan francophones see themselves either way, as part of a francophone nation or part of an ethnic group.

Two other issues further complicate the identity puzzle. One is the status of being bilingual. Some people, regardless of where in Canada they live, are legally both French and English Canadians. Still, following Thériault, some in this group might identify more strongly with their province or region than with their country, while others in this same group might emphasize more the French or the English side of their bilingual status (possibly giving priority to the province or region as well). Additionally, living in a minority society could easily encourage a bilingual person to identify more strongly with the majority language and with the province in which he or she is residing than with Canada. Such an orientation is perhaps most likely to develop in those provinces where talk is heard from time to time about separating from Canada, notably Alberta, Newfoundland, and British Columbia.

The other issue hinges on the interprovincial migration of francophones and bilinguals. In some cases, they have moved to another province, but do not, or at least do not yet, identify with it.

For example, a man might move to Halifax in Nova Scotia but continue to identify himself as Québécois, because he believes he will return in the next few years to Québec. His desire to return hinges in part on the fact that living in a majority anglophone society with poorly developed English is not easy. Moreover, the multitude of cultural differences can be disconcerting.

This emphasis on personal linguistic distinctiveness should be allowed to mask the distaste of Canadian francophones for being thought of as an ethnic group. They argue, with irrefutable logic, that they are no more an ethnic group than the country's anglophones, for both helped found Canada. In their minds (and in the minds of many anglophones) they are members of one of the nation's two charter groups, whereas immigrants from outside the country raised to speak other languages and steeped in other cultures are properly considered ethnic. With reference to these feelings, Bernard Bocquel (1990: 118) argues that "the French of the future is condemned, if it is associated, whether closely or remotely, with an ethnic group. French is not Ukrainian, it is not a heritage language. It is official" (translation). Be that as it may, I shall occasionally use the terms ethnic and ethnicity for the convenience they afford in communicating the perspective of sociology as applied to this area of social life.[5]

The question of linguistic identity, it is clear, is enormously complex and, at present, by no means wholly understood. Part of the problem, which will be considered in later chapters, is that identity is simultaneously collective and personal. It is collective when "the notion addresses the 'we-ness' of a group, stressing the similarities or shared attributes around which group members coalesce [e.g., language]" (Cerulo, 1997: 386). It is personal when individuals use the collective identity to place themselves and others, saying in effect "I am francophone," "you are anglophone," and the like. Whether collective or personal, identity cannot be ignored. It has extensive political implications everywhere in Canada, while it simultaneously influences personal involvement in the francophone society in which the individual lives. For once a person is competent in a language, he or she can choose to claim or reject active membership in the linguistic community that has grown up around it, to identify publicly with it, and even to work for its survival and development.

As if the question of identity were not complicated enough, the cultural geographers at Laval University devoted to the study of francophone identity throughout North America have observed that North Americans who trace one or more of their ancestors to Québec often identify themselves by this geolinguistic heritage (e.g., Waddell, 1994: 221-224). They are Québécois in the same sense as many later-generation Germans and Italians, for example, who hold they are German or Italian, even though they were born in Canada and never learned their heritage language. For these Quebeckers, Québec is their mother country (Louder in Louder, Trépanier, and Waddell, 1994: 194, n.5). Some of them have lost, or never even acquired, the ability to speak French, while others are fluent in that language. Most of the latter live in Canada, however, where they incorporate the mother-country element in a complex identity also containing, in the typical case, provincial, bilingual, and international elements.

The linguistic identity of contemporary Canadian francophones is now more complicated than ever. But the history of francophone Canada shows that simpler forms of it have been present and salient from the beginning.

Chapter 2
A Short History of Francophone Canada

I pursue three goals in this chapter. The first is to show that francophones do truly qualify as a charter group, as one of the founders of Canada as a nation. The second is to show that francophones have helped establish many of Canada's regions and communities, and not just Québec. The third goal is to trace the proportional decline of francophones everywhere in the country except Québec, where they have enjoyed a proportional increase. Accomplishing these three goals will give sufficient historical background for understanding the present situation of Canada's francophone societies as examined in this book. More detailed historical information with reference to particular events and situations will appear in subsequent chapters.

The French Charter Group: Québec[1]

In nation-building terms, a charter group is a set of people, distinguished by certain ethnic characteristics, who, possibly along with other charter groups, create a nation's constitution or its equivalent. It is commonly held that Canada's two charter groups were composed of people from France and England. Both countries took an interest in the New World at about the same time, with France making its first official contact with it through Jacques Cartier, who on his maiden voyage to North America, sailed into the Bay of Gaspé in 1534. Cartier recognized the rich natural resources that could belong to France if only she would establish herself there permanently, a decision she refused to take, however, until early the next century when Samuel de Champlain built settlements in 1604 at Port-Royal (near Annapolis Royal, N.S.), in 1608 at Kébec (Indian word for narrow place in the river, site of today's Québec City), and in 1634 at what is now Trois-Rivières, Québec. France hoped to realize three objectives with its permanent settlements: trading furs, evangelizing native peoples, and exploiting natural resources.

In pursuing these objectives, the French ranged widely over North America, venturing as far south as Louisiana and as far west as the Rocky Mountains, while prudently avoiding the eastern seaboard of the present-day United States, territory held by

England, its arch-rival for control of the continent. Many a town and city in this vast expanse owes its origin and, in some instances, its present name to an enthusiastic and courageous gang of settlers, explorers, and fur traders who, in departing from one point or another in present-day Québec under the aegis of either the King of France or the Roman Catholic Church, established there forts, trading posts, and sometimes even the community itself. Thus, Kingston, Ontario, got its start as Fort Cataraqui, a French stronghold and trading post; Windsor, Ontario, was initially a French settlement; and The Pas, Manitoba, began as a French fur trading centre named Fort Paskoyac. Their founders were *Canadiens*, the francophones from France who resided permanently in North America, a term also used up to the Treaty of Paris to identify the *habitants* of Québec, descendants of the *Canadiens*.

But the French dream of a francophone North America was destined to become a nightmare, for the British came to severely outnumber the French on land and strategically outmanoeuver them at sea. In 1763, with the Treaty of Paris, France ceded the vast majority of its North American holdings to England. This did not, however, spell the end to francophone existence on this continent. Particularly in the Maritime Provinces and Québec (in 1763 the name was applied by Royal Proclamation to the entire province), where there were and still are large concentrations of francophones, francophone life continued under British rule in the forms of Québec society and Acadian society. In the early period of the English regime, which began with the Treaty of Paris, francophone Québec consisted mainly of farmers, crafts workers, and small business people, virtually all being guided by Roman Catholicism and nearly all living on the fertile lands bordering the Saint Lawrence River, itself sandwiched between the Laurentian and Appalachian Mountain chains. Large-scale commerce, public administration, and the liberal professions were almost exclusively the domain of anglophones, usually of British extraction and for the most part Protestant. This class structure did not change significantly until well into the twentieth century.

But circumstances – particularly the American Revolution (1776) – forced the British to placate the francophones of Québec with a variety of blandishments. Prominent among them was the division in 1791 of its remaining North American colony into Upper Canada and the West and Lower Canada and the East as separated by the present-day Québec-Ontario boundary. The first was comprised

mostly of anglophones, the second mostly of francophones. Each
had its own parliament, and in Lower Canada, French could be used
in governmental functions, even though English was the official language. Other legal and religious concessions had been granted earlier, which combined to make life attractive enough among the
Franco-Québécois to stem any significant tendency to side with the
Americans in their struggle against France's nemesis, England. But
that threat passed, and in 1840, after francophone Quebeckers led by
Louis-Joseph Papineau failed in their attempt in 1837-1838 to acquire
more autonomy through civil insurrection – the famous Patriot
Rebellion – Lord Durham united the two Canadas. Now for the first
time, francophones were a minority within the larger political sys-
tem, even while they constituted a majority within Québec itself.
Instead of gaining more autonomy, they lost a significant amount of
what they had. Much of today's political tension over the place of
Québec in Confederation has its roots in this turbulent period.

Confederation itself occurred in 1867, bringing in many changes
whose overall effect was to dilute still further Franco-Québec's influence. Possibly the most momentous of these was the addition
between that year and 1949 of eight dominantly anglophone
provinces. Nevertheless, the British North America Act, which made
all this possible, did separate federal and provincial powers; this
included for Québec, as for the others, the right to look after its own
civil law, education, and linguistic rights. Québec could also direct
its own affairs in the spheres of religion and culture. But since 1867,
as a member of Confederation, it has been perpetually at logger-
heads at the federal level with the other provinces, who have only
rarely understood its unique linguistic and cultural position in
North America and who have been preoccupied with their own
interests, many of which have been incompatible with those of
French Québec.

The period between 1840 and 1940 in French Québec is commonly described as one of extreme Church control; during this time
the Catholic hierarchy co-operated with the elite anglophone minority to keep francophone farmers, laborers, and small shopkeepers in
a subordinate position. Over the years and with the connivance of
anglophone leaders, the Church gained official control of French
Catholic education, matters pertaining to social welfare (e.g., hospitals, orphanages, services for the needy, residences for the elderly),
and civil registrations, notably births, deaths, and marriages. This is
the period that most directly fits the observation of Jean-Charles

Falardeau: "the history of French Canada, is the history of the Church in Canada" (translation). In return, the Church defended capitalist values and the status quo in class relations. So perhaps it was to be expected that, during industrialization, when thousands of French-Catholic laborers migrated to the cities in Canada and New England, they would turn out to be docile, efficient employees in the factories owned and managed by anglophone Canadians and Americans. The Church did remain faithful to the French language, however, using and promoting it everywhere and under all conditions within its ambit.

As the twentieth century unfolded, the number of francophones in the ranks of the elite began to grow; French-speaking professionals and wealthy entrepreneurs benefited much as their anglophone counterparts did from the cozy relationship with the Church. Notwithstanding this "internal" collaboration, cracks began to appear in the walls of the institutional fortress that the Church had become by this time in history. For example, its rural values clashed increasingly with the urban values and attitudes of many of its parishioners, whose numbers were swelling rapidly in response to the voracious personnel needs of urban industry, particularly that in Montréal. The suspicion of religious authority was one such attitude; it was exacerbated when the Church joined with the federal government in opposing the many Franco-Quebeckers who refused to be drafted into service during World War II. Not long after, the credibility of Church authority suffered another blow when the hierarchy sided with management against the workers during the asbestos strike of 1949. Moreover, attendance at services had been declining for some time – still more evidence that Church influence was waning.

The tide officially turned in 1960, when Jean Lesage and his newly elected Liberal government took power, ushering in the broad social transformation that soon came to be known as the "Quiet Revolution" (*la Révolution Tranquille*). In the course of the next 15 years, new action-oriented Québec governments, as their premier goal, transformed the educational system, which had deteriorated seriously under the conservative governments that held office between 1920 to 1959, particularly the regime of Maurice Duplessis and his party, the Union Nationale. Behiels (1985) describes the deplorable situation that had developed by 1960 in Québec in a broad range of areas. By that time, it had the lowest average number of years of schooling in Canada; housing programs were non-existent; sanitary conditions were deplorable; vocational training was hard to find; modern medical equipment was rare; welfare programs varied widely from city to city; and only those students from the private, fee-paying classical colleges could enter the universities. Yet little change was possible as long as the Union Nationale was in power, for the rural districts were over-represented in the National Assembly, while the urban districts were most acutely afflicted with these problems.

Fuelled by the slogan of *maître chez nous* (master of our own house), the new Lesage government took control of health, social, and educational services, all of which previous governments had left to the Church. But with no significant financial support from those governments, the Church could only provide minimal, and increasingly outdated, help in these areas, each of which had evolved into a complicated technological and scientific field of its own. None of this, however, prevented the Church from amassing its own resources, which became an embarrassment after 1960 when it found itself with an enormous surplus of personnel and buildings it once needed to perform these functions.

In broad terms, the Quiet Revolution gave francophone Quebeckers a tremendous boost of confidence. This came about in part through educational reform designed to improve the quality of French taught there and to educate in French a much broader spectrum of the population. This has been achieved, though not without certain setbacks. Additionally, the Quiet Revolution had the effect of channelling more capital into francophone enterprises, with the result that Québec now has a reasonably strong industrial and financial base substantially controlled by francophones, a base anchored primarily in its considerable natural resources (most notably hydro-electric power), its manufacturing sector, and its co-operative movement, particularly the Mouvement Desjardins. Bélanger (1993: 391) sums up Québec's contemporary economic situation:

> The most recent evaluations put local francophone control over the province's economy at approximately 60 percent. In recent years, Québec entrepreneurship has undergone major transformations and is now made up of large industrial and financial firms that closely resemble those controlled by large anglophone capital. Many Québec francophone firms have acquired significant international status, after bypassing the Canadian market.

What was once an economy based almost exclusively on family enterprise, as seen in the period before the Treaty of Paris, has evolved into a much broader economy that includes numerous businesses of major proportions, two of the most celebrated being Bombardier and Hydro-Québec, a state-owned corporation.[2]

In 1976, the Parti Québécois (PQ), with René Lévesque as leader, gained power on, among other issues and promises, the pledge to seek sovereignty for Québec. During the following year the celebrated Bill 101 was adopted; it legislated French as the official language of Québec. Yet, in voting in May, 1980, in the first referendum, Quebeckers decided by nearly 60 percent to deny their government the mandate to negotiate "sovereignty-association" with the federal government. Nevertheless, the PQ was re-elected in 1981, served another four years, and then lost in 1985 to the Liberal Party and its leader, Robert Bourassa. The PQ was returned to power in 1994 under the leadership of Jacques Parizeau, who was subsequently replaced by Lucien Bouchard.

The marginality of Québec vis-à-vis the rest of Canada stands out in relief in the history of the constitutional struggles that have plagued the nation since 1981. The First Ministers Conference on the Constitution held that year in Ottawa ended in failure to persuade Québec to sign the accord. Thus the Constitution Act of 1982 – it brought the Constitution to Canada from Great Britain – was implemented without the approval of Québec, the actual and spiritual home of one of the two charter groups who founded the country. The attempt at Meech Lake in 1990 to bring Québec into the new Act likewise failed, as did the Charlottetown agreement in 1992. The latter was rejected by six other provinces and the Yukon. Discouraged by this time with constitutionally-related conferences, Québec absented itself from the framing and signing of the 1996 Calgary Declaration, whose intent was to signal that the other provinces now recognize Québec's unique character. This question is examined further in chapter 4.

Acadia

Although Acadians have been in Canada as long as any group of francophones, it is logically impossible to classify them as part of the French charter group. For as the following history shows, many were expelled in the eighteenth century, and of those who remained or returned, most lived in severe poverty until the third decade of the twentieth century. Therefore, they were in no position to do anything other than survive; they were unable to work at founding a nation, as did their counterparts in Québec. Only later were the Acadians able to organize themselves socially and economically at a level where they could be considered a society, albeit a minority society in Nova Scotia and Prince Edward Island and a parity society in New Brunswick.

The etymology of the word "acadia" reveals a case of linguistic blundering. According to Daigle (1993: 2), the original name – "Arcadia" – which initially referred to an area near the contemporary state of Delaware, was mistakenly applied by sixteenth-century cartographers to the region of today's three Maritime provinces. Eventually the r disappeared, leaving Acadia as the name for the region and Acadian as the name for the people from France who helped settle it. Although Jacques Cartier had visited Acadia on the same voyage of 1534 that took him to the Bay of Gaspé, the first French colonists did not arrive until 1604 with Champlain and Pierre du Gua de Monts. The British, who also had an interest in the region, took possession of it in 1613 and in 1621 changed its name to Nova Scotia. The French got it back in a treaty drawn up in 1632.

Both France and England wanted Acadia. As a result, with neither country possessing sufficient military strength to hold the area, it passed back and forth between them, accompanied by name changes, until the Treaty of Utrecht in 1713. At this time France ceded to England a triangular territory bounded approximately by the Strait of Canso and the present-day Nova Scotian communities of Amherst and Digby. Still, this accord failed to settle completely the question of who owned Acadia. Although the English did not agree, the French believed they had the right to develop areas outside the ceded portion, such as Île Saint-Jean (P.E.I.) and Île Royale (Cape Breton Island). On the eastern coast of the latter, the French established the fortress of Louisbourg to protect the seaway entrance to New France. Meanwhile, Acadia, as a French society, was expanding.

In fact, the Acadians greatly outnumbered the British until the 1750s, when England decided to bring more colonists to the area. During that period, some 7000 Britons arrived to take up residence in Nova Scotia. The French responded to this menace by constructing Fort Beauséjour (near Sackville, N.B.), the purpose of which was to try to prevent the English from crossing the isthmus that separates present-day New Brunswick and Nova Scotia. The English countered by building their own fort less than three kilometres away. Trouble was brewing, and the English decided to settle the matter in a definitive way, a way that would, however, be transformed into a permanent rallying cry of Acadians everywhere.

The principal bone of contention at the time was the Acadians' refusal to swear unconditional loyalty to the British crown; they would only commit themselves to neutrality, to agreeing to avoid taking up arms against either France or England. In reaction to this stance, England decided to deport them, a process that began in 1755 and lasted to 1762. During the *Grand Dérangement*, as it has come to be known among Acadians, an estimated 13 000 people, or three-quarters of the population, were put aboard ships bound primarily for England or her colonies. Others were imprisoned, escaped to Québec, or sought refuge in outlying areas of the region, most importantly, northern New Brunswick and western Prince Edward Island. Among the deported, untold numbers died from hunger, disease, and shipwreck. Many who wound up in the American colonies were unhappy with their lot there and so returned to Acadia (restrictions eased somewhat after 1764) or moved on to such places as France, Québec, Martinique, Louisiana, Santo Domingo, and Saint-Pierre and Miquelon.

The remaining Acadians (fugitives, returnees, released prisoners), once they took the oath of allegiance, were permitted to resettle themselves. The English, however, would allow them to locate only in scattered groups in certain remote parts of the region: western and southern Cape Breton, the tips of the Nova Scotian peninsula and Prince Edward Island, along the eastern and northern shores of New Brunswick, and along the Saint John River. This is basically the linguistic geography of modern Acadia, except that francophones in these areas subsequently developed some of the hinterland behind their new coastal communities. The object of this policy was to retain the best farm land for British subjects, including those who came to New Brunswick as loyalists in the aftermath of the American Revolution. The land on which the Acadians were allowed to settle was good only for subsistence farming, thus forcing them into fishing as a livelihood.

This was the beginning of a period of great hardship for the majority of Acadians, a period that lasted until the co-operative movement began to gain momentum in the 1930s. Most were compelled to earn their living in the fishery, in which, however, they were unmercifully exploited by the English merchants through whom they had to sell their catches. For many decades, the aim of

the typical Acadian was to survive. And this explains why it is difficult to regard the Acadians of the late eighteenth and early nineteenth centuries as part of the French charter group, especially when
compared with the more numerous and socially- and economically-
developed Quebeckers. Léon Thériault (1993a: 47) describes the situation:

> The temporary and local character of their institutions is
> then a dominant trait. They do not establish collective insti-
> tutions. Thus their priests, in general, are missionaries, not
> *curés* [parish priests], at least until around 1840. They have
> few schools and often the teachers are *maîtres ambulants* [itin-
> erant teachers], that is, teachers who impart their meagre
> knowledge sometimes in one village, sometimes in another.
> They have no newspaper, no lawyer, no physician, no insti-
> tution of higher education. There is not even, properly
> speaking, a middle class. (translation)

Thériault qualifies the years between 1763 and 1864 in Acadia as a
period of "silence."

From these humble circumstances, a new Acadia emerged, characterized in part by an ever-mushrooming population. Chiasson
(1998: 7) reports that, at the dawn of the nineteenth century, 9500
Acadians existed in the three Maritime Provinces compared with
87 000 at the time of Confederation in 1867. Such numbers were
bound to have an effect. In the 1840s and 1850s a handful of
Acadians got elected to the three provincial legislatures. Then in
1846 Henry Wadsworth Longfellow published his poem
"Evangeline," which in French translation gave poignant literary
expression to the rallying cry of the *Grand Dérangement*. Abbé F.X.
Lafrance, a Québécois by birth, established in 1854 in Saint-Joseph,
New Brunswick, Acadia's first francophone institution of higher
learning – Séminaire Saint-Thomas – which was renamed Collège
Saint-Joseph in 1864 and then, in 1963, through an amalgamation
with two other francophone colleges, became the Université de
Moncton. In 1859 Edme Rameau de Saint-Père published the first
French-language history of the Acadians. *Le Moniteur Acadien*, a
weekly and Acadia's first French-language newspaper, started coming off the presses in Shédiac, New Brunswick, in 1867. It, too, was
founded by a Quebecker, Israël-D. Landry. This newspaper was the
first in a string of 40 weeklies, semi-weeklies and dailies that would
be published locally, provincially, or regionally up to the present
(Beaulieu, 1993: 530).

Collège Saint-Joseph was the catalyst for creating an Acadian middle-class, from which leaders began to emerge who could speak for the Acadian cause, mobilize opinion, and organize the people to solve their unique problems. Starting in 1881 these leaders held throughout the Maritimes a number of "national" public assemblies for the purpose of discussing the future of Acadia and Acadians. Among the products of these assemblies were the founding of the Société nationale des acadiens, whose mandate was to promote the French fact, and the creation of a distinctive flag, the French Tricolor with a yellow star in the blue strip. A national holiday was also chosen – 15 August, the day of the Feast of the Assumption – as well as the Acadian slogan, *l'union fait la force*, or unity makes strength. The hymn *l'Ave Maris Stella* was selected as the Acadian national anthem.

Some of the problems Acadians face today emerged during the latter half of the nineteenth century. Two of them – one revolving around primary and secondary education in French and one centred on assimilation and migration out of Acadia to other parts of Canada and to the United States – will be covered in chapter 6. A third problem, however, has been solved. Centred on the lack of a Catholic religious structure expressly organized to serve Acadians, this problem worsened as Acadia became an identifiable society (more than a mere extension of Québec or France). Léon Thériault (1993b: 448) describes the hurdles that had to be surmounted to correct this deficiency and how this was accomplished:

> On the local level, it is necessary to create parishes where Acadians constitute the majority, even if this means dividing parishes where anglophones are in the majority. As for the episcopate [the level of the diocese], there is a double objective: first obtain the appointment of an Acadien priest to head the diocese and then restructure the dioceses to create one that will be constituted of a majority of francophone Catholics. As for the parishes, the objective was accomplished in 1914, but for the dioceses, the *lutte* [struggle] will continue until 1953. (translation)

The efforts of Acadia's Catholics paid off, for between 1935 and 1953 Rome instituted an archdiocese and two dioceses in Nova Scotia and New Brunswick.

Newfoundland

Today, Newfoundland has three concentrations of franco-phones, none of which was significantly populated by the deported Acadians. The concentration in Saint John's, on which little histori-cal or sociological research exists, appears to be a typical urban francophone migrant community. By contrast, the francophone community in Labrador City is indigenous, being composed mainly of Franco-Quebeckers who helped found the town in 1961 as a cen-tre for the iron ore mining industry in the area (Barla, 1991). Here, too, francophones have yet to come under the scrutiny of social sci-ence research. Studies have been conducted, however, on Newfoundland's largest concentration of francophones: those resid-ing on the Port-au-Port Peninsula on the west coast of the island.

Magord (1995: 32-35) writes that, in the seventeenth and eigh-teenth centuries, French fishers worked the coasts of western Newfoundland and, although illegal according to the Treaty of Utrecht (1713), some of these men and their families nonetheless managed to remain there (often with the connivance of local anglo-phones) and even establish small communities. Early in the nine-teenth century, five fishing stations, all in Saint George's Bay, still had no year-around residents, although French fishers from Saint-Pierre who had been given permission in 1815 to fish the area soon arranged to stay in it permanently. A number of them settled in the station at Cap-Saint-Georges (Cape Saint George), which by 1860 consisted of some 20 families. They in turn helped further populate four other communities on the Peninsula: La Grand'Terre (Mainland), Maisons-d'hiver (Winter Houses), L'Anse-à-Canards (Black Duck Brook), and La Barre (Long Point). In the 1890s, these predominantly francophone settlements attracted another and final wave of immigrant French fishers, who contributed further to the Frenchness of the Port-au-Port.

The Port-au-Port was therefore largely francophone until the 1940s, when it started coming out of its isolation, a process initiated by the construction of a major American military base at Stephenville, situated near the entrance to the Peninsula. Dilution of the francophone way of life continued when Newfoundland joined Canada in 1949 and, like their anglophone neighbors, French-speak-ing Newfoundlanders began receiving monetary hand-outs from the federal government. Somewhat later roads were built to the Port-au-Port communities, and in 1962 they began receiving electricity.

These changes spawned rampant assimilation to English, with the result that French nearly disappeared in this area of Newfoundland. Magord (1995: 111-137) found in his study, conducted in the early 1990s, that the parents of the Peninsula's youth could speak little or no French. Yet, the grandparents of these same youth remembered French (their mother tongue) well enough to communicate with them. This curious generation gap was in part created by the youth themselves who, proud of their heritage, took advantage of various educational and community services made possible by the 1969 Official Languages Act to develop a mastery of both French and English. In chapters 7 and 8, we examine the present and future of francophone Cap-Saint-Georges, l'Anse-à-Canards, and La Grand'Terre, the three communities where French language and culture is still alive.

Ontario

Jaenen (1993) writes that, up to 1821, what was to become Upper Canada and later Ontario was, for francophones, little more than a desultory collection of forts, trading posts, and encampments established for exploiting the fur trade and controlling this vast territory, both operations being directed from headquarters based in Québec. In 1821, the year the fur trade declined definitively in Central Canada (Gervais, 1993: 49), the few francophones actually living in Upper Canada constituted but a small minority of the total population: 4000 out of a total of 120 000 inhabitants (Jaenen, 1993: 39). These francophones gathered in small communities well removed from the centres of economic and political activity, which were anglophone in any case, communities spread across a vast hinterland and geographically isolated even from each other. Here they farmed, lived by the creed of the Catholic Church, and followed their cultural traditions.

Gervais (1993) holds that significant francophone colonization of Ontario began only in the latter half of the nineteenth century when the forest industry came into its own, stimulated by a burgeoning market for wood in Britain and the United States. By 1910 more than 200 000 francophones were living in the province, concentrated in three geographic areas: the extreme east, or what is today Ottawa and the federal riding of Glengarry-Prescott-Russell, extreme southwest around Windsor, and northeast, in and near such cities as Hearst and Kapuskasing. The Ottawa River and the city of Ottawa (known as Bytown until 1855) became the social and cultural centre of the earliest concentration.

Most of the lumbering was carried out close to the Ottawa River, with some also being done along other tributaries to the Saint Lawrence River, itself the starting point for shipping wood overseas or down the eastern seaboard of the United States. Francophone males were regarded by their employers as ideal for the job of *bûcheron* (lumberjack); these men were mostly rural, knew how to handle an axe, were living close by in Québec, if not in Ontario itself, and knew the various rivers and passages. They were also reputed to be docile, reliable workers. The forestry, along with other resource-based activities, soon transformed Ottawa into the commercial centre of the Ottawa River valley and the francophone centre of Ontario.

For much of the history of the city, its francophones have been concentrated east of the Rideau Canal in Lower Town, which includes the districts of Orléans and Vanier. This area became the cultural capital of French Ontario, for here were located many of its most important institutions, including a hospital and a number of churches and Catholic religious orders (notably the Oblates and the Grey Nuns of the Cross). This was also the home of several schools, numerous French-language newspapers, and various francophone organizations as well as the bilingual Collège de Bytown (later to become the Université d'Ottawa) and the Institut canadien-français, a cultural establishment. In 1886 the Diocese of Ottawa was elevated to the status of archdiocese. Together these establishments provided the financial, intellectual, and religious support for francophone colonization to the east of Ottawa, especially in Glengarry-Prescott-Russell, and eventually across the entire province of Ontario.

The last half of the nineteenth century in Canada and the United States was a period of tremendous geographic expansion, when governments at all levels were encouraging people to buy virgin land, sold at bargain prices, then clear and farm their purchase. In the meantime, the seigneuries in the Saint Lawrence valley in Québec had become full, forcing young people to seek work elsewhere. Some, as already mentioned, found their livelihood in the textile factories of New England, others found it on farms in the American Midwest, and still others found it in Canada by heading west to Ontario and the prairies. Many French-speaking migrants took advantage of colonization programs operated by the Church, the model for which was developed in Québec by the *curé* Antoine

Labelle. The clergy supported these programs by establishing diocese- and parish-based colonization societies, whose functions included disseminating information about opportunities, recruiting people eager to take advantage of them, and financing some of their initial costs. The *curés* sometimes held annual recruitment meetings (Gervais, 1993: 66).

Many a francophone region in Ontario got started through such programs, including especially the area east of Ottawa and the counties of Essex and Kent in the Windsor area, where agriculture was the principal occupation. Yet over the years, the majority of Ontario's francophones settled farther north in the Canadian Shield, whose alternatively rocky and swampy composition is unfit for any farming other than the subsistence variety. Mining and forestry reigned supreme here, especially after the period of railway construction between 1880 and 1930. First the forest industry in the region, then the copper and nickel mines around Sudbury, brought francophone workers to this part of Ontario. In the Lake Timiskaming (Lac Témiscamingue) area on the Québec border, forestry and later selected agriculture in the Little Clay Belt surrounding the Lake attracted still more francophones. And as numerous silver mines were built in that area in the early twentieth century, another wave of French-speaking migrants arrived to avail themselves of this new economic opportunity.

As construction of the transcontinental railway proceeded westward, new resource-based communities sprang up. Kapuskasing is a case in point. It was founded in 1910 as a train station, but since the 1920s, it has been a lumbering, agriculture (in the Great Clay Belt), and pulp and paper centre. Hearst, located farther west along the same rail line, has a similar history. Both communities became destinations for large numbers of Québec francophones during the first half of the twentieth century. Still other francophones, most of whom came from the Ottawa Diocese (Gervais, 1993: 92), migrated to the Lake Nipissing area, particularly to Sturgeon Falls, to work in its pulp and paper industry and to North Bay to take up a variety of urban occupations.

Up to approximately 1910 Franco-Ontarians as a group were primarily working class, poorly educated, and thus without occupational speciality. Many were employed in marginal agriculture or one of the resource-based industries and lived in rural areas and small cities on the periphery of the province's economic centre. Still, thanks to the francophone elite in Ottawa, there was an identifiable institutional basis to their communities, albeit one primarily centred on religious and cultural establishments, since Protestant anglophones mostly controlled their economic institutions. Against this backdrop the Catholic Church managed to ensure a coherent lifestyle in the spheres of education, spirituality, social assistance, and the family, while striving to keep French language and culture as the glue that could hold this institutional structure together.

But the twentieth century has brought considerable change to this profile. Ouellet (1993: 149-155) shows that, particularly in central and southwestern Ontario but also in the east and north of the province, francophones, much as anglophones, are distributed across the entire range of occupations and in similar proportions. Today, francophones work not only in agriculture, mining, and forestry but also in sales, service, administration, and the professions. Some work in the clerical occupations, others own their own businesses.

This emergence of this new occupational profile parallels some important changes in the demographic profile of Franco-Ontarians. Everywhere in Canada except Québec and parts of New Brunswick, there has been a significant drop in the proportion of francophones, with assimilation being widely cited as the principal cause of this trend. Nevertheless, the communities in northern Ontario have lost significant numbers of francophones and anglophones. Since 1971, the Census of Canada has consistently recorded net losses of francophones from that region to the east, centre, and southwest of the province (Ouellet, 1993: 185). The decline of the mining and forest industries has left many workers with no choice but to migrate.

The Prairies

In many ways, the early history of francophones in western Canada is the same as that for New France and Ontario: first adventurers explored the land, then somewhat later some of them turned to the fur trade. Later still, the voyageurs – the French-speaking canoe men and workhorses of the fur trade – arrived to perform contractual labor for the trading companies. Unusual, however, was their tendency, when their contracts were finished, not to return to the East but to remain in the West and marry Indian women, doing so in such numbers that a distinctive society of Métis soon arose on the prairies. Although the term Métis is variously defined, the definition most appropriate for the purposes of this book describes a French-speaking, Roman Catholic half-breed of French-Indian or

Scots-Indian descent.[3] Grant MacEwan (1984: 125) sketches the nine-teenth-century Métis way of life:

> For the most part, the Métis clung tenaciously to the lan-guage and church of their French parents and the primitive outdoor life of the Indians. But instead of travelling with the Indians, they chose their own company and formed fairly compact hunting communities, creating another clearly defined group in prairie society drawing its livelihood from the pursuit of the buffalo and trapping.

By the early 1880s the supply of buffalo had virtually run out, forc-ing some Métis to take up farming and pushing many others north and west to Catholic missions in central Saskatchewan and Alberta.

The Métis were centrally involved in establishing a number of communities in western Canada, including Lord Selkirk's Red River Colony (the precursor of the Province of Manitoba), Saint-Boniface, Manitoba (the cradle of western Canadian French culture; Saint-Pierre, 1992: 87), and Duck Lake, Saskatchewan, and Saint-Paul, Alberta (both originally Métis missions). They also worked in vari-ous capacities to help settle the West in a more general way, some-times as entrepreneurs in the haulage business using their red-river carts, sometimes as interpreters, and sometimes as bull team opera-tors. Louis Riel, by far the most celebrated Métis, was born in Saint-Boniface.

Riel led the Northwest Rebellion (1885), which pitted Métis, Indians, and white settlers in armed conflict against the federal gov-ernment over a range of issues, including food rations and land claims for the starving Indians and Métis and default on the prom-ise of a railway for the whites. Riel became president of a provision-al government formed to press Ottawa for, among other things, recognition of a "Revolutionary Bill of Rights." Riel's forces were defeated, however, and in November, 1885, he was hanged in Regina for high treason. Although mother-tongue francophones across the country supported suppression of the rebellion, wide-spread and long-lasting outrage occurred in Québec over Riel's exe-cution. Just another example, they reasoned, of the cynical regard of the English in Canada for their French compatriots.[4]

The Métis were not, however, the only francophones to help set-tle the West. For example, Manitoba was the destination in the late nineteenth century of a francophone Belgian immigration; they set-tled in their own small communities and in Saint-Boniface. For much of the nineteenth century, Saint-Boniface was the archbishopric for the West, and its archbishop, Mgr. Alexandre Taché, was alarmed at the influx of anglophones and the strong possibility they would numerically overwhelm the francophones in the region. Following the example of Père Labelle, as others had, he formed a colonization society in Saint-Boniface, through which he recruited francophones from eastern Canada, New England, and France to establish themselves on the lands abandoned by the Métis (MacEwan, 1984: 195). He envisioned a "chain" of francophone communities across the West (Saint-Pierre, 1992: 78). And, whereas the result was not as dramatic as he would have liked, a number of communities, nearly all of them based on farming, did spring up between approximately 1875 and 1940. In Manitoba these included Letellier, Saint-Jean Baptiste, and Sainte-Agathe, all just south or southwest of Saint-Boniface.

Although perhaps inevitable that breaks would occur in the chain, francophone communities did nonetheless take root from approximately 1880 to 1915 in parts of southern Saskatchewan, among them Ponteix, Gravelbourg, and Willow Bunch, and in parts of central Saskatchewan in such towns as Debden, Saint-Denis, and Zenon Park (Anderson, 1985). Particularly in Alberta, the settlers moved into former mission communities, such as Saint-Paul, Saint-Albert, and Morinville, and when all the farm land was claimed, moved on to establish other communities, among them Legal, Beaumont, and Villeneuve. Still later, from 1912 to approximately 1940, several Catholic priests led Canadian francophone settlers into the Bonnyville area in east-central Alberta and the Peace River country in northwestern Alberta, establishing here the communities of Falher, Tangent, Girouxville, and several others. These villages and small towns were commonly organized in what Anderson (1985: 7) calls "*blocs*," or clusters of communities, also a common practice among many of the other ethnic groups who helped settle the prairies.

Francophone settlement, as might be expected, was distinctly different in the large cities. There French-speaking migrants tended to concentrate in neighborhoods and parishes. Thus Edmonton, known first as Fort des Prairies and whose population in 1870 was 60 percent French, has retained down through the years many of its indigenous francophone families in the district of Bonnie Doon and the Parish of Saint-Joachim. Calgary was on a similar trajectory in the 1890s with its own francophone suburb known as Rouleauville, named after two brothers from Québec who rose to prominence in that city (Stebbins, 1994). But Rouleauville was soon overwhelmed by anglophones, after which assimilation claimed nearly all the indigenous francophones in the area and left development of the Calgary French community primarily to migrants.

British Columbia

Recorded historical knowledge of francophones in British Columbia is sparse. The present-day French community in Vancouver is symbolic and composed mainly of migrants (see chapters 9 and 10 for details). So, from what is known about francophones in this province, it seems safe to argue that the most distinctive communal development there took place in Maillardville.

Maillardville, named after its first parish priest, *abbé* Maillard from France, is a French-speaking enclave within the District of Coquitlam in exurban Vancouver. The enclave emerged between 1908 and 1910 near Fraser Mills, a saw mill on the Fraser River, which initially recruited its workers from Québec (Villeneuve, 1983). At the height of francophone development in Maillardville, several hundred families – most of them concentrated along a couple of streets – carried on daily life largely in French aided by the usual francophone institutions: church, school, convent, credit union (*caisse populaire*), and the like. Later, the need for more workers was met by francophones from Willow Bunch, Saskatchewan. But after World War II, several forces combined to push the community into decline, one of the most powerful being assimilation to English. Another was company policy: the workers and their offspring were guaranteed positions at the mill whereas the third generation was not. Consequently, during the 1950s and 1960s, this group sought work in nearby anglophone communities, so that today many of Maillardville's francophone residents are elderly retirees.

Conclusion

Historically, the richness and texture of Canada's francophone societies has always weakened as the distance increases east or west from Québec. The New Brunswick and Ontario societies have been robust on their western and eastern edges, respectively, but have lost some of their strength thereafter. Gilbert (1998) calls this the centre-periphery model. It was pioneered by Louder, Trépanier, and Waddell (1994: 198), who metaphorically described Québec as the purely francophone central mountain; Acadia, Ontario, and New England as the bilingual foothills; and Louisiana and the rest of francophone Canada as a culturally and racially mixed (*métissé*) sea dotted with islands and clusters of islands of francophone communities, a linguistic archipelago. We should note, however, that francophone life gets something of a new lease in Saint-Boniface, even if it weakens noticeably west of there and even if decline is less, or least rather uneven, mainly because Saint-Boniface never had the richness and texture of francophone life enjoyed in Québec. In other words, Saint-Boniface is not the linguistic mountain Québec is. In this book, to describe the geographic distribution of francophones in Canada, I use both Gilbert's centre-periphery metaphor and Louder and Waddell's (1983) "archipelago" (*l'archipel*) metaphor as conceptually linked earlier in this paragraph.

As previously stated, considerable rural to urban migration is evident within each francophone society in parallel with significant immigration of international francophones to all parts of Canada. Moreover, the Official Languages Acts have helped valorize to a noticeable extent French and francophone activities across the country, while globalization is accentuating the importance everywhere of world languages. And very much in harmony with all this is the steady growth of the international French community. In short, history and demography might seem to paint a pessimistic picture of the survival and development of Canada's francophone societies, but the contemporary portraits framed in the next several chapters cast doubt on its validity for the reasons just given, among many others.

Part II
Majority Societies

Chapter 3
Québec Society

This chapter and the chapters on Canada's other francophone societies center on the unusual and unique aspects of the society under consideration. In the pages ahead it will become evident that each of these societies is in diverse ways both unique and distinct. Nevertheless, among them, only Québec has been publicly and politically described in these terms. Although space requirements limit treatment of the distinctive aspects of Québec society, this chapter should still convey a solid sense of what being distinct and unique means in concrete, everyday life terms. The commonsense view is that Québec's distinctiveness rests primarily on linguistic differences. True, language is clearly one of its important distinguishing features, but it is by no means the only one.

Geographical Features

The map of Canada reveals that Québec, Canada's largest province, is also a peninsula (Tétu de Labsade, 1988: 21). Apart from being an island, there is no better geographic means of ensuring cultural distinctiveness than being surrounded on three sides with water. Unless, perhaps, it is ensured through isolation by mountain ranges, of which Québec has two: the Laurentians paralleling the north shore of the Saint Lawrence River and the Appalachians paralleling its south shore. Historically, both acted as barriers to movement and communication. Even today, 80 percent of Quebeckers live on the relatively flat terrain bordered by these two chains, or more precisely, in the giant square of land bounded by the cities of Montréal, Sherbrooke, Québec City, and Trois-Rivières (Tétu de Labsade, 1988: 24).

Running approximately through the middle of this square is Le fleuve Saint-Laurent, or simply, Le fleuve, from the time of European exploration a major transportation route into the heart of North America. It consists of freshwater at Montréal, but becomes progressively more saline down river from Québec City, where tides are also evident. Although a considerably less serious problem today than in the past, the Saint Lawrence, because of its great width and fast current, has always been a barrier to direct communication, except when frozen. Tétu de Labsade (1988: 24) writes that, given these qualities,

> it is therefore natural that it is one of the favorite themes of cultural expression, whether it occurs in literature, painting, or film. Le fleuve carries with it some heavy emotional charges: it is the umbilical cord of the native peoples; artists understand well the place it holds, as much psychologically as physically, in the life of Quebeckers of yesterday and today. (translation)

Furthermore, it is likely that Québec could be described as Canada's most regionalized province, in the sense that, in comparison with the other provinces, it has significantly more distinctive cultural-geographic areas within it. Québec is commonly divided into 21 such regions, counting Anticosti Island, the Magdalene Islands, Nouveau Québec (approximately the northern half of the province between James Bay and Labrador), and the two main urban agglomerations of Montréal and Québec City. Montréal is Québec's economic and cultural metropolis and Canada's second largest city with a CMA of 3 326 510 people in 1996 (Statistics Canada, 1998a) . Québec City is the province's political capital and historical center (the walled section of the town is a UNESCO world heritage site), its second largest city, and Canada's seventh largest. Its CMA consisted of 671 890 people in 1996. The main regions lying beyond the aforementioned square with their own outstanding economic features are Saguenay-Lac Saint-Jean (agriculture, aluminum manufacturing) to the north, Gaspésie (formerly fishing, presently tourism) to the east, Outaouais (federal government civil service), and Abitibi-Témiscamingue to the northwest adjacent to Ontario (forestry, mining).

Political-Economic Portrait

An enduring legacy of the Quiet Revolution, Quebeckers came to realize that they had in their provincial government a powerful means of development enabling them to ameliorate the festering problems of the earlier Duplessis era and thereby join the modern world. *Rattrapage* (catching up) quickly became the watchword of the day. A most important change was to redirect the provincial government from its passive involvement in the affairs of the society, including the areas of culture and welfare once looked after by the Church, to becoming actively involved in them. Thus, a vast civil service was created to administer the newly expanded and restructured systems of health, welfare, and education. Also inaugurated was a program designed to nationalize the energy industry (e.g., Hydro-Québec) and establish various quasi-public organizations in the fields of finance and investment with a mandate to stimulate the growth of francophone Québécois capital. It has been estimated that, all told, the new regime created 23 new governmental departments, 55 consultative bodies, 63 economic management institutions, 9 administrative tribunals, several social service institutions, and a good number of state-owned enterprises. It also created a system of junior colleges and another of provincial universities, both set up to serve all parts of the province (Lachapelle et al., 1993: 79). As Reginald Whitaker (1993: 24) put it: "locked out from both the corporate world [it was virtually anglophone] and the national [federal] state, the francophone middle-class would build a state in Québec that would be open to its talents." This middle-class, largely an urban movement, was highly critical of the Duplessis government.

This was the time in francophone Québec when the nationalists began to shun the identity of French Canadian, favoring instead that of Québécois. They grew increasingly convinced that, for Canadian francophones outside Québec, it was *point de salut*, not a hope, as Sheila Arnopoulos (1988) once described their plight. Efforts would therefore be best directed to saving their own territory where, aided by a greatly transformed provincial government, they could truly be *maître chez nous*. This, it turns out, was more a middle-class than a working-class outlook, since the beloved state of the former was the suspected employer of many of the latter, raising for them the all-too-familiar spectre of labor-management problems. Moreover, it was the emergent middle class of Québec who benefited the most from the changes, for it fell to them to fill the complicated professional and technical posts in the health, welfare, and educational bureaucracies of the new state.

As could be expected, perhaps, being master of one's house has meant different things to different people. For some it has meant the kind of control enjoyed by an autonomous nation. Quebeckers with this orientation have tended to be *indépendantistes*, many of whom have joined the Parti Québécois. And a few of them, most notably the terrorist group known as the Front Libération du Québec, went much further, fomenting the October Crisis of 1970 by kidnapping James Cross, a British diplomat, and later by kidnapping and ultimately killing the Québec minister of labor, Pierre Laporte. For others, however, including Prime Minister Pierre Elliot Trudeau, being master of one's own house has meant gaining sufficient control within the federal government to ensure the survival of Québec as a francophone society. These are the *fédéralistes*, and they have tended to become members of the Liberal Party of Québec or that of Canada, if not both.

An intermediate position, pioneered by the Parti Québécois, is to seek "sovereignty-association" with Canada; its adherents are *souvereignistes*. This arrangement envisions full political sovereignty in parallel with an economic association formed along the lines of the North American Free Trade Agreement or the European Economic Union. Nonetheless, the *souvereignistes* argue that it would be prudent to collaborate at the federal level in the largely non-controversial areas of government such as defense, currency, transportation, and the administration of tariffs and customs.

Turning next to the trade union movement, the expansion of government in Québec in the 1960s led to at least a couple of distinctive developments in this realm. One was the phenomenal growth in the number of organized workers employed in the service industries, mainly in the schools, hospitals, and the civil service. Moreover, with a significant proportion of all union members in the province working for one branch of government or another, it should come as no surprise that union-management relations occasionally get politicized. For example, the government might argue that it is holding the line on wages for the benefit of taxpayers or a union might claim that public interests will be threatened if certain positions (e.g., nurses, teachers) are cut to save money for the government.

Without going into the myriad details about the relations between unions and government and their political alliances since 1960, note more broadly that these relations have been stormy enough to generate considerable suspicion on both sides. The response in recent decades to this situation, a response unique in Canada, has been to engage in *la concertation*:

> [*La concertation*] is not a formal structure of participation but depends instead on the willingness of various authorities to participate. . . . It aims . . . to align independent social action with policies being promoted by the state, and to coordinate the activities of autonomous community groups and public social support in the pursuit of those policies. . . . The auton-

omy and equal position of each group of organizational participants is ostensibly respected . . . . Consensus, often stated to be the ultimate objective of *la concertation*, is an elusive goal. (White, 1997: 32)

Thus confrontation and cooperation coexist in the same process of discussion. White (1997: 33) says the "Québec model" of *la concertation* is a unique blend of the Anglo-Saxon tradition of autonomous social groups in confrontation with the state and the Continental tradition of autonomous social groups working through the state.[1]

The process of *la concertation* has become even more conspicuous in the 1990s because of its role in the development of Québec's social economy (*l'économie sociale*), known these days in anglophone North America as the "third sector" or the "nonprofit sector." This is the world of not-for-profit, non-governmental organizations. These entities are formally independent of government, even though they may receive grants from it. They provide socially desirable services in a range of areas, including health, welfare, education, and recreation, as well as religion, human relationships, the arts, and community development. In an era of widespread economic upheaval caused by the far-reaching consequences of globalization and the rule of computer technology, the social economy has emerged as a major way of solving the many problems generated by these forces, among the most prominent being stress, boredom, overwork, and unemployment. The following remarks by Jean Panet-Raymond (1998: 3), Director of the École de service social de l'Université de Montréal, show why the Québec model of *la concertation* is important in this situation:

> While the Québec government historically has had a monopoly in the provision of welfare programs, it is now moving towards more reliance on the community sector, whose social mission must increasingly include an economic mission if it wishes to retain public financing. The community movement is oscillating between the hope that a "solidarity government" will act as a partner that is open to local initiatives, and the fear of being dictated to by a government that is itself facing economic constraints due to the imperatives of globalization.

The willingness to discuss issues, as developed earlier in labor relations, now has wider application. Furthermore, it distinguishes Québec's approach to these problems from the approaches favored by many of the other provinces: privatization of third sector services or retention of them but only to the extent that they will return a profit.

A portrait of the distinctive facets of the Québec economic and political scene would be seriously incomplete without a discussion of the *caisse populaire*, Québec's version of the credit union. Alphonse Desjardins established in 1900 the first of these organizations as a cooperative savings and loan company for the working class. His strategy, the implementation of which he had observed in Europe, was to encourage working men to save and plan for the future and to provide credit for them as they struggled to succeed financially. Desjardins's vision was that, through this mechanism, French-speaking Canadians might achieve a significant degree of economic independence. By 1920, the year Desjardins died, there were 206 *caisses populaires* in Québec, Ontario, and the francophone communities in New England (Roby, 1988: 314). Today over 1200 of these organizations are in operation under the umbrella of the Mouvement Desjardins. From the beginning they have had the strong and enthusiastic support of the Catholic clergy.

Education

As indicated earlier, the Catholic Church was largely responsible for education in New France and, later, in Québec. Throughout much of the history of denominational schooling there, the actual teaching was done by either the clergy themselves or the members of one or two religious orders. Lay teachers, who were almost always women, were uncommon and very poorly paid (Tétu de Labsade, 1988: 183-84).

After 1850 an educational administrative structure was put in place that would endure until the late 1960s, when the reforms recommended by the Parent Commission were implemented. This structure consisted of two systems, one public, one private. Responsibility for running the public system fell to two autonomous committees, one Catholic, the other Protestant. The Catholic public system, which provided free education, grew much more and much more quickly than the Protestant public system and was best developed at the primary level. The Catholic private system charged tuition and expanded mostly at the secondary level. It included the classical colleges, which were often seminaries as well, several industrial arts schools, and eventually a couple of universities. Université Laval in Québec City was the first of these. Later it opened a branch in Montréal, which subsequently became the Université de Montréal.

The inferior educational position in which francophone Québec found itself on the eve of the Quiet Revolution was an unwanted child of this administrative structure. Since most francophones in the province were relatively poor, few could afford schooling in the private system, while schooling in the public system was limited, for the most part, to primary education. Moreover, the Catholic Committee found little appeal in compulsory education; it was adopted 80 years after adoption by the Protestant Committee. Additionally, until the reforms of the 1960s, very little money was available for public schools and public schooling, even though the number of students in both languages grew rapidly after World War II (Fournier and Rosenberg, 1997: 124). Even the private Catholic system was deficient in certain ways; for example, women were first admitted to McGill University in Montréal in 1885, but were barred from francophone higher education until over 50 years later (Tétu de Labsade, 1988: 186).

Still, the Catholic public system did evolve somewhat, to the extent that a small number of students could obtain a secondary education and, if qualified, attend a teachers college, a technical school, or even a university, although here only in certain faculties. The public and private components of the Catholic System are compared in Table 3.1.

Table 3.1 Catholic System of Education in Québec (before Parent Commission)

Level	Public	Private
Elementary	7 years	7 years
Secondary	5 years (a classical option after 1945 in some places)	8 years (classical college diploma: BA)
Post-Secondary	2-3 years (teacher college) diploma: certificate	No equivalent
University	Accessible only in certain faculties	Entirely accessible

Source: adapted and translated from Tétu de Labsade (1990: 189)

The needed reorganization of education in Québec followed closely on the release in 1966 of the report of a royal commission headed by Mgr. Alphonse-Marie Parent. But even before this the Lesage government had established free schooling for all in the first eleven grades. Then, guided by the recommendations of the Parent Commission, the government undertook a set of changes of tremendous scope. They applied, in the main, to the Catholic system, both its public and its private components. First, the government established a ministry of education, signaling thus its intention to direct the educational interests of Quebeckers. Then, following North American convention, it cut primary education to six years, to which five more were added at the secondary level to equal 11 years of basic schooling. Third, the number of small primary and secondary schools was reduced by developing large, consolidated, multipurpose, regional schools.

Compared with education at this level elsewhere in Canada, creation of the CEGEPs, or *Collèges d'enseignement général et professionnel*, was the most radical of these reforms. All students graduating from grade 11 are now required to attend a CEGEP program at one of over 40 colleges spread across the province. Those in the three-year technical programs are prepared for immediate entry into the labor force, while those in the two-year program are trained to enter one of Québec's universities. Here, assuming a full-time program, they spend another three years earning a bachelor's degree. The goal of these changes, which are still in effect, was to make education much more widely available than heretofore.

University education was also revamped in accordance with the same ideal of increased availability. Thus, in 1968 the provincial government instituted the Université du Québec, the main constituents of which are located in Hull, Montréal, Abitibi, Chicoutimi, Rimouski, and Trois-Rivières. Before this, francophone Quebeckers had access to only three universities: Université Laval, Université de Montréal, and Université de Sherbrooke. The same legislation created the anglophone institution of Concordia University by amalgamating the Montréal colleges of Loyola and Sir George Williams. Students pay a modest tuition at the CEGEPs and the universities. Table 3.2 contains an outline of the Catholic system of education restructured according to the recommendations of the Parent Commission.

Table 3.2 Catholic system of Education in Québec, both public and private (after Parent Commission)

Level	Public and Private
Elementary	6 years
Secondary	5 years
CEGEP	2 years (to university) 3 years (to labor force)
University	3 years (BA) and beyond (MA, Ph.D.)

Source: adapted and translated from Tétu de Labsade (1990: 191)

Language

As every Québec demagogue knows, nothing in that province arouses emotion and stirs action like the question of the survival of the French language. And well it should, for mother-tongue francophones in North America, according to 1990 and 1991 American and Canadian census data, constitute a mere eight percent of the population of this continent, a serious under-representation even if, after English and Spanish, they are its third largest linguistic group (extracted from Louder, 1996: 413). Fortunately, over 25 percent of these 22 million francophones are concentrated on the peninsula of Québec where, even then, it has not always been easy to ensure survival of *la belle langue*. In 1996, 5 792 635 unilingual and multilingual mother-tongue francophones lived in Québec (Statistics Canada, 1998a). There they constituted 85.8 percent of the overall population, while most of the rest were second-language francophones whose mother tongue was English.

Seeing to the survival of French is a profound and never-ending challenge, even in Québec and even with its institutional completeness, in good measure because English-language radio and television are readily available, as is a great range of English books, magazines, and newspapers. Much of this material has widespread appeal; it is popular culture, an art at which Americans have excelled for most of the twentieth century and for which, in recent decades, the Franco-Québécois have shown a nearly unquenchable thirst. Television alone accounts for the partial French-English bilingualism of many a Quebecker. Of course, other conditions also threaten French in Québec; they include the dominance of English in the commercial world, the appeal of English language popular song among francophone youth (Pronovost, 1997: 162), and the desire of many francophones of all ages to take part in the broader scene in which they live, Canada, in particular, and North America, in general.

What is the nature of the French that Quebeckers are trying to protect? Québec French has several distinguishing properties. One, compared with French spoken around the world, that spoken in Québec has several distinctive accents. A popular display at the Musée de la civilisation in Québec City presents six accents (from Montréal, Québec City, Gaspésie, Gatineau, the Saguenay, and the Beauce), each with its own variants.[2] These accents owe their existence to the former insularity of the different regions of Québec; once the colonists from France settled in a region in North America, there was little interchange with colonists in the other regions.

Two, Québec French contains a number of archaic words as well as a number of local terms and expressions. The archaic words have survived because they are familiar, facilitate everyday communication, and the aforementioned isolation prevented adoption of alternatives. So certain archaisms have endured, at times long after they went out of vogue in francophone areas of the world more susceptible to change. The oft-heard locution *barrer la porte* is archaic because North Americans no longer bar doors, but lock them instead. Still, nothing is wrong linguistically with such a phrase, even if it is old and sounds strange to francophones from Europe or Asia, for example.

The same may be said for many local terms and expressions in Québec. They are often linguistically above reproach, even while having a foreign ring for francophones whose vocabulary does not include them. These terms and expressions arise to deal with local phenomena that lack a referent in the standard language. For instance, francophone Quebeckers invented the word *la poudrerie* to refer to a blizzard (related to *le poudre*, or powder), a climatic condition unknown in France, which for this reason alone invariably provoked a great deal of concern and discussion among the *Canadiens*.

Three, Québec French, as employed by the typical speaker, contains a sizeable number of anglicisms: French words and expressions borrowed from English. This practice is inevitable given the pervasiveness of English in everyday life in Québec society, not to mention its even greater pervasiveness in the lives of francophones in the parity and minority societies outside Québec. Moreover, in both the present and the past, the two languages have intermingled in commerce, politics, popular culture, and the work place. But given the dominance of English on this continent, the anglicism is much more problematic in North American French than in, say, European French and, for that matter, much more problematic than the gallicism is in Québec English.

Some anglicisms are obvious, as when a woman announces her intention to *canceller* a subscription to a magazine or, while in the hotel, her desire to speak with *le bell-boy*. Other anglicisms are subtle, however, and therefore far more threatening to the logic and integrity of French, because they masquerade as indigenous elements of the language. When Quebeckers say *je mets l'emphase sur quelque chose*, they mean they are accenting something. The problem is that the French noun *l'emphase*, though its spelling is similar to the English noun "emphasis," nevertheless has a very different meaning. It refers to pomposity, or bombast.

While living in Québec City one summer, I went to a service station to have the tires rotated on my car. As a second-language francophone, I had not yet had to deal with this procedure in French, but now had to try to communicate what I wanted done. I knew that in French the noun *la rotation* means something is rotating, as I rotate the steering wheel when turning a corner, and that I was in no need of having my tires rotated in this sense. After several minutes of linguistic sparring, I said in exasperation, in French, that I would like to have my tires rotated, realizing at that very moment that I was committing an anglicism. But *voilà*, I had communicated; the *mécanicien* knew precisely what I wanted, and duly rotated the tires. When I read the bill later that day, the computer print-out, designed and worded in Shell Canada's home office, said that the tires on my car had received a *permutation*, a changing of the positions of the tires. Perfectly good French and, I should like to add, perfectly good English, too, except that the illogical usages of "rotate" and "rotation" have become so entrenched in the latter that asking anglophone service station personnel to permute your tires would most likely bring a blank stare and a request for clarification.

Four, contact with anglophones in areas of life where Québec francophones have had little experience is especially fertile breeding ground for anglicisms. Work was one such place during the first half of the twentieth century, when rural Québécois moved to the cities in search of employment in manufacturing. Here the "boss" usually spoke English, using that language to refer to objects and procedures the migrants had scant familiarity with. As a result, over the years, a unique oral language emerged within the otherwise linguistically sound French of these workers, that was nevertheless peppered with English terms and expressions. During the 1960s it came to be known in certain intellectual circles in Québec by the derisive term of *le joual* (Bergeron, 1980; Bélisle, 1969), it being especially prominent in Montréal, the great industrial city of Québec. *Le joual* is a form of colloquial French, more particularly a form of *l'argot*, or slang (Smith, 1990: 49-50). Since nearly everyone occasionally uses slang, whatever the language, *le joual* is still heard on the street in Québec, in certain spoken forms of popular culture, and in those social circles where slang is the main way or the only way of communicating verbally. It is, however, considerably less prominent today than formerly.

Given the precarious situation of French in overwhelmingly anglophone North America and the fear of many francophones that the language will disappear there unless protective measures are found, it was only a matter of time before legislation designed to deal with the problem began to appear. Motivated by a multitude of conditions – e.g., decline in the birth rate to well below replacement level (a crude rate of 1.4 births per 100 000 people in 1998), threat of continued incursions of English, poor quality French in the general population – Québec governments in the post-Duplessis era began to act. In 1961, the Lesage regime established l'Office de la language française to look after the quality of the language. Various governments from then to 1976 toyed with and sometimes passed legislation favoring the use of French in one way or another, including Bill 22, passed in 1974. It established French as Québec's official language.

It remained, however, for the Lévesque administration and the Parti Québécois to give birth in 1977 to the celebrated Bill 101, the Charter of the French Language (*la Chartre de la langue française*). With this act, French became the official language of work, commerce, and teaching as well as legislation, administration, and communications. Moreover, the Charter included legislation for setting up a body – le Conseil de la langue française – whose mission was to ensure that French is routinely used in these areas. The Charter turned out to be unconstitutional in certain ways and so had to be modified in places, but its basic principles remain in force to this day. In 1989, using the notwithstanding clause to circumvent a Supreme Court ruling, Robert Bourassa's Liberal government passed Bill 178, the contentious sign law. It regulates public signs for all commercial enterprises with 50 employees or less, requiring that any such sign must be totally in French, or if it also contains English, the English portion must be presented in letters of no larger than half the size of the letters in the French portion.

These laws have the support of the majority of francophone Quebeckers, who feel they must create a dominantly French environment in their society if it is to persist linguistically, even while some observers remain unconvinced of the necessity (e.g., Guindon, 1988: 169-70; Dion, 1987: 64). Few francophone Quebeckers, however, quarrel with the assumption that the French language itself is vital to the survival of Québec as a francophone community. As Léon Dion (quoted in Tétu de Labsade, 1989: 106) observed: "The French language has been above all the principal integrating force in Québec society. To renounce this principle would be to undermine the very foundation of that society in its secular form" (translation). And today, formal French in Québec has evolved into a grammatically and linguistically correct form all of its own, referred to by some as "standard Québec French" (*le français québécois standard*), which is neither the French of France nor that of any other country or district, but rather a genre of French adapted to the demands and realities of life in North America. Say Martel and Cajolet-Laganière (1995), standard Québec French warrants its own dictionary, albeit one that would exclude *le joual* and other forms of familiar, or popular, French.

Culture

The Quiet Revolution consisted as much of vast cultural changes as it did of changes in politics, education, language, and the economy. Before 1960 folk and rural traditions dominated the cultural scene, which was a principal reason for establishing in 1961 the Ministry of Cultural Affairs. This unit would help organize the fine and popular arts, and where justified, financially aid them. As a result, Québec has since excelled in a number of cultural areas, all centered in Montréal, the acknowledged cultural capital of the province and, in certain areas, all of Canada.

One of these areas is film, where according to Tétu de Labsade (1988: 379), Québec is especially strong in comparison with the other Canadian provinces. For example, she notes that, in 1981, two-thirds of the Genie awards went to artists in Québec's film industry. Véronneau (1988: 768) writes that Québec French-language film was supported in its infancy by the National Film Board, when the latter moved from Ottawa to Montréal in 1956 and began to attract a number of talented filmmakers from that area. Two of them, Gilles Groulx and Claude Jutra, produced in 1958 *Les Racquetteurs*, a documentary that helped give expression to the emerging nationalist aspirations of francophone Quebeckers. Jutra went on to make *Mon Oncle Antoine* (1971), said by Véronneau to be "one of the finest Québec films every made." It was Pierre Perrault, however, who dominated documentary film making during the 1960s, with many of his productions also being based on nationalist themes.

Now a Québec specialty, the documentary film movement (*le cinéma direct*) lost some ground in the early and mid-1970s, partly because it was surpassed at that time by an interest in fictional film, with *Mon Oncle Antoine* as its most renowned exemplar. But the late 1970s and early 1980s saw renewed enthusiasm for the documentary, which has retained its supremacy ever since. Perrault directed two major film cycles, one on Abitibi, the other on the Montagnais-Naskapi, while other documentarists concentrated on subjects in ethnology, nationalism, and popular culture. Several female filmmakers received acclaim for documentaries made during these years, including Anne-Claire Poirier's *Mourir à tue-tête*, an analysis of rape, and Iolande Cadrin-Rossignol's *Laure Gaudreault*, a film about a courageous schoolteacher in difficult times.

Tétu de Labsade (1988: 390) notes that notwithstanding its superiority in the documentary field, Québec is actually best known internationally for its animated films. Working primarily during the 1960s and 1970s, Norman McLaren became Québec's (and Canada's) most renowned director of animated film. He became widely respected for his pioneering techniques in animation. Frédéric Back also enjoys a world reputation, primarily for his short film *Crac!*, a fetching, animated history of francophone Québec, and *L'homme qui plantait des arbres*, an illustration of a text written by Jean Giono. Both won Oscars (1982 and 1988). Back creates his animations by drawing on translucent transparencies with wax crayons.

Montréal, with its 200 commercial cinemas, has become a world showcase for American and European films (Latouche, 1988: 1800). Founded in 1972, the annual Festival des Films du Monde (Montréal World Film Festival) is a widely-acclaimed exhibition of new films produced in every corner of the globe. Additionally, Latouche writes that in Montréal "as many as 30 full-length features of various types are produced locally each year."

Starting in the 1960s, Montréal has also gained a reputation for making exceptional contributions to dance, particularly to the field of modern dance, where several public and private schools train performers. It is also the home of Les Ballets Jazz de Montréal, which was founded in 1972 and has since performed in 40 countries (Bishop, 1988: 168) and La La La Human Steps, an experimental group established in the late 1970s by Eduoard Lock. The annual *Festival International de Nouvelle Danse* was first held in 1987; it has greatly enhanced Montréal's image as a world center for modern dance.

Notwithstanding the previously-mentioned appeal of English-language songs, songs sung in French have a special place in Québec, in considerable part because they constitute an important basis for cultural identity and a powerful vehicle for expressing themes unique to francophone life in that province (Bélanger, 1996-97). A renowned *chansonnier* first in Québec and then in France as well, Félix Leclerc (1914-1988) wrote and sang his own material, making use of such themes as love, humor, and nature in ways that endeared him to French-speaking people in Canada and abroad. He, Jean-Pierre Ferland, Clémence Desrochers, and others formed a group called "Les Bozos," who entertained in Montréal cabarets around the time of the Quiet Revolution. Gilles Vigneault, who joined Les Bozos in the 1960s, became in the 1970s and 1980s in both song and speech an articulate spokesperson for the French language and the nationalist cause. Earlier, however, he worked with others in the group in the popular *boîtes à chansons*, evening nightclub programs featuring these singers as individual entertainers. Somewhat later, Robert Charlebois would sing to Quebeckers using witty French lyrics conveyed in tunes carried along by the rhythm of American popular song. The distinctiveness of Québec popular song and singing is still evident in the late 1990s, finding its most notable expression at this time in the interpretations of world-famous performer Céline Dion.

Tétu de Labsade (1988: 337-38) explains the capacity of Québec popular song to bring together francophone Quebeckers. Sometimes this is achieved by describing in lyrics an aspect of the natural environment in Québec or a well-known place there. Alternatively, some songs draw people together by treating familiar sentiments such as love, friendship, or tenderness. Still other songs relate to the common tendency among French Quebeckers to react with humor and *la joie de vivre* to problems and awkward situations, not in the least their status as a linguistic minority in Canada and North America.

Québec has also excelled in several other popular arts, one of which is the circus. Montréal is home to one of the very few North American circus schools, the École Nationale de Cirque, some of whose graduates find work in either the Cirque du Soleil or the Cirque Éloize, both based in Montréal. The first, a world-renowned one-ring circus, was founded in 1984 with an emphasis, not on animals, but on clowning, acrobatics, and imaginative theatricality. Students of the circus school occasionally work as buskers in the streets of Montréal and Québec, where they acquire additional performing experience while providing onlookers with some unusual entertainment. Although neither Montréal nor Québec can be described as Canadian centers of jazz, the summer *Festival International de jazz de Montréal* nevertheless now ranks as one of the world's five largest festivals of this art. More than 350 indoor and outdoor shows are presented during this ten-day event.

No tour of the prominent cultural features of Québec would be complete without examining its comedic tradition, arguably the most distinctive field of theatre in the province (unless it is circus). Elsewhere (Stebbins, 1990: 27-29), I describe the rise of Québec stand-up comedy, a unique art form that evolved, in part, from a blend of three other arts – those of the monologist, the impressionist, and the mime – that began in eighteenth century Europe and continued in Québec during its lengthy period of social, political, and cultural isolation from France and anglophone North America ushered in by the Treaty of Paris. Among the unique aspects of Québec stand-up comedy are the inclination of many performers to develop one or more *personnages*, build acts around them, and dress in costume to present them. The *personnages* are not impersonated real persons as in the imitations of André Philippe Gagnon; rather they are fictional, albeit richly stereotyped characters. Popular examples in the past have included Marc Favreau as a tramp, Yvon Deschamps as Ti-Blanc Le Brun, a rustic Québécois of yesteryear, and Claire Jean as a bride.

Since this kind of stand-up comedy differs dramatically from the kind performed in English in Canada and the United States and since the French version of the art is not typically presented in comedy clubs, special arrangements have emerged so that it can be observed publicly.[3] The most prominent of these is the *Festival Juste pour Rire* (held mainly out of doors and in the theaters along

Montréal's rue Saint-Denis), the first and possibly still the only festival in the world devoted purely to stand-up comedy and related arts. It was conducted entirely in French from 1983 through 1985, after which, when language is used, it has been constituted of a mix of French and English routines. Although performers from French Québec always occupy a prominent place in this event, a great variety of French and English acts are also presented by artists from several other countries. Most of the Québec artists in this Festival are trained in the province's École nationale de l'humour. And after performing in the *Festival*, many join touring groups under the banner of *La tournée juste pour rire*, a circuit that enables them to present shows in local theaters across the province, in New Brunswick, and in other francophone communities across Canada. Individual comedy stars such as Yvon Deschamps, Marc Favreau, and Clémence Desrochers also tour, presenting concerts in the theaters and better nightclubs. Montréal's reputation as a world capital of comedy was further enhanced with the opening in 1996 of the Musée Juste Pour Rire, the only international museum devoted to humor.

Even if Montréal is the uncontested center of Québec's approximately 350 festivals (the city's tourist office promotes it as the "City of Festivals," Lavallée and Lafond, 1998), Québec City, it should be noted, does organize two very prominent events of its own that, for years, have served as major attractions for francophones throughout the province. The Québec Winter Carnival is Québec's and Canada's most famous winter festival; it was launched in 1894, died six years later, and was revived in the 1950s. Its talking snowman, mascot *Bonhomme Carnaval*, is now as emblematic of Québec City as the Citadelle, the Hôtel Château Frontenac, and the old city wall. The other event is the *Festival d'été*, held annually for ten days in early July. It features, among other things, indoor and outdoor concerts in the fine and popular arts, street performances in the variety arts, and widely-diversified displays of Québec foods and crafts. But not to be outdone in this regard, Montréal now holds each summer its own popular culture equivalent called *Les FrancoFolies de Montréal*.

Turning next to painting, François-Marc Gagnon (1988: 123) observes of Canadian art that "in many respects the Canadian experience in art may seem to parallel the American one, but the French influence, completely lacking in the US, is too overwhelming in Canadian art not to maintain an essential distinction between the art forms of the two countries." James Wilson Morrice, a Montrealer who studied with individual masters in Paris, is considered the father of Canadian modernism, which began around 1900. Ozias Leduc belonged to the same school, but also chose to express himself at times in still-life and landscape paintings inspired by the Saint-Hilaire region. Leduc thus joined certain other Québécois painters, among them Clarence Gagnon and Aurèle de Foy Suzor-Côté, to produce a truly distinctive regional art with which Quebeckers could easily identify, a style centered on the land, the people, and the traditional ways of life. Upon his return from Paris in 1940, Alfred Pellan brought to Canada the influences of cubism (particularly Picasso). A few years later Québec art took a political turn, when Paul-Émile Borduas organized a group of younger painters (*Les Automatistes*), including Jean-Paul Riopelle and Fernand Leduc, who in 1948 signed a manifesto known as *Le Refus Global*. The document challenged traditional Québec values, while refusing with anarchistic reasoning any ideology that cramped creative spontaneity. Gagnon (1988: 122) indicates that, after this liberation, several successive movements occurred in which painting tended to be more "theoretically defined" than in the other provinces. Such a climate must surely have contributed to the rise in the 1960s of the Fusion school in Montréal, known for its loose groupings of artists who produced works made up of combinations of different media (e.g., film, dance, music, poetry). Many other groups and schools have since sprung up, again chiefly in Montréal.

Gagnon says that part of the strength of Canadian art, both French and English, is that painters in Canada have not isolated themselves from influences originating in other countries, even if they have been freed by distance from the weight of tradition in those countries. In this respect, art in Québec benefited enormously from the easy contact with art in France.

Architecture is the final cultural form covered in this chapter. Some of what is distinctive about this art in Québec stands in the countryside and small towns. Here, within the framework of the built environment, Québec society finds unique expression in the ubiquitous, charming *maison Québécoise* (Québec-style house). It is one or two floors high and fitted with a combined roof and overhang that resembles a ski jump covering a porch, or *galerie*, running the length of the building at the front. Many of these dwellings have claimed the attic as supplementary living space, which usually involves installing dormer windows (*lucarnes*) in the roof, both front and back. Additionally, at the center of the typical francophone village or the center of each parish in the cities, stands the parish church. Almost always an imposing edifice, many are distinguished by two great towers at each end of the transept. Convents and presbyteries also abound throughout French Québec (though most no longer serve their original purposes), many being identifiable by their mansard roofs.

In addition, both Montréal and Québec City have their heritage sections where these communities first began. Many interesting and well-preserved specimens of urban commercial and residential colonial architecture are available here, with the collection in Québec City being the more spectacular, and for this reason and the reason of its central role in Québec history, possibly the one more likely to be frequented by vacationing Quebeckers and other tourists. Otherwise, urban architecture in Québec, although frequently interesting and imaginative, is nevertheless unexceptional given what is found in other large Canadian cities. Still, many a Montrealer, were he or she to move out of town, would feel the absence of the omnipresent Montréal staircase that links the sidewalk and second floor of many of its six-unit apartment buildings. Viewed as a set, these staircases give the residential street where they are found a special visual effect, not unlike being in a vast trough.

Conclusion

The main goal in this chapter has been to describe a number of the distinctive geographic, political, economic, educational, linguistic, and cultural features of Québec society. Yet, because space is limited, it has been impossible to consider in this survey all that is distinct about this society. Nonetheless, the contents of this chapter should suffice to put into concrete terms politicians' often glib qualifications of Québec as "distinct" or "unique." Its contents also show what francophone Quebeckers are struggling to preserve, and that language is an important, but not the only important, consideration in their lives. But if it is not the only important consideration, it is certainly the first important one. For without French as the language of everyday life, much of the rest that was covered in this chapter loses its significance as something distinct, something ineluctably Québécois. This, then, is the justification for opening the next chapter on issues in Québec society with the language question.

Chapter 4
Contemporary Issues in Québec Society

If maintenance of the French language is a critical issue in Québec, it is not, however, an isolated matter. It is intimately linked to the province's low birth rate and its rates of francophone immigration and emigration. It is a major force behind the quest for sovereignty-association and Québec's relationship with the rest of Canada. It is further tied to the question of sufficiency of economic independence and, of course, to that of identity. These issues are considered in this chapter in the order just presented.

Language

In the final analysis, Guindon and Dion (referred to in the preceding chapter) are right: French will not survive in Québec if its francophones prefer another language. For in a free country, no amount of legislative persuasion can alter the fundamental sociological principle on which their observation stands, a principle first put forward by Emile Durkheim (1951: 372): "when the law forbids acts which the public considers inoffensive, we are indignant with the law, not with the act it punishes." As Guindon (1988: 169) notes:

> Nothing is more effective as a language "cop" than the unilingual citizen who feels at home, and who refuses both to speak a language other than his own and to be addressed in a language other than his own. The unilingual person is the most political of individuals when it comes to language enforcement, the most adamant and unyielding, and yet that person need not be politically conscious. Becoming unilingual is a sign of full membership, if not for the immigrant who is "transitionally" bilingual, then for his offspring who will achieve unilingualism.

In the 1970s many francophones in Montréal, one of the few communities in Québec where they have routinely had the opportunity to learn English and use it, did in fact reject that language.

But now, at the dawn of the twentieth-first century, the linguistic scene in Montréal and most of the rest of Québec is far more complicated than ever before. Today, across the world, many people feel they must learn English if they are to succeed in certain walks of life, most notably commerce, science, tourism, and international politics. English itself has become global (*The Economist*, 1999: 85). In this respect, many Quebecers are no different from many other people the world over. Moreover, people who want to learn a complex modern language to the point where it will be truly useful in the aforementioned areas have their work cut out for them. They must build vocabulary, perfect accents, familiarize themselves with the main idioms, and master an involved linguistic structure. These goals cannot be realized without a great deal of reasonably regular practice in the language to be learned.

In other words, although a sign law and similar legislation may not be absolutely necessary, it is also now clear that many modern francophones will not always try to protect the French language using the alternative approach suggested by Guindon. Today, a significant number of French-speaking Quebeckers, as they go about their daily lives, are going to want to, indeed are going to have to, "practice their English." And evidently, a number of them have been doing exactly that, for in 1994, approximately 32 percent of francophone Quebeckers were bilingual in French and English (Commissioner of Official Languages, 1994: 10). Bilingualism is defined here as in the Census of Canada as the ability to hold in both languages a conversation of some length on a variety of subjects. The same source reports that nearly half the labor force in Québec is bilingual. Given these facts, it perhaps no surprise that Premier Bouchard, as leader of the incumbent Parti Québécois, recently described Québec to a group of American business people meeting in Philadelphia as "the most bilingual region in North America, an asset we intend to take full advantage of" (*Calgary Herald*, 1998a).

The principal threat of bilingualism, its critics argue, is that it leads much too often to assimilation to the second language and its culture. Indeed, it will become evident later that assimilation of this kind does take place, but also that it is by no means an inevitable outcome of learning a second language. One of the most celebrated disadvantages of bilingualism, at least from the standpoint of social science, is the possible or real loss of a person's capacity to speak his or her mother tongue, a condition that Lambert (1975: 67-68) has dubbed "subtractive bilingualism." This term describes the linguistic situation of language minorities who, in the course of learning the tongue of the majority group, gradually lose their ability to speak their own tongue. In other words they develop extensive faults in grammar, syntax, spelling, vocabulary, pronunciation, and related areas of speech.

But French-English bilingualism for mother-tongue franco-phones in Québec is like that of many second-language franco-phones living in Canada's minority societies; it is an "additive bilingualism," wherein the second language is learned with little or no loss to the mother tongue. The additive form develops as a person learns a second language while participating in the social world of the linguistic majority as a first-language member (speaking French in the francophone majority societies, speaking English in the francophone minority societies). The learner nonetheless values and respects both languages and the settings in which each is used. Additive bilingualism does not lead to significant assimilation, whereas the subtractive variety does.

Census data indicate that additive bilingualism is growing in Québec, since its proportion of francophones has been either increasing or holding steady since 1971 (Langlois, 1998: 15). Nevertheless, it can be argued that measures requiring use of French on all public and commercial signs and in all schools and public installations, help maintain the dominance of francophone culture in Québec. In doing so, they also help ensure that bilingualism there will never be other than additive.

When they are not worrying about bilingualism, guardians of the French language in Québec worry about its quality. Yves Berger (Therrien, 1997), writer, literary director of Éditions Grasset, and member of the Conseil supérieur de la langue française, says French is suffering terribly from a case of anglicisms, bad spelling, misuse of foreign words, grammatically incorrect syntax, and other debilitating weaknesses that, if not cured soon, could be its death. Something must be done to restore it to reasonable health, not only in Québec but also in France where, Berger says, the language is in possibly even worse shape. He does not, however, prescribe any remedial measures for the linguistic maladies he has diagnosed.

Birth Rate and Immigration

Although Québec's population of francophones and its numerical superiority over the speakers of all other languages are more than enough to sustain French dominance at present, many francophone Quebeckers worry that their ever-declining birth rate, already well below replacement, will eventually eclipse francophone presence in the province. Their birth rate slipped below replacement between 1970 and 1975 (see Table 4.1) and, with the exception of a small, temporary rise in the late 1980s, has continued its decline through the 1990s.

Table 4.1 Birth rates in Québec 1965-1996

Year	Number of Births	Average Rate per Woman
1965	123 279	3.07
1970	96 512	2.09
1975	96 268	1.75
1980	97 498	1.62
1985	86 008	1.39
1990	98 013	1.63
1995	87 258	1.58
1996	85 298	1.57

Source: Langlois (1998: 9).

Québec has one of the lowest birth rates in the Western world.

Immigration, which is guided by policies set in the Department of Immigration, a unit of the Québec government established in 1968 in the spirit of the Quiet Revolution, is seen as one way to compensate for the contemporary Quebecker's low enthusiasm for having children. In this respect, in 1978, the federal government granted Québec the power to select its own candidates from among those intending to immigrate to the province. And in 1991 an agreement between the two levels of government enabled Québec to receive financial compensation for the reception and integration of immigrants into Québec society as well as up to 30 percent of the total immigrant flow to Canada. In fact, apart from a constitutional guarantee that these arrangements will forever be in force, Québec now has all the power it can obtain to control as it sees fit immigration to the province.

The big challenge now is to establish a consensus on how this might best be done, how to arrive at the optimum number and mix of immigrants to be admitted. In principle, at least, new francophones are most welcome these days, but since most contemporary migrants come from Third World countries, their presence in Québec raises serious questions about how to integrate them into that society and its First World culture. This goal of integration is complicated by the fact that, in 1996, only 39 percent of Québec's immigrants spoke French compared with 33 percent who spoke English (Langlois, 1998: 18). Whatever their language, these newcomers are often racially, culturally, religiously, and even linguistically different from *"pure laine"* francophone Quebeckers. Moreover, as Black and Hagen (1993: 294) point out, there has been an "aggressive courting of immigrant investors," a practice started by the Parti Québécois when it was in power and continued subsequently by the Liberals. Neither compatibility of language nor that of culture has been of much concern in these cases. Nevertheless, Anctil (1996: 151-152) believes that today "francophone Québec has become in a very short time and for the first time in its modern history, a society open to streams of migration of world-wide diversity that therefore reflect religious, cultural, and linguistic realities hitherto unknown in this country" (translation).

There is furthermore the twin problem of retaining the immigrants who do come to the province as well as the Quebeckers who yearn to move from it. In 1996, for example, 28 577 immigrants chose Québec, but after counting all emigrants from Québec to foreign lands (whether immigrants returning home or Quebeckers leaving for another country), the province had a net gain through international migration of only 18 778 people. That same year it suffered a net loss to the other provinces of 15 154 people, some being immigrants, some being Quebeckers, with Ontario, British Columbia, and Alberta as their main destinations. Thus, in 1996 Québec had a net population increase through population movement of only 3624 people (Langlois, 1998: 12). Net population increase was substantially higher, however, at other times during the 1990s: 30 165 (1993), 5401 (1994), and 16 182 (1995).

Québec's population has nonetheless been rising over the years, from 5 259 211 in 1961 to 7 407 700 in 1997 (Langlois, 1998: 4). Given a rate of birth far below replacement, immigration has been by and large the main force driving population increases and softening the decreases. But this has come at a cost. In much of the First World there is concern about the obtrusive foreignness of recent Third-World immigrants (earlier immigrants become progressively more familiar), and it is no different in Québec. Here, too, clashes of cultures have occurred, and the ethnic population helped the "no" side eke out its narrow victory in the 1995 Referendum, suggesting that the slogan of the 1960s *maître chez nous* may be becoming effete. It is also well-established that most immigrants to Québec want to learn English, and that to reach this goal some migrate to other provinces or to the United States. This opportunism is resented by many Franco-Quebeckers.

Sovereignty-Association

Sovereignty-association was defined in the preceding chapter. Although an invention of René Lévesques' Parti Québécois when confronted with the fact that full independence, or separation, was politically unpopular even with many francophone Quebeckers, the idea has since been embraced with equal enthusiasm by the provincial Liberals. At bottom, it has two broad dimensions, one political, one economic.

The political dimension revolves around constitutional concerns. Were Québec to remain part of Canada, both political parties would insist on a major overhaul of the structure and principles by which Canadian federalism has been operating since 1867. This "renewed federalism" has so far been opposed by the provinces and the federal government, although they have softened their positions somewhat since the late 1970s when sovereignty-association was first proposed. Ottawa's initial reaction, however, under Prime Minister Trudeau, was to repatriate the Constitution from Britain, a project that ignored Québec's concerns.

And what are those concerns? In 1985, in an atmosphere of improved relations between the Parti Québécois and the new federal Conservative government, the former submitted a statement containing 22 conditions for Québec's agreement to a constitutional accord. These included:

- Recognition in the constitution of Québec as a distinct society
- Limitation of the application of the Charter of Rights and Freedoms in Québec to democratic rights
- Recognition of Québec's control over employment
- Recognition of Québec's control over its economic and regional development
- Guarantee that Québec has the constitutional right to veto, including the establishing of new provinces and the reform of certain national institutions

⚔ Granting of increased power in the field of communications

⚔ Sole authority over the selection and settlement of immigrants

⚔ Special role and status in international relations

A considerably scaled-down and therefore heavily criticized version of this list prepared by the Québec Liberal Party, which regained power late in 1985, did manage to get enshrined in the Meech Lake Accord drawn up in June, 1987. All provinces but Manitoba ratified the Accord by the deadline of 23 June 1990, which was nonetheless insufficient and it became null and void.[1] Once again Québec found itself marginalized from Canada and the other provinces.

Lachappelle et al. (1993: 49) note that a number of polls taken after the Meech Lake failure consistently indicated that close to two-thirds of Quebeckers supported the principles of sovereignty-association. Given the mood of the public, then, Liberal Leader and premier Robert Bourassa could hardly ignore the sovereigntist position, especially when the Bloc Québécois was formed in 1990. In the 1993 federal election, this new federal party took nearly all the seats in Québec having a high proportion of francophones. The Bloc's platform has been that sovereignty is the only workable alternative for Québec. Bourassa tried to strike a compromise between that position and unalloyed federalism (Québec as just another province, *une province comme les autres*), by accepting the recommendations of the Bélanger-Campeau Commission calling for a renewed federalism, a new relationship between Québec and the rest of Canada. The National Assembly (Québec's provincial government) endorsed the Commission's deadline of October 1992, by which satisfactory changes had to be made or there would be another Québec referendum on the question of sovereignty.

In July of 1992 leaders of the provinces and the federal government huddled in Prince Edward Island to try to frame an agreement that would satisfy all parties. The outcome of these deliberations was the Charlottetown Accord, described by Louis Balthazar (1997: 55-56) as "the result [of] a series of hasty discussions leading to vague and irrational compromises mixed with a few good proposals like the recognition of self-determination for the aboriginal populations." Perhaps predictably, the Accord failed to get the support of Canadians in a federal referendum held in October of 1992. Once again Québec was left out in the cold and the stage set for the return to power of the Parti Québécois in the provincial election of September 1994.

The new government, under its leader Jacques Parizeau, moved quickly to organize for 1995 a provincial referendum on sovereignty, for the time seemed ripe for success. One early sign of this was the dramatic change in the political landscape of the House of Commons after the 1993 election. The Progressive Conservative Party, in part because it became associated with former prime minister Brian Mulroney and the failed accords, was virtually wiped out. The federalist Liberals under Jean Chrétien won a majority, while the opposition was broken up along regional lines, between the western-based Reform Party and the separatist Bloc Québécois, who formed the Official Opposition. In preparation for the referendum, Parizeau's government drafted legislation and held a series of public consultations. The referendum, originally scheduled for spring, 1995, was delayed until 30 October of that year. It was then held on the following question: "Do you agree that Québec should become sovereign, after having made a formal offer to Canada for a new economic and political partnership, within the scope of the Bill respecting the future of Québec and of the agreement signed on 12 June 1995?"

The Bill in question was Bill 1, known as the Act respecting the future of Québec; it included a declaration of sovereignty in its preamble. Furthermore, an agreement was struck on 12 June 1995 between the Parti Québécois and the Action Démocratique du Québec, a new provincial political party advocating confederation with the rest of Canada. This agreement, centered on the sovereignty proposal, stated that, following a referendum victory on the question in the preceding paragraph, Québec would proceed with a formal offer of partnership with the rest of Canada.

At the beginning of the referendum campaign, the so-called "No" side, which opposed separation, enjoyed a substantial lead in the polls. But as the campaign progressed the "Yes" side gained momentum, particularly after assumption of its leadership by Lucien Bouchard, who had taken over for Parizeau a mere three weeks before the voting date. In the end, after an emotional and somewhat controversial campaign (e.g., there were complaints that the referendum question was vague), the "No" side won a narrow majority of 50.56 percent of the vote.[2] Throughout all this, political expediency ruled the day in the Parti Québécois, for it was promoting partnership with Canada by way of its version of sovereignty, crafted in response to an electorate that clearly rejected complete separation, or independence. The "No" side was comprised of federalists, who wanted to remain fully a part of Canada, but with options for negotiation on matters of concern to Québec, particularly the previously mentioned 22 conditions.

Since this event some steps have been taken outside Québec to try to meet some of those conditions. Shortly after the 1995 Referendum, the House of Commons passed a motion recognizing Québec as a distinct society and granting to the large provinces veto power on future constitutional change. There is even talk about a general devolution of authority from Federal to provincial levels and about the possibility of incorporating a distinct society clause in the Constitution. The Calgary declaration of September 1997, stating that Québec is a "unique society," is another sign of compromise.

Still, none of these measures has teeth; a federal government or influential coalition of provincial governments hostile to Québec's interests could ignore them all. So, although the political climate at century's end is moderately propitious with respect to those interests, Québec still has no choice but to continue to talk sovereignty because it still has no constitutional guarantees protecting its French language and culture as expressed in the 22 conditions. As many observers have argued of late, constitutional change is the only way to break the deadlock (e.g., O'Neil, 1997; Resnick, 1991). Even former Prime Minister Trudeau, who tried to stem the tide of Québec separatism with his bilingual programs, has recently been discovered to have been of the opinion as early as 1977 that only a decentralized federal system would work to keep Québec in the fold (Aubry, 1998).

In the meantime, manoeuvres such as the federal government's decision to ask the Supreme Court to rule on whether Québec can legitimately separate from Canada, are unlikely to enhance conciliation. The Court did decide on 20 August 1998 that Québec has no right under the Constitution to secede unilaterally. The federal government and provinces do, however, have a duty to negotiate secession if a majority of Quebeckers support separation in a referendum. Apropos of this judgement, CROP polls taken in Québec in its wake revealed that 58 to 60 percent of those polled view a majority of 50 percent plus one person as too small a plurality to justify starting separation procedures (*Calgary Herald*, 1998b: A3; 1999: A6).

Economic Independence

As affirmed in chapter 2, Québec is already reasonably independent economically. What remains to be described is how closely aligned nationalism and economic success have become in that province. Lachapelle and his colleagues (1993: 64) explain this relationship:

> Quebecers have realized the limitations of efforts to satisfy their individual material wants through the use of the State and cultural affirmation. To be master in your own home is not especially satisfying if your house is a small one. The international market was far bigger and far more attractive than what the domestic market had to offer. As well as providing even greater space for French-speaking Quebecers to enhance their own material interests, an international outlook would enhance their own culture. Québec's nationalism is now more than ever rooted in a deep-seated will to economic success.

Consistent with this change in economic orientation is the exceptionally warm welcome Québec gave to the North American Free Trade Agreement, vis-à-vis the reactions of the other provinces. American trade and private investment are defined in Québec as especially desirable, so understandably, every political party there worries about America's views of Québec's possible separation. Although the *péquistes* (followers of the Parti Québécois) have been guided over the years by somewhat more socialistic policies than the liberals, both camps have firmly embraced the merits of individual initiative and private enterprise at all levels of life: local, provincial, regional, federal, and international.

Québec also represents itself abroad through strategically-placed offices established to disseminate information about trade, culture, tourism, and education. Their numbers have been severely reduced, however, as part of the government's battle with its deficit. It operates only six offices today, whereas in 1991 it operated 30 offices in 20 countries on four continents (*Financial Post*, 1991). In the Government of Québec, these offices and other international matters fall within the jurisdiction of a separate ministry, the Ministère des relations internationales, a unique department in Canadian provincial government.

The stress on individual initiative and private enterprise harmonize well with the neo-conservative ethic prevailing nowadays in Québec and in all the other Canadian provinces and industrialized countries of the world. Everywhere the public sector has reached its limits and is undergoing reductions in size. Like other governments, the ones in Québec lack the resources to provide many of the services they once did. Still, as noted in the preceding chapter, solutions to this problem, such as privatizing these services and trying to make them profitable, have generated noticeably less interest in Québec than elsewhere in Canada.

Where does all this change leave the French language? Many francophone Quebeckers believe that it is absolutely essential to the survival of their culture (Lachapelle et al., 1993: 68), even as they are being bombarded these days by English film, radio, television, and various printed media. Given the love many Franco-Quebeckers have for *les affaires*, for doing business, and the fact that the world over business is being conducted more and more in English, it is reasonable to ask if French will survive, even in Québec. My conclusion, which is founded on my assessment of the chances of French surviving in the minority societies (see chapters 6 through 12), is that it will survive in Québec and do so very well. As in the past, additive bilingualism will continue to grow, favoring the English side of the linguistic equation and equipping the speaker with a vocabulary that enables him or her to "do business" or science or tourism, whatever his or her work and leisure interests. And it is entirely possible that some mother-tongue francophones in Québec will reach a point where, because they work exclusively in English, they become unable to do so in French, even though they lead the rest of their lives in their first language.

This bilingual lifestyle is possible because, for nearly all mother-tongue Franco-Quebeckers, work in English (or in French for that matter) is but one part of their existence. Elsewhere in their weekly round – at home, at school, at church, during leisure, while carrying out non-work obligations, etc. – French dominates by and large. In other words, a week has 168 hours. If, in a typical week, a person devotes 40 of them to work and work-related obligations and 74 to sleep and other body maintenance requirements (e.g., showering, exercise), 54 hours of free time remain for pursuing leisure activities or non-work obligations. Of course, to the extent the person is forced to work longer hours or chooses to do so out of love for the job, the amount of free time decreases, unless the additional hours of employment are taken from time used for sleep or body maintenance.

Lachapelle et al. (1993: 70) observe that Québec nationalism has evolved a great deal during this long period of economic change. Once an insular, collectivist, highly conservative orientation resting on rural religiosity, nationalism was transformed with the Quiet

Revolution into a confident, functional statist orientation. That is, nationalism came to be anchored in the Québec state, which provided for the material wants of its citizens. But more recently, the state's provider role has shrunk dramatically, leaving the field open for the entrepreneurial business person to come to the fore and give nationalism an individualist foundation rooted in economic liberalism. Quebeckers believe that French language and culture are as well served by the present nationalism as by its two earlier versions. Given the new nationalist ideology of today, what then can be said about the identity of the contemporary Franco-Québécois?

Identity

First, let it be clear that this book primarily treats of two general, or overarching, identities, one linguistic and one national, and not of the many particular "role-identities" (McCall and Simmons, 1976) people have in the modern world. The latter are exemplified by identities associated with an occupation (e.g., physician, secretary, truck driver), family role (e.g., father, daughter, grandmother), religion (e.g., Jew, Moslem, Catholic), leisure activity (e.g., stamp collector, cross-country skier), and the like. Linguistic and national identities are more inclusive than these role-identities; the first two add another layer of meaning to the third, while placing them in a broader cultural and political context.

When observers of francophone life in Canada write about identity, it is usually the general variety they discuss. Léon Dion (1995) sets out seven aspects of general linguistic identity: personal name, geographic territory, history of the language group, the group's political status, its dominant religion, the language itself, and the larger society with which the first six are associated. Thus, alone, the names Dominique Michel and Yvon Deschamps identify these two Québécois popular culture stars as francophone, as does the fact that they live in Québec where French dominates. Although less precise than the first two, being Roman Catholic at least strengthens the possibility of being identified as francophone, although it is also plausible that the Catholic person in question is Irish or Italian, for instance. We have already examined some of the history of francophones in Canada, the political status of French in this country, and its relationship to Canadian society, and more will be said on these three aspects in subsequent chapters. What, then, about the language itself as an aspect of linguistic identity?

For contemporary francophone Quebeckers, their linguistic identity is normally more clear-cut than their national identity. That is, it is usually fully evident to a person whether he or she is mother-tongue or second-language francophone, unilingual in French or English or bilingual in those two languages, these being the most common linguistic identities in Québec. Somewhat less common is the linguistic identity of allophone, a general category that is broken down on a personal basis by language spoken, such as Chinese and French or Arabic and French. French in these instances is a second if not a third language. There are also trilinguals, the most common combination in Québec possibly being mother-tongue francophone and second-language anglophone and hispanophone.

For unilingual speakers living and working in communities where their language overwhelms all others – the situation of most anglophones in North America and most francophones in Québec – it is highly unlikely that they think much about being unilingual anglophone or francophone. They have thus only a **demographic** linguistic identity, the kind used in census counts for example, rather than a **working** linguistic identity, the kind that people are sometimes conscious of and therefore that sometimes influences their everyday life activities. Bilingual, trilingual, and allophone people have working linguistic identities; they are often aware of them, particularly at the moment they switch languages to communicate with someone. Under these conditions, when a certain language is chosen to facilitate communication or achieve some other goal (e.g., to show competence in the language, to speak privately with someone), the speaker's linguistic identity is of the working variety; it is part of his or her definition of the ongoing situation. In this capacity it helps guide the speaker's behavior as the situation unfolds.

Consider now national identity. Before the Quiet Revolution most francophone Quebeckers identified themselves as French Canadians, much as this label was defined in chapter 1. But with the heightened consciousness that emerged around the many changes that took place just before 1960 and for many years after, the large majority of them came more and more to see themselves as Québécois. Francophones in Québec who want to be part of the federal system in Canada, many of whom are believed to have voted "No" in the 1995 Referendum, also see themselves as French Canadian, even uniquely so among some of the older generations. Those opting for sovereignty logically reject the appellation of

French Canadian, preferring instead to identify themselves exclusively as Québécois. Their nation is Québec, while Canada is in effect another country. Their flag is not the Maple Leaf but rather the distinctive blue and white *fleurdelisé*. It was ratified in 1958 in the National Assembly as the official flag of Québec ten years after it was hoisted for the first time atop the central tower of the parliament building in Québec City (Paulette, 1997: 27-28).

Nevertheless, as long as the separation issue remains unsettled, the national identity of Franco-Quebeckers cannot be established on firm ground. Those preferring to identify themselves as French Canadian can do so at the moment, though they must realize that, for them, the future of this identity is shaky. Those preferring to identify themselves exclusively as Québécois can also do so (and many do exactly that), but at present they must nonetheless qualify from time to time this status as an aspiration not yet juridically realized and possibly one that never will be realized in this manner. In this regard, a variety of practical procedures force a certain Canadian character on all Canadians when, for example, they travel abroad with their passport, operate an export or import business, or apply for an entry visa to another country. In short, national identity for francophone Quebeckers is at present a fluid orientation at times inconsistent with everyday affairs.

Are linguistic identity and national identity invariably linked? I believe that they are not, and further that such a link, where it exists, could be weaker in the future for some francophones. To be sure, the foregoing discussion suggests the opposite; that being francophone and living in Québec (Québécois) and being francophone and living in Canada (French Canadian) **are** linked. But globalization has brought together francophones across the world, and as noted later, many francophone Canadians and Quebeckers are deeply involved in this movement. As a result they are also beginning to see themselves as members of the international francophone community. The point, then, for the present discussion of identity among Franco-Quebeckers is that globalization may undermine to some extent, perhaps eventually even a considerable extent, both its Québec nationalist and its French-Canadian foundations. This proposition suggests that internationally-oriented francophones will come to value their linguistic identity more than their national identity. Nevertheless, because the effects of globalization on national identification and international linguistic identification among francophones remain to be examined, it is only possible at this time to speculate about them.

Conclusions

This chapter and the preceding one help give substance to the observation that Québec is by far the most francophone of all francophone societies in Canada, even though parts of some of the others are themselves heavily francophone. As such, Québec has become the yardstick by which the others (including the francophone societies in the United States) measure themselves, doing so in myriad ways. Québec is also used from time to time in this book as the benchmark for, or ideal type of, North America's francophone societies. Still, it will soon become apparent that francophone societies operating in parity and minority circumstances cannot always be realistically compared with *la Belle Province* and that many francophones living in these circumstances would often reject such a comparison in any case.

But even more important than sporadic comparisons with Québec is its role as rallying point for other Canadian and American francophone societies. This is not a role that Franco-Quebeckers have always embraced, especially during the 1960s and 1970s when statist nationalism reigned supreme on their soil. The prevailing sentiment then was that French and francophone culture were rapidly losing ground everywhere else in North America, and that all effort should therefore be directed to saving these values where victory was most likely to be assured, namely in Québec. Today, at this *fin de siècle,* many Quebeckers are still sceptical of the survival of French outside their province, even though many now also believe they should nevertheless try to ensure that as many of the francophone communities on this continent as possible do survive and develop as such. Indeed, they are beginning to see how they could benefit mightily from success in this endeavor.

This new sense of responsibility for the linguistic and cultural welfare of francophones outside Québec is concretely expressed in, for example, the Parc de l'Amérique Française, which occupies an entire city block near the parliament building in Québec City and in the Musée de l'Amérique Française, a branch of the Musée du Séminaire de Québec located in the same city. Additionally, The federal Liberal Party now recognizes Québec's special responsibility in its slogan identifying Québec as the *foyer principal de la langue, de la culture, et de la tradition juridique française* (the main home of French language, culture, and legal tradition). This slogan was adopted in April, 1996. The province has also developed numerous cultural and educational programs for the francophone societies and communities lying beyond its borders (see chapter 12). Still, many a Quebecker is astounded to learn that French is spoken and viable francophone communities exist in such anglophone bastions as Calgary and Vancouver. The next six chapters show where this impression of a lack of French is justified, or soon likely to be, and where it is not justified and not ever likely to be.

Chapter 5
Acadian Society

Acadian society, which comprises the francophones of New Brunswick (Nouveau-Brunswick), Nova Scotia (Nouvelle-Écosse), and Prince Edward Island (Île-du-Prince-Édouard), has to this point in this book been treated as a unitary social and cultural entity. Although most of the time I will continue with this approach, it will nevertheless be necessary, especially in this chapter and the next, to occasionally analyze Acadia according to its constituent provinces and even according to certain regions within them. The provincial boundaries were established to meet British needs and interests, not those of the minority Acadians, and today considerable variation is evident among the three provinces with respect to the lifestyles and life chances of their francophone populations qua francophones.

This having been said, it is possible to paint a reasonably complete descriptive picture of Acadian society as a whole by examining five areas of everyday life: geography, community structure, education, language, and culture. Throughout this chapter and the next, Acadian society in New Brunswick is examined first, followed by an examination of the Acadian societies of Nova Scotia and Prince Edward Island. This sequence affords comparison between the first, the most developed, and the second two, which are less well developed.

Geography

Figure 5.1 shows the areas where New Brunswick's Acadians are concentrated. More than 90 percent of the province's francophones live in its northern and eastern regions (Canadian Heritage, 1994). The southern part of the province has comparatively few francophones, although as has happened everywhere in Canada, those living there have gravitated to the cities, Saint John and Fredericton. The largest and most perceptibly francophone area in New Brunswick is the Acadian Peninsula, especially the part containing the communities of Caraquet, Shippagan, and Inkerman. For example, Caraquet, with a population of 4653 in 1996, of whom 96.8 percent were mother-tongue francophones (Statistics Canada,

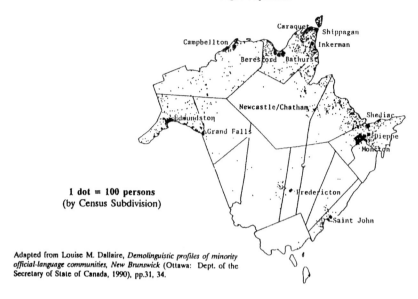

NEW BRUNSWICK
French Mother Tongue Population

1 dot = 100 persons
(by Census Subdivision)

Adapted from Louise M. Dallaire, *Demolinguistic profiles of minority official-language communities, New Brunswick* (Ottawa: Dept. of the Secretary of State of Canada, 1990), pp.31, 34.

Figure 5.1

1998b), is widely-regarded as a main centre of Acadian culture and religion. From my own brief observations of life in that city, where French signs dominate and only French is heard in public places, I got the impression that the town and its surroundings are as thoroughly francophone as many Québec communities of similar size. Seventy-five thousand first-language francophones reside on the Acadian peninsula.

Moreover, many of the communities along the Northeast coast between Moncton and the Acadian Peninsula have proportions of mother-tongue francophones similar to or only slightly lower than Caraquet. The same may be said for the cluster of communities around Edmunston, a city of 11 033 people in 1996, of whom 92.7 percent have French as their first language (Statistics Canada, 1998b), as well as Kedgwick and Saint-Quentin, two villages located between Edmunston and Campbellton, each with a proportion of mother-tongue francophones exceeding even that of Caraquet. Nevertheless the two largest cities in northern New Brunswick – Bathurst and Campbellton – only had populations of approximately 50 percent francophone. Moncton was even lower, being 33.9 percent francophone in 1996 (Statistics Canada, 1998b), although suburban Dieppe, a community of 12 497 people, and neighboring Shédiac (pop. 4664) were 76.5 and 80.8 percent francophone that same year.

Figure 5.2 indicates that Nova Scotia's francophones are concentrated mainly along the "French Shore," in the municipal districts of Clare and Argyle at the southwestern tip of the province, on western and southeastern Cape Breton Island, and in Halifax. Nowhere in this province do mother-tongue francophones dominate numerically as they do in parts of northern New Brunswick. The largest and most fully francophone community in southwestern Nova Scotia is Pointe-de-l'Église, or Church Point (pop. 500). It is located in Clare, which was 69 percent francophone in 1996 (Statistics Canada, 1998b).[1] The next largest concentration is found in neighboring Argyle, the population of which is 54.4 percent francophone. Most francophones on Cape Breton Island live in parity circumstances either in two western counties, one of which contains Chéticamp (pop. 1000), or on Île Madame in the southeast corner in the communities of Petit-de-Grat and Arichat. Chéticamp is the economic and cultural centre of the two counties; it lies in the Inverness Subdivision A (administrative unit), 44 percent of which is mother-tongue francophone. The Île Madame villages are found in Richmond Subdvision C; 52.1 percent of its population is francophone.

Figure 5.2

NOVA SCOTIA
French Mother Tongue Population

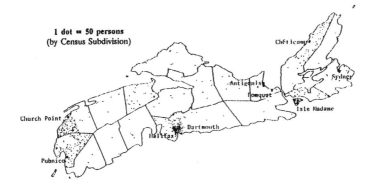

Adapted from Louise M. Dallaire, *Demolinguistic profiles of minority official-language communities, Nova Scotia* (Ottawa: Dept. of the Secretary of State of Canada, 1990), pp.30, 33.

PRINCE EDWARD ISLAND
French Mother Tongue Population

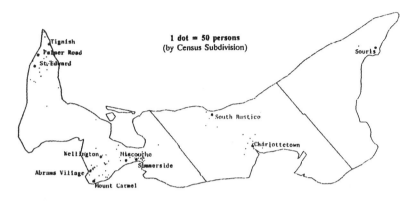

Adapted from Louise M. Dallaire, *Demolinguistic profiles of minority official-language communities, Prince Edward Island* (Ottawa: Dept. of the Secretary of State of Canada, 1990), pp.31, 34.

Figure 5.3

The largest concentrations of Acadians on Prince Edward Island are found in the western half of the province, notably the Évangéline area, which includes the towns of Wellington, Abram-Village, and Mont Carmel, and the north west tip of the island in such communities as Tignish, Palmer road, and Saint-Edward (see figure 5.3). Laforest (1991) writes that, of the two regions, Évangéline is the more solidly francophone and for that reason can be qualified as the stronghold of French culture on the Island. Table 5.1 presents population and language data pertaining to the three most important communities in this region.

Table 5.1 Population profile of Selected Évangéline communities, 1996

Communities	Population	Percent francophone
Abram-Village	328	85.4
Wellington	427	62.6
Mont Carmel	1178	76.0

Source: Statistics Canada (1998b)

Abram-Village contains the region's educational institutions, while Wellington is the governmental administrative centre for Acadian services, which are normally provided in French (Cormier, 1994: 263-64).

Community Structure

This section, and its counterpart in succeeding chapters, centres on the institutional and organizational structure of the francophone society being examined. Such sections are necessary in an assessment of the francophone societies outside Québec, because nearly all are institutionally incomplete. It is therefore important to show how incompleteness manifests itself and how, despite this weakness, these societies still constitute viable milieux for the survival and development of French language and francophone culture. This section and the following one on education show in concrete terms, then, why and how French language and culture in minority circumstances can exist cheek by jowl with English, presently the world's most influential language.

French education, although undeniably part of francophone community structure, is treated separately in this chapter and the others, primarily because it plays a central role in survival and development and relates in complex ways to a particular provincial government, which has the constitutional right to direct educational affairs within its jurisdiction. Finally, in our examination of Acadian Society, little will be said about the community structure of the virtually homogeneous francophone towns and cities in northern and eastern New Brunswick. They, as nearly all their counterparts in Québec, are institutionally complete, linguistically speaking, thereby rendering irrelevant, at least for the present, the questions of linguistic survival and development so important elsewhere.

The incomplete institutional structure of a minority francophone society in Canada revolves around the areas of life where French is frequently used, possibly more often than English, possibly even exclusively so. These areas are leisure, education, religion, and the family. Beyond them English dominates, especially in the spheres of commerce, health care, politics, government, and the work place (Hébert and Stebbins, 1993: 151-152; Stebbins, 1997: 70-71). To give substance to the first four, francophones have created sizeable networks of francophone friends and relatives, as well as numerous informal small groups and formal organizations such as clubs, societies, and associations. Individuals use French in different ways within this structure. For example, Pierre speaks it exclusively at home, participates in both a francophone theatre society and a local social club, but has no contacts with any school or church (being childless and a non-practicing Catholic). Mireille, on the other hand, speaks only English at home, but belongs to a French parish and volunteers frequently for francophone events.

What are the principal organizations in Acadian society? The history of Acadia showed that, from the outset, the Catholic Church was heavily implicated in preserving and fostering the French language. Modern Acadia is still dotted with Catholic parishes, which focus the attention of their parishioners on a range of church-related events from masses to church picnics. To be sure, some Acadians have no affiliation with a parish, or if they do, they participate little in its activities. These people find other ways of getting involved in the social structure of their society.

In this respect, most Acadians have nuclear and, often, extended family ties with other francophones. For instance, compared with some other francophone societies in Canada, Acadian society, depending on the province examined, has a low or moderately low rate of linguistically exogamous marriages, or marriages where the partner's mother tongue is other than French. In North America this tongue is highly likely to be English. The following figures, calculated from 1996 Canadian Census data (Statistics Canada, 1998a), show by province the proportion of marriages composed of mother-tongue francophone husbands and wives wedded to mother-tongue anglophone spouses.

- New Brunswick   25.5%
- Nova Scotia   63.6%
- P.E.I.   65.7%
- Québec   05.3%
- Saskatchewan   71.4%
- Alberta   75.4%

Here, as in so many other areas of francophone life, northern and eastern New Brunswick stands out as more purely Acadian than either Nova Scotia or Prince Edward Island.

Still, many of the things people do in Canada's minority francophone communities can be conceived of as leisure, a sphere that often overlaps those of family and religion and, to some extent, even that of education. Leisure, although it covers a vast range of human interests, can nevertheless be classified according to two basic forms: casual and serious (Stebbins, 1992; 1999). Casual leisure can be defined as immediately, intrinsically rewarding, relatively short-lived pleasurable activity requiring little or no special training to enjoy. Its types include play (including dabbling), relaxation (e.g., sitting, napping, strolling), passive entertainment (e.g., TV, books, recorded music), active entertainment (e.g., games of chance, party games), sociable conversation, and sensory stimulation (e.g., sex, eating, drinking). It is considerably less substantial and offers no career of the sort found in serious leisure. In broad, colloquial terms, it could serve as the scientific term for the practice of doing what comes naturally.

By contrast, serious leisure is the systematic pursuit of an amateur, hobbyist, or volunteer activity that participants find so substantial and interesting that, in the typical case, they launch themselves on a career centred on acquiring and expressing its special skills, knowledge, and experience.[2] Amateurs are found in art, science, sport, and entertainment, where they are inevitably linked in several ways with their professional counterparts. Hobbyists lack this professional alter ego, even if they sometimes have commercial equivalents and often have small publics who take an interest in what they do. Hobbyists can be classified according to one of five categories: collectors, makers and tinkerers, activity participants (in non-competitive, rule-based pursuits), players of sports and games (where no professional counterparts exist), and enthusiasts in one of the liberal arts whose hobbies centre largely on reading in such areas as philosophy, science, history, and the languages. Among the activity participants we find hunters, bird watchers, and cross-country skiers.

Volunteering is a special kind of helping action valued by both the volunteer and the beneficiary of this action that is not coerced, mandated, or remunerated, but is rather done for its own sake. Serious leisure volunteers help in a wide variety of ways in 16 different types of organizations. Career volunteers, as they are known in leisure studies, work in health, science, religion, politics, education, recreation, civic affairs (advocacy projects, professional and labor organizations), spiritual development, economic development, government (programs and services), human relationships, and the arts. These volunteers also serve in the fields of safety or the physical environment, while others prefer to provide necessities (e.g., food, clothing, shelter) or support services. Although much of career volunteering appears to be connected in some way with an organization of some sort, the scope of this leisure is possibly even broader, perhaps including the kinds of helping devoted individuals do for social movements or for neighbors and family. Still, the definition of serious leisure restricts attention everywhere to volunteering in which the participant can find a (non-occupational) career, in which there is more or less continuous and substantial helping, rather than one-time donations of money, organs, services, and the like.

Francophones in majority, parity, and minority societies partake in these activities, just as anglophones do, with the members of both language groups tending to do this with linguistically homogeneous partners. Compared with francophones living in Québec and northern and eastern New Brunswick, however, those living elsewhere do commonly have during their leisure somewhat more contact with the English language. But in every type of francophone society in Canada, French-speaking Canadians spend significant amounts of leisure time in French, for example, singing in a choir or acting in a play (amateurism), skiing with the family or hiking with friends (hobbyist activity), or attending a dinner party or meeting for drinks with friends (casual leisure). Some activities are carried out in the world of formal groups and organizations, as theatrical work and choral singing are; some are carried out in the informal world of friendship networks and family relations, as exemplified by going on a picnic and watching a French film.

These days, because of government cutbacks, nearly all francophone organizational activity in the minority societies is conducted by volunteers, with some of the volunteering being casual leisure and some being serious leisure. Whichever form, these volunteers pursue it primarily in six of the 16 types of volunteer organizations: education, religion, recreation, civic affairs, human relationships, and the arts (Stebbins, 1998b). Francophones volunteering in the French schools in their communities, most of whom are parents, commonly serve on one or two school committees or contribute their time to a parent-teacher organization or, rarely, even do both. Those working in the area of religion may be members of one or more parish committees or help out in a chapter of the Chevaliers de Colomb (Knights of Columbus). Turning to recreation, francophones in some provinces have formed sports organizations for their youth, two of which are found in Acadia: Société des jeux de l'Acadie (New Brunswick) and Comité provincial des jeux de l'Acadie (Nova Scotia). One main objective here is to hold annual francophone games. There are also many local francophone chapters of the Scouts and Guides. This emphasis on youth is well founded, for they are widely-recognized by francophone adults as their replacement in the local sub-community – *la relève* – a special resource to be nurtured with great care.

Francophones living in minority circumstances seldom participate in French in the civic organizations of the larger community. Yet in a way, they have their own civic organizations, whose missions, in broadest terms, are to relate local and provincial francophones to each other, the three levels of government, and the general (mostly anglophone) public. In every province and territory, an overarching association exists for these purposes, frequently extended through numerous branches (*régionales*) operating in the larger cities. In Acadia these organizations are the Société des acadiens et acadiennes du Nouveau-Brunswick, Fédération acadienne de la Nouvelle-Écosse, and Société Saint-Thomas d'Aquin (P.E.I.). Managing them and staffing their many projects is a veritable sponge of volunteer time.

Additionally, many francophone sub-communities in the minority societies also maintain a cultural centre or community centre, sometimes combining the two in the same building and organization. Whereas the director of one of these is likely to be remunerated, his or her staff are usually not. From a classificatory standpoint, these centres are both recreational and civic affairs organizations. Museums and historical sites emphasizing local francophone history and culture – e.g., Musée de la mer (Shippegan, N.B.), Village historique (Caraquet, N.B.), Port-Royal (N.S.), Musée acadien (Miscouche, P.E.I.) – serve both functions, besides being tourist attractions.

A good number of organizations have sprung up in the field of human relationships, most of them being small clubs. Depending on the size of the community, it is common to find francophone clubs for women (sometimes affiliated with a parish), men (often a chapter of the Chevaliers de Colomb), youth (not infrequently part of a provincial federation of such organizations), senior citizens (usually only a provincial organization), and groups established according to the principles of friendship, good works, and commercial activity, as exemplified in Richelieu International. This organization has 246 local clubs in Canada, of which 32 are located in Acadia (Guindon and Poulin, 1996: 44-45). In all these clubs volunteers are the only

source of help, including the executive of the group, who are classi-
fiable as career volunteers, and the rank-and-file, who mostly serve
as casual volunteers performing a variety of functions (e.g., serving
meals, selling tickets, publicizing events).

The arts have given rise to their own set of organizations.
Theatre is perhaps the most evolved of them all and therefore plays
the most significant role in community structure. At least theatre
societies are common throughout francophone Canada, and members are not required to be actors. Furthermore, some communities
have musical groups, dance troupes, and writers organizations,
although these tend to restrict membership to the artists themselves.
It is likewise with craft groups. These organizations may be linked
provincially in an overarching entity that represents them to the
francophone and anglophone communities and to federal and
provincial sources of funding for the arts. In New Brunswick this
group is known as the Conseil provincial des sociétés culturelles, in
Nova Scotia it is Conseil culturel acadien de la Nouvelle-Écosse, and
in PEI it is Fédération culturelle de l'Île-du-Prince-Édouard. Here,
too, there is plenty of scope for volunteer work, both serious and
casual.

One last note on community structure: all the minority francophone societies also include some professional, work-related francophone organizations. The more institutionally complete the society,
the more such organizations flourish and proliferate. But most
provinces have an association for schoolteachers who teach French
and a francophone jurists association that organizes legal aid for
francophone clients. And local and provincial co-operative organizations dealing with fisheries and agricultural products are common
in Acadia. Moreover, many communities whose francophone populations are large enough have their own *caisse populaire*. And most
provinces also have some kind of inclusive economic organization
for francophone operators of small businesses, the most common of
these being restaurants, bookstores, day care centres, and translation
services. The Conseil économique du Nouveau-Brunswick, which
was founded in 1979, organizes over 1200 francophone business
people in that province. Now there is talk among them about the
tourism potential of the francophone regions, an as yet insufficiently exploited sphere of French business activity (Guindon and Poulin,
1996: 30-31).

Working in French in the minority societies makes for an
uncommon livelihood. When it does happen, it happens in the pro-

fessions and businesses discussed in the preceding paragraph, in certain federal government positions deemed bilingual by the Official Languages Acts, and in certain provincial government positions deemed bilingual because of local need. In all these lines of work, it would be rare for the worker to spend an entire day on the job without speaking English. Indeed, in a typical day, they are likely to speak more English than French.

Education

The locution "French education" refers to primary and secondary schooling conducted entirely in French except for English; it is taught as a subject like history or mathematics. Down to the present, proponents of French education have had to confront four issues: One, acquiring the right to have French education for their children. Two, once the right was won, establishing French education from kindergarten through grade 12. Three, obtaining the authority to manage French schools and educational programs once they were established. Four, securing provincial funding for their schools equal on a per capita basis to that granted to other publicly-supported schools. Francophones want French education for their children because anything else is flatly inadequate, including the French immersion programs. These are inadequate because they are designed for anglophone children with no family or cultural background in French.

The first issue was definitively settled throughout Canada for both official languages with the adoption in 1982 of the Charter of Rights and Freedoms, whose relevant section reads as follows:

Minority Language Educational Rights

23. (1) Citizens of Canada

(a) whose first language learned and still understood is that of the English or French linguistic minority population of the province in which they reside,

or

(b) who have received their primary school instruction in Canada in English or French and reside in a province where the language in which they received that instruction is the language of the English or French linguistic minority population of that province,

have the right to have their children receive primary and secondary school instruction in that language in that province.

This right applies only where "sufficient" numbers of children are present to warrant provision of such instruction. If numbers are sufficient, then instruction and the facilities used to provide it must be supported with public funds.

Having this legal right does not imply, however, that it will automatically be implemented by every province in the country, a maxim many minority francophones soon experienced first-hand. In varying degrees the provinces dragged their feet, for the right, being a minority right, was unpopular with majority-filled legislatures. Frequently, francophones had to take the matter to the courts to obtain the legal clout needed to get their province to respect their educational rights. In New Brunswick this approach was unnecessary, however, for its Ministry of Education had recognized linguistic duality in 1973 and had established two parallel, linguistically-homogeneous school systems by 1981 (Canadian Heritage, 1994a). Acadian schools were also legally recognized in Nova Scotia in 1981, but in Prince Edward Island compliance with Section 23 came only in 1989. Nevertheless, minority schooling is now available in appropriate facilities in all provinces, though not in all communities, since some fail to meet the condition of sufficient numbers.

Even the third issue – management of the schools – has finally been settled in every province. Although it was different in New Brunswick, minority French schools elsewhere, once they became available, were placed under the jurisdiction of anglophone school boards; these were Catholic in some provinces, non-sectarian in others. This arrangement generated an assortment of difficulties, not the least of which was lack of sympathy for francophone educational interests and procedures. Non-sectarian systems and francophone Catholic curricula and practices did not always mix either. But today, except for Newfoundland where a school board has been promised (see chap. 7), francophones living in the provinces manage their own school systems.

The fourth issue is of much more recent birth than the first three. A news release from the Association de la presse francophone published in *Le Franco* (1997c) indicates that this struggle, as the previous ones, is likely to wind up in the courts in many instances. This is how equivalent funding was won in 1996 in British Columbia. At the time of the press release, parents' groups in New Brunswick, Nova Scotia, and Prince Edward Island were considering whether to follow suit.

The question of education in French in Canada's minority francophone societies is by no means confined to the years between kindergarten and grade 12 or 13. The *prématernelle*, or francophone pre-school, is found everywhere in Canada.[3] At the other end of the educational spectrum, most minority francophones have reasonable access to a French or bilingual technical college, community college, and university. New Brunswick has four francophone community colleges, all located in the northern and eastern parts of the province. In Nova Scotia, francophones can take advantage of the small network of institutions incorporated in the Collège de l'Acadie. French post-secondary education in Prince Edward Island is available only by videoconferencing (Canadian Heritage, 1994b).

The Université Sainte-Anne, a four-year francophone school located in Pointe de l'Église, Nova Scotia, offers several bilingual programs in conjunction with two of its main specialities: the training of French teachers and specialists in French language and literature. Established in 1890 as a college, it enrolled 437 full- and part-time students in the academic year 1996-97. In the academic year of 1997-98, the Université de Moncton in Moncton, New Brunswick, a unilingual francophone institution, enrolled 6016 students (full- and part-time). This institution offers a wide variety of undergraduate programs as well as a number of programs at the masters level. It was founded in 1963 when l'Université Saint-Joseph, itself founded in 1864, agreed to become an affiliate of the new Université de Moncton.[4]

French and bilingual universities in the minority francophone societies of Canada make several unique contributions to those societies. For one, these universities, along with those in Québec, train Canada's future francophone elite. Furthermore, they constitute a major source of French teachers for the French immersion programs, French schools, and core French programs in English schools (where French is taught as a subject). Third, these universities are important because they serve as centres for local and regional francophone life. This occurs, for example, when they offer adult education courses, present concert series, organize arts shows, or hold conferences. Moreover, professors in these institutions strive to maintain high linguistic standards. Here is where the war on anglicisms is most fiercely fought. Finally, the large majority of researchers on francophone communities in minority circumstances, whose data have helped make this book possible, are affiliated with these universities.

Language

The proportions of francophones in Canada's provinces and cities are reported in this book using 1996 census data (Statistics Canada, 1998a; 1998b) gathered using two measures: mother tongue and knowledge of French. Both concepts were defined earlier. The second measure is always the higher of the two, because it includes a substantial number of mother-tongue anglophones who have become second-language francophones. By knowing the number of people who know French as a first or second language, we gain a more accurate understanding of the real size of the parity and minority francophone societies than if, as a measure, we rely solely on the number of mother-tongue francophones living there. As argued throughout this book, these societies function with both types of speakers, and the latter should therefore figure in quantitative estimates of the linguistic vitality of those societies.

Statistics Canada also offers a great deal of census data on still another measure of language: language spoken at home. In Canada, this measure is invariably lower than that of mother tongue and is therefore generally regarded as the most conservative measure of presence of a language. The census data on the numbers of people speaking French at home are not reported here, because they are misleading. For instance, it has already been shown that, for Acadian society, the home is only one place where French is spoken, that the spheres of leisure, religion, education, and for some people, even work offer other important opportunities for speaking it. Moreover, speaking a language is by no means the only way to use it. Thus, a person might read French at home and speak it with colleagues at work or with friends during leisure. Another person might watch several hours of French television at home and perform volunteer work in the local sub-community, but never speak French at home because he or she is the only francophone in the household. No one has measured the full extent of French language use in a typical week by the typical Canadian francophone, whether he or she is first- or second-language. Until such research is undertaken, it is best to rely on measures of broad scope capable of giving a more realistic picture of the use of French in **all** facets of everyday life than the language-at-home measure does.

Table 5.2 contains the raw population figures and their percentages of the total population for each province constituting Acadian society, as based on the measures of French as mother tongue and knowledge of French.[5]

Table 5.2 Proportions of Francophone Acadians, 1996

Province	No. of first-language francophones	Percentage of Provincial population	No. of people who know French	Percentage of Provincial population
NB	245 095	33.6	311 180	42.7
NS	37 595	4.2	85 355	9.5
PEI	5885	4.4	14 740	11.1

Source: Statistics Canada (1998a)

Péronnet (1996: 201-02) concluded after extensive research that the traditional vocabulary of Acadians is presently undergoing considerable change, with the greatest rate of change occurring in the least isolated areas of their society. She noted three major tendencies: movement toward standard French, incorporation of English terms in French speech, and usage of regional words and expressions, whether created locally or borrowed from other French-language regions. On the other hand, she found that usage of traditional words and phrases is declining everywhere in Acadia.

Culture

The goal of this section is not to inventory all the cultural activities in Acadia, but rather to cull a reasonably representative sample of those of note, those that lend distinctiveness to this society. In other words, the routine expressions of art, dance, music, theatre, and literature will not be covered other than to mention straight away that they certainly exist and that, together, they amount to a significant set of shared symbols that serve as pegs for a francophone identity and as rallying points for Acadian causes. This is possible, in part, because many Acadian artists, composers, writers and playwrights, both past and present, have incorporated Acadian themes in their creations. This section does, however, look briefly at Acadia's major festivals and communications media.

It is quite possible that Antonine Maillet, born in 1929 in Buctouche, New Brunswick, is the best known of all Acadia's fine artists. Her two most successful novels – *La Sagouine* (1971) and *Pélagie-La-Charette* (1979) – brought her widespread fame (especially in France) and were instrumental in establishing her as a dominant force in Acadian literature (Boudreau and Maillet, 1993: 725-26). Her imagery – she expresses it as a storyteller of Acadian themes – exemplifies well the observation made in the preceding paragraph about using the society's symbolism to create rallying points for its people. Maillet's success as a novelist parallels the Acadian cultural revival of the 1970s and 1980s.

Acadia is also well-known for its musicians. Arthur LeBlanc, born in 1906 near Dieppe, New Brunswick, is frequently referred to as the "Acadian poet of the violin." By the time he died in 1985, he had performed throughout Europe and North America. Anna Malenfant, a classical singer, was one of the first Acadian singers to gain national and international renown. Rose-Marie Landry of Caraquet and Roland Richard of Rogersville, New Brunswick, have since followed in her footsteps. Benoît Poirier from Prince Edward Island has made his career as an organist working in Montréal. Édith Butler, born in 1942 in Paquetville, New Brunswick, helped disseminate Acadian culture through her own popular music, first a genre of folk music, then later, a fusion of folk and rock and roll. By 1987, she had 11 albums of Acadian material in circulation (Plouffe, 1988: 307).

When reviewing the culture of Acadia, it is also important to examine its folk art, the most noteworthy today being the music and the stories and legends. Acadians know and still sing melodies unique to their society, for example, "l'Évangéline," "le Reveil de l'exile," and "le Pecheur Acadien." The most powerful myth in Acadia, whose influence persists to this day, is a popular adaptation of the poem "Évangéline," wherein Grand-Pré (the community in the poem that the British deported) retains its idyllic image and the themes of endurance and suffering are underscored (Finney, 1996: 227). The New Brunswick legend about the tree of life illustrates this tendency (taken from Dupont, 1994: 17):

> During the days of the *Grand Dérangement*, 15 Acadians were imprisoned in a *"cave à patates"* [potato cellar] dug in the earth at Beauséjour. Pierre à Pierre à Pierrot, who was part of the group and its leader, attempted to maintain the morale of his friends who were perishing daily. Thus isolated in darkness, they dug earnestly in the dirt with bare hands to escape from this small cave. By the time they had managed to do this, they had lost their fingernails.

> Exhausted, they then undertook a long trek in the forest, which would lead them to Memramcook. But Pierre à Pierre à Pierrot was no longer able to give them energy.

> They had just buried the oldest of the group when, upon looking up at the sky, they saw a large tree laden with beau-

tiful fruit that none of them had seen before. After treating themselves to the fruit, they reached a building spared by the enemy, where they stayed long enough to recover their strength before setting out to rejoin their families.

Later, these Acadians and their descendants made several attempts to search the forest from Beauséjour to Memramcook, but they never found the strange fruit tree. (translation)

Also current is the myth of an Acadia lost, as expressed in the loss of identity occasioned by the wrenching injustice of the *Grand Dérangement*, the attendant break-up of families, and the subsequent years of wandering in search of a new home – a sort of collective destiny.

Turning briefly to the diverse artistic and cultural festivals that abound in Acadia, first mention goes to the "oldest and most important" of them all (Cormier, 1994: 181): the annual *Festival Acadien de Caraquet*. It celebrates the culture and joie de vivre of the Acadians. As so many others held in the Acadian areas of the maritime provinces, this festival also features traditional art, dance, crafts, cuisine, and music. And each year throughout Acadia, a number of other fairs, events, and festivals take place as well, although these happenings tend to offer comparatively little Acadian art and culture.

One of the two French-language dailies available outside Québec – *l'Acadie nouvelle* (founded in 1984) – is published in Caraquet and distributed across New Brunswick, while five other communities in the province are further served by francophone weeklies. Additionally, Franco-New Brunswickers can choose from three francophone magazines, two of them reporting analysis and opinion of current events and issues of interest to Acadians. The media scene is much sparser in Nova Scotia and Prince Edward Island, however; here Acadians have access to only a single province-wide weekly apiece: *Le Courrier de la Nouvelle-Écosse* (founded in 1937) and *La Voix Acadienne* (a P.E.I. publication founded in 1974). Neither province has a French-language magazine.[6]

The Société Radio Canada (S.R.C.), the French branch of C.B.C., operates a station in Moncton to serve the Maritimes. As for the other radio stations in the region, two are private (both in N.B.) and several are community-owned and operated. In addition to the radio and television of S.R.C., which also provides programming from Montréal, Acadians can receive by way of cable several of Québec's

French-language TV channels. One of these is TV5, an international French chain whose multinational programming is broadcast to all of Francophonie.

Conclusion

Acadia, and especially northern and eastern New Brunswick, is an area of Canada rich in francophone pride and heritage. Nevertheless, since external appearances can often be deceiving, this fact is not always evident to non-francophone outsiders touring the region. My own travels through the area revealed an overtly anglophone presence in many localities, as manifested in English signs, notices, advertising, and the like. But when I entered commercial establishments in the regions of heaviest francophone concentration, I often heard people speaking French. As mentioned earlier, in Caraquet, Edmunston, and many other francophone communities in northern and eastern New Brunswick, and to a lesser extent in Pointe de l'Église in Nova Scotia and Abram-Village in Prince Edward Island, external appearances are unquestionably francophone. But, apart from these areas, francophone society in Acadia is mostly imperceptible, a crucial issue with which Acadians are now trying to grapple. Thus, although Acadia is classified in this book as a majority francophone society, it is evident that this descriptor applies best to northern and eastern New Brunswick.

Chapter 6
Contemporary Issues in Acadian Society

This chapter begins with the issue broached in the final paragraph of the preceding chapter: the imperceptible character of much of Acadian society. Theoretically at least, imperceptibility can lead to problems. For instance, is a francophone identity possible when French is hidden? And does imperceptibility strengthen the tendency to marry an anglophone? After tackling these two questions, the chapter moves on next to examine the changing role of the volunteer in Canada's francophone communities lying outside Québec, and then to assess the recent decline in enrolment in Acadia's two French universities. It ends by considering the problem of the quality of French in this society.

The fourth issue raised in the section on education in chapter 5, the issue about equivalent educational facilities and programs, will not be further discussed in this book, chiefly because it is still too new to have generated much to report. Nevertheless, the snail's pace at which this question is emerging and being dealt with does give further weight to the observation that change often comes slowly in the world of minority francophones, perhaps because many of its problems are complex, sometimes divisive, and frequently related in some way to financial resources, to mention but a few possible explanations. When an issue gets into the courts, the rate of change seems to slacken even more.

Acadia's Imperceptible Francophones

Always the exception, francophone life is anything but imperceptible in northern and eastern New Brunswick. Elsewhere in Acadia, however, francophone perceptibility is a matter of degree, and it turns out, a good measure of the vitality of the French language there. Giles, Bourhis, and Taylor (1977: 308) hold that "ethnolinguistic vitality" results from a set of structural factors influencing the probability that the language group in question will conduct itself as an active and distinctive entity in inter-group relations. Of the three components of vitality identified by the authors – status or prestige of the language, demographic presence of those who speak it, and institutional support – it is the latter that bears most directly on the question of its perceptibility in a given community. Institutional support refers to the extent that a language receives formal and informal representation in the community's institutions. One measure of this is how much and how often written French is visible in public places in the community. Another is how much and how often spoken French can be heard here.

To the extent French is aurally and visually perceptible in the public spaces of Canada's francophone minority and parity societies, where in those spaces is it likely to be found? In the Preface I described my tour of some of Canada's francophone communities, one of my interests being to systematically search there for French in or on the following:

- Community welcome and farewell signs
- Street signs
- Stop signs (stop, stop/*arrêt, arrêt*)
- Signs on the property of the Catholic churches
- Commercial signs (e.g., billboards, store signs, window advertising)
- Signs on the property of public institutions (e.g., parks, town hall, library, hospital)
- Signs on the property of schools and day care centres
- Signs on the property of seniors' residences
- Notices posted on the town notice board and in the supermarkets)
- Brochures and flyers locally available

In addition, I looked for the presence of *caisses populaires*, chapters of the Chevaliers de Colomb, francophone clubs, and francophone cultural and community centres. Oral perceptibility was measured only occasionally, by eavesdropping momentarily on talk in local supermarkets, restaurants, and drug stores, or on the street and, when purchasing something in these places, by waiting to see in which language the clerk would address me.

Most of the time, I will not report my observations on a community-by-community basis. Instead I wish to present only my general impressions of each francophone society and, where differences exist, of its regions. As for Acadia, everywhere I went outside northern and eastern New Brunswick revealed what could be called **scat-**

tered bilingualism; that is, some of the foregoing measures were in French and English or, very rarely, in French only and some were in English only. The latter tended to be the most frequent. Pointe de l'Église in Nova Scotia and Abram-Village in Prince Edward Island were partial exceptions, showing a rather more predominantly francophone presence than the other towns in their regions. Otherwise, it was necessary to carefully scrutinize the local setting, looking for commercial signs, which dominate numerically in most communities, as the type of measure with the highest probability of being worded exclusively in English, or less often, in some proportion of French and English. In this regard, signs on the property of the local Catholic Church, the most common being the announcement of Sunday mass, were the most likely to be at least bilingual if the parish had a significant number of francophone members. Signs on school property were also good measures, although many small communities now send their children to a regional school located some distance away. Indeed, a number of villages were too small to support a francophone club, community centre, *caisse populaire*, or chapter of the Chevaliers de Colomb.

In short, geographically-speaking, much of Acadia consists of towns and cities where francophones live as a minority and where aural and visual proof of this fact is scattered. Based strictly on these two measures of ethnolinguistic vitality, French would have to be described as weak in these places. Fortunately for the questions of survival and development, however, vitality is also measured in several other ways. O'Keefe (1998: 10) discusses four, which revolve around identity, education, utility, and symbolic considerations. Each will be covered at appropriate points in this chapter and succeeding ones, for the matter of ethnolinguistic vitality touches all minority francophone societies in Canada.

Identity

In chapter 1, I indicated, following Thériault, that linguistic identity among Canadian francophones living outside Québec is largely anchored these days in the province in which they reside. Yet in this chapter and the preceding one, discussion has centred on Acadians as a singular, homogeneous group living not in a particular province, but in a region composed of three provinces. In fact, when it comes to the question of identity, the approach I have taken is justified more by the historical circumstances of Acadia than by its contemporary situation. Allain, McKee-Allain, and Thériault (1993: 382) describe what has happened over the years:

> One will have no doubt observed that the boundaries of this Acadia have shrunk with time: if they refer in the first instance (the traditional period, 1860-1960) to the set of the three maritime provinces, the contours of Acadia are identified more and more with those of New Brunswick starting with the period that follows (the modernizing period, 1960-1970) . This phenomenon is only accented in the course of the last two periods (the critical period, 1970-1980 and the fragmented organizational period, 1980-1990). (translation)

Put otherwise, the "Acadia of the Maritimes" (*l'Acadie des Maritimes*) is now a myth, says Cécyle Trépanier (1996). After conducting 120 interviews and several periods of extensive participant observation in six areas in Acadia, she concluded that being Acadian means that people feel a sense of belonging first to their local town or city, then to their region, and then possibly to their province. As further evidence of this tendency, she notes that the Société nationale de l'Acadie, which originated in 1881 under another name, has had to adjust to it by becoming a federation uniting the three provincial associations mentioned earlier and using as common ground the mission of representing Acadians on the international scene. Clarke's (1998: 84) analysis of Acadian identity squares with Trépanier's conclusion, wherein he observes that identity is linked with community of residence. In Acadia this is very likely to be a community founded on the fishing industry employing both men and women. Clarke says that the typical Acadian finds a main identity in his or her occupational role in this industry, where the industry itself is the economic mainstay of the local community. Meanwhile, the importance of language and ethnicity is diminished when people identify themselves this way.

Nevertheless, language is always a part of this identity, even if it fails to distinguish on its own francophone Acadians from francophones in Québec and elsewhere in Canada. When joined with language, living in a particular community within a particular province has been shown to serve as an important identifier that sets Acadians apart. But except for those in northern and eastern New Brunswick, being Acadian in and of itself now seems to be receding in significance as an identifier, even if it is still informative to speak of Acadia as a historical and cultural entity. Bear in mind, however, that all this refers to Acadians' personal, or role, identification of themselves while living in Acadia. Those living outside that region often form Acadian societies, suggesting that, under these circumstances, self-identification as Acadian becomes an important way of differentiating themselves from francophones of other origins.

Exogamous Marriages

Discussion here is confined to families formed from three main types of marriage according to language: the all-French endogamous marriage (two francophones), the type-1 French-English exogamous marriage (female francophone-male non-francophone), and type-2 French-English exogamous marriage (male francophone-female non-francophone).[1] The non-francophones are usually anglophone, although some of them who routinely speak English have a mother tongue other than French or English.

The Calgary study (Stebbins, 1994) sheds light on some of the problems that can boil up from the exogamous unions, problems that are common to many if not all the francophone minority societies in Canada. Fourteen of the exogamous marriages in the Calgary study were type-1, the remaining four were type-2. The interviews with the francophones in these relationships strongly suggested that their children are much more likely to develop a facility in French and a commitment to the language and culture of the francophone parent when that parent is their mother, a finding that squares with national research on the matter (Churchill and Kaprielian-Churchill, 1991: 48; *Le Chaînon*, 1993: 2; Turcotte, 1993: 17). As a general rule, the mothers in the families contacted in the Calgary study, whether anglophone or francophone, whether employed outside the home or not, appeared to spend significantly more time with their children than the fathers. This is especially likely to happen when children are young.

This lopsided relationship gives the first-language mothers a singular advantage in inculcating their first language, which, by the way, the second-language francophone mothers in the Calgary study tended not to use. The first spoke French with their children much if not all of the time. As for the purely anglophone mothers – those in a type-2 relationship – they had no choice but to speak English, although it seems they regretted this limitation. In the interviews their francophone husbands described them as highly sympathetic with their own desire to raise their children as francophones (with a working knowledge of English as well). These mothers were trying to learn French, and all had enthusiastically endorsed the plan to send their children to either a French school or an immersion school.

The linguistic question was at its prickliest in families founded on type-1 exogamous marriages (see also Heller and Lévy, 1992: 11-13). Here the mothers had in significant degree succeeded or were in the process of succeeding in raising their children as francophones, at least up to the teen-age years. But according to the interviews the anglophone fathers were a constant hindrance in this mission, for they, when compared with the type-2 anglophone mothers, were less sympathetic toward French, in general, and toward French in their home, in particular. True, each accepted his partner's wish to send their children to French schools, when he might have reached a compromise on an immersion school or dug in his heels and insisted on an English school. But only one anglophone father signalled a genuine commitment to learning French, and very few were interested in the bilingual activities of the local francophone community.

Faced with this attitude the francophone mothers uniformly concluded they must tackle "the French question" with diplomacy (or politeness, as some put it), whereas the francophone fathers never mentioned the need for such an approach with their anglophone wives. In practical terms, diplomatic francophone mothers, when father is present, try to speak largely if not exclusively in English with the children so he can participate in the interaction, however brief it may be. One francophone mother observed that "when my family from Québec visits us we have to speak in English when he [her husband] is around, even though he is the only one in the room who cannot understand French. If we do not he gets upset."[2] Another mother with one pre-school child discussed a different problem: "Since my husband is anglophone we talk nearly all the time in English. Although he can understand French to some extent, it is much easier to deal with the problems of everyday life in English. With both of us working there is enough stress without adding language difficulties." In short, for families founded on type-1 exogamous marriages, French talk is often limited to situations where the francophone mother is alone with her children.

One area of life where diplomacy and compromise reached their maximum expression was in naming the children. In the mixed marriages of this study, the most desirable names were those with which members of the extended families of both parents could identify. The names also had to be pronounceable in both languages, with minimal variation between the two languages in the pronunciations themselves. Furthermore, respondents wanted names with a modern "ring" to them in contemporary francophone and anglophone society. With a few exceptions these rules of naming were followed.

But, by faithfully adhering to such rules, the number of remaining names from which to choose becomes annoyingly small for some respondents,. Nevertheless those chosen, for example Paul, Marc, Philippe, Julie, Mélanie, and Stéphanie, were regarded as having solved a potentially thorny family problem, particularly with reference to their own parents, who were sometimes less than enthusiastic in the first place about the cross-language marriage. One respondent described the persistent difficulty his parents, brothers, and sisters had with Jason, his son's name: "In French the pronunciation is quite different. Moreover it is extremely rare to meet someone in Québec whose name is Jason. As a result my relatives always have difficulty when they refer to him by his name [points to the baby in his mother's arms]. We never thought about such complications when we chose the name."

All exchanges between the parents in the exogamous marriages were carried out in English, a practice that significantly affected the linguistic atmosphere of the home. Most of the respondents in these marriages, when asked to consider all the talk done at home, estimated that English was spoken 75 to 80 percent of the time. Nonetheless, the francophone mothers spoke proudly about how they persevered at keeping French alive as the language of communication with their children. They did this in good part by being tenacious, by refusing to interact with them unless addressed in French, that is unless their own fluency in English led them to respond inadvertently in that language.

In sum, the Calgary study suggests that in Acadia and elsewhere in Canada's minority francophone societies, the domestic part of the linguistic lifestyle of francophone parents in mixed marriages is founded chiefly on their relationships with their children. "The dominant language around here," one mother noted, "is English. I speak in French with my children, but that is all." Another observed that "my only chance to use my French at home is in talking with my children. Of course I read some in French and watch some French television, but speaking it, well, there are no other opportunities unless my relatives or francophone friends visit us."

Volunteers and Volunteering

I have suggested elsewhere (Stebbins, 1998b) that in the medium- and large-sized cities outside Québec in Canada, and even in some of those in the United States, francophone volunteers play a crucial role on the local level maintaining and advancing the French language and one or more francophone cultures.[3] Research on key francophone volunteers in Calgary and Edmonton (Stebbins, 1998b) reveals that these people make substantial contributions to the maintenance and growth of their linguistic communities, which similarly to those in minority Acadia, function more or less imperceptibly within the dominantly anglophone climate. Today, these communities, when considered together, help make up what Louder and Waddell (l983) described as a linguistic archipelago. The Calgary-Edmonton study suggests that francophone volunteers in North America have done a great deal to keep this archipelago from sinking forever in the demographic and cultural sea of the English language in which most of this continent has been awash for approximately two centuries.

Still, volunteers, indispensable as they are for the maintenance and development of the urban francophone communities in minority circumstances, are not all of a kind. Some are highly skilled and knowledgeable, (e.g., club president, association treasurer, theatre society fund-raiser), whereas others provide a needed but simpler service (e.g., taking tickets at the door, serving food at the annual *cabane-à-sucre*, addressing envelopes for a mass mailing). Some work long hours week after week, whereas others spend no more than an evening or two each year performing a certain activity. Even in the second category, the volunteers may be highly skilled or knowledgeable, as exemplified in the handful of people who are engaged each year in Calgary to judge an annual science fair for francophone students, which takes approximately seven hours of their time during two days. All these volunteers help maintain and develop their linguistic community, but the knowledgeable, highly skilled, long-working variety contributes most substantially to these two goals. I have coined the term **key volunteer** to identify this type.

The key volunteers in the urban minority francophone communities of North America serve in one, or sometimes two or three, official posts within one or more established "grassroots" groups or organizations there. I paraphrase David Smith (1997) here, who defines "grassroots associations" as local, formal, and semiformal organizations which are commonly composed purely of volunteers and which he contrasts with "volunteer programs," the latter being created and run by work organizations. President, vice-president, treasurer, and secretary are the most common posts in the grassroots groups and organizations, but chairing an important committee or directing a major program, for example, can also contribute greatly to the maintenance and development of the local community. None of these positions is remunerated, although in increasingly rare circumstances, a president or director may receive a minor honorarium. The organizations, which in these communities are often small, are legally chartered, whereas the established groups are not, even though they have existed long enough to have become highly visible on the local scene. While most urban francophone collectives are organizations in this legal sense, some clubs and friendship groups find it is unnecessary to establish themselves formally.

Key volunteers are distinguished from other types of volunteers by at least four criteria. First, presidents, treasurers, and the like have complex and extensive responsibilities whose execution affects in important ways the functioning of their group or organization. Second, such positions are enduring. Officers are usually elected for a year, and chairs and directors may serve even longer terms. Third, the success of the groups and organizations where they serve contributes significantly to the maintenance and development of the local francophone community. Fourth, key volunteers have a high degree of commitment to their collectives and through them, the Calgary-Edmonton study clearly shows, to these two community goals.

At first blush, activity of this kind might look more like work without pay than anything else. But, as explained in the preceding chapter, career volunteering, of which key volunteering is an important subtype, is still most accurately understood as a special kind of leisure, as a form of career volunteering.

The Calgary-Edmonton study revealed that the key volunteers themselves, given their central positions in the local francophone community, see those positions and the people who fill them as absolutely indispensable for the survival and development of the collective. Moreover, they see a general shortage of these critical people in the two communities, a proposition that received additional support from the responses of the overall sample to the question of whether the number of available volunteers is sufficient or insufficient. Only three respondents said the number of volunteers was sufficient, suggesting that, in their organizations (in religion, education, and one of the arts), they had no difficulty finding people to help with routine activities and assume key positions. The others, in referring both to their own group or organization and to their language community as a whole, left no doubt that they see an acute and widespread shortage of francophone volunteers.

Different respondents cited different causes for this situation, among them pressure at work, indifference toward the local francophone community, complexity of the volunteer post to be filled, and dissension in a particular organization or in the community as a whole. Organizations with a large proportion of elderly members must sometimes struggle with greater shortages of volunteers than organizations of the same type composed mostly of younger members. Old age, these days around 75 to 80 years, eventually leads to a decline in volunteering, as poor health, low income, transportation problems, and for some, reduced mental acuity start to curb their effectiveness (Fischer and Schaffer, 1993: 15-18).

This problem, it turns out, is hardly unique to Canada's urban minority francophone communities. Putnam (1995) has observed it on a far more general level in the United States, where the number of members is declining in voluntary organizations requiring high levels of face-to-face interaction with people outside the person's own family and friendship circles. The reverse is true, however, for voluntary mass membership organizations, which he calls "tertiary organizations" and which are exemplified by the Sierra Club and the American Association of Retired Persons. They seldom, if ever, require this level of contact with strangers. The vast majority of groups and organizations in the urban francophone sub-communities are grass-roots rather than tertiary organizations.

All this suggests that the urban francophone communities functioning in minority circumstances, including those in Acadia, are now facing, or are about to face, a full-scale volunteer crisis rooted in a combination of reduced public and private grants, shortages of volunteers, burnout of some key volunteers, and the need to gain more complete control of their own groups and organizations. Paquette (1997), speaking for all of Canada, holds that these minority communities are, at present, highly fragile and that the aforementioned conditions are contributing mightily to this situation. Everywhere, then, the sharp sense of urgency is prodding francophone leaders to try to ameliorate the volunteer crisis.

The Universities

The discussion of francophone universities continues in this chapter about issues, because these institutions play a strategic role in the parity and minority francophone societies. To repeat briefly what was said earlier, the large majority of the leaders of these societies are educated in these universities. And be they leaders or followers, their graduates eventually enter the upper echelons of francophone society, where they coalesce into the primary force pressing for further culturo-linguistic survival and development.

Throughout the decade of the 1990s, Université Sainte-Anne (located in Pointe de l'Église) has enjoyed continuous growth in enrolment, in good part because several new French secondary schools were established in Nova Scotia during that period (Lépine, 1992). This institution has trained many of the French teachers now working in the province. The University also traces its success to its bilingual bachelor programs; they draw students from as far away as Québec, where such programs are in short supply. Nonetheless, the fact that many first-year students have a poor mastery of French has forced Université Sainte-Anne to offer a remedial program, a problem well known to all francophone universities in Canada (and, for that matter, most anglophone universities, who must try to ameliorate the weak English of many incoming students).

The situation is less optimistic at the Université de Moncton, where annual enrolments climbed moderately during the early and middle 1990s and then began to drop moderately after that. One difficult problem, says Marc Poirier (1992), is that many of New Brunswick's Acadian families are still poor and cannot afford to send their children to university, even though tuition at the Université de Moncton is lowest of the 14 maritime universities. Poirier cites data indicating that 60 percent of the students at this University support themselves with student loans. Moreover, those who do find the means to enter the institution often get immediately channelled into French remedial classes. Many students do nonetheless manage to surmount these obstacles and earn a bachelor degree. But if they want to pursue graduate work, they must once again confront the limitations of living in minority circumstances, for the University has only 25 master programs and no doctoral programs.

All francophone universities in Canada, those in Québec included, have had to face the problem of insufficient course material in French. In the past, it was often solved by assigning material in

English, understandably an unpopular approach with students since many of them read with difficulty books and articles written at the university level in that language. To make matters worse, the few French texts available were inordinately expensive. This situation has improved substantially in recent years, but if sociology – one of the author's specialities – is typical of most university subjects, choice is still limited, even if most of the time professors may now choose from at least a couple of textbooks in a given area.

Language

The preceding section identified weak French as a problem in Acadia, not only among would-be university students but also among Acadians in general. Partial assimilation into English is a major cause of this problem, for in the typical case, it leads to partial anglicization of the assimilated person's French. That is, some Acadians are acquiring a subtractive bilingualism.

Louise Péronnet (1993: 471) says that considerable linguistic change is evident in the Acadia of today, fuelled in the main by its transformation from a society once closed and isolated to one now open and increasingly involved economically and politically with the dominant group, anglophone maritime Canada. Nevertheless, today as in the past, Acadians remain a linguistic minority, even in New Brunswick.

Péronnet (1993: 474) treats of two common types of minority language problems found in modern society. One type centres on the status of the language, the right to use it and its prominence among other languages; the other centres on spoken and written aspects of the language, what linguists call its "corpus." The first type of problem has already been considered in earlier discussions of ethnolinguistic vitality, Canada's two official languages, and the minority status of French and francophones virtually everywhere outside Québec and northern and eastern Ontario and New Brunswick. Suffice it to say at this point that, throughout Canada, French in minority circumstances is generally not valued as highly as English, but that it is not at the same time generally regarded as irrelevant or despicable. Many an anglophone Canadian recognizes French as a major world language and one he or she would like to master, even without the opportunity to use it locally.

In contemporary Acadia, the problem of the corpus of Acadian French revolves around three important themes: assimilation to

English, standardization of French, and teaching French as a mother tongue.

> In this social context [changing Acadian society], the hottest question at the moment from the standpoint of the identity of the Acadian community is without doubt the one of maintenance and development of the French language, and its obverse, the threat of linguistic assimilation (translation) (Péronnet, 1993: 472).

If the threat of assimilation is real, not only in Acadia, but across the land (excluding the majority societies), then how powerful is it? Harrison (1996: 12), working with Statistics Canada data, reports a 35 percent drop between 1971 and 1991 in the number of youth (people aged 15 to 24) whose first language was French. This despite the fact that during this period the overall number of first-language francophones in Canada rose by five percent. Between 1971 and 1991, New Brunswick saw a decline of 27 percent, while Nova Scotia and Prince Edward Island saw declines of 46 and 61 percent. Note, however, that a significant part of this decrease was caused not by assimilation per se, but rather by migration from Acadia, for the proportions of anglophone youth living there have also declined, their rates ranging during the same two decades from 10 and 17 percent depending on the province.

The picture is even more complicated than this, however. Thus between 1971 and 1991 the percentage of bilingual youth rose by approximately eight percent in New Brunswick and Nova Scotia and approximately five percent in Prince Edward Island. The national average (again excluding the majority societies) was approximately six percent for the same period. Moreover, no data exist on the question of whether this bilingualism is predominantly additive or subtractive. It is known, however, that the tendency to abandon the mother tongue generally increases from early adulthood to about 35 years of age, after which personal change of this sort is uncommon (O'Keefe, 1998: 40). Additionally, exogamous marriages tend to spawn a degree of assimilation among children of these unions.

Even with all this weighing of evidence, it is still impossible to arrive at a definitive estimation of the threat of assimilation, whether in Acadia or in the other minority and parity francophone societies. As observed in the preceding chapter, this is because the very operational definitions of francophone employed in Statistics Canada's quinquennial censuses are too loose and narrow to lead to clear-cut conclusions.

The second theme – the standardization of French – raises another set of prickly questions. Should the French striven for be the most prestigious, say that of Paris, or a version of the language that incorporates aspects of Acadian regional French, which is a vernacular language? Attempts to standardize French do not necessarily lead to linguistic development, for if regional elements are replaced by those of a standard language and the standardized elements are rejected by ordinary speakers, this situation may spell the death of the language in that region. Péronnet (1993: 478) cites evidence showing this can be the outcome of any program of French standardization in Acadia when the common person refuses to accept the standardized elements.

In short, linguistic standardization must evolve to some extent, a process wherein the majority of speakers in the local community become willing to drop old traits for new ones, doing so because they see major advantages in using the latter. This could be a tall order in eastern New Brunswick where *chiac*, a sort of Acadian counterpart to Québec's *joual*, is a common form of slang. Nevertheless, one argument for standardization that might win over many Acadians, as their society opens up and contacts grow more national and international, is that a standard French reasonably free of regionalisms and therefore usable in formal situations constitutes a major advantage in communication in, for example, business, tourism, and entertainment.

This leads to the third theme in the problem of the corpus of Acadian French: the quality of the French taught in Acadian schools. Péronnet (1993: 473) raises such questions as the efficacy of oral instruction in French compared with its written form, the structure of sentences over and against the principles of spelling, and the textual forms of examination in preference to multiple-choice instruments. She also criticizes the nature of the grammar taught in Acadia's francophone schools, noting further that in heavily bilingual and anglophone regions, perhaps too much English is given too early to students. Furthermore, primary and secondary teaching, whether in French or English schools, is continuously being evaluated and French teaching in Acadia and elsewhere in the francophone communities of Canada is no different. But inferior teaching can generate special problems for the survival and development of minority and parity communities, because it puts francophones receiving it at a disadvantage when trying to enter francophone universities and communicate on an extra-regional scale. It is no wonder that the issue of the quality of teaching stirs significant concern among Acadia's leaders.

As Boudreau (1995: 136-138) observes, the French language in Acadia can be both divisive and unifying. It is divisive when, *à la* Péronnet, it is seen as difficult to learn and an embarrassment to the person who fails to speak and write it correctly and when in reaction to this weakness, he or she resorts to English. It is divisive when some Acadians call for French to prevail in all spheres of life, while others are content to let the language find its own level in competition with English and American culture in the local Acadian community. On the other hand, French leads to unification when Acadians regard themselves as special people who can speak another world language in dominantly unilingual, anglophone North America. It is also unifying when they see themselves as members of a group who struggled against all odds to make this possible.

Conclusion

The significant level of institutional incompleteness, the low to moderate perceptibility of French, and the feeling of belonging to a minority not only characterize many francophone communities in Nova Scotia and Prince Edward Island, but also describe well the situation of minority francophone societies across Canada. No equivalent of northern and eastern New Brunswick exists in this vast territory, though it will soon be apparent that certain areas in Ontario come close enough to be considered majority regions. But Acadians have something special in comparison with the others, including even Québec, since they share the collective memory of the *Grand Dérangement*, the poem "Évangéline"; and the decades of poverty, isolation, and commercial exploitation. When combined, these experiences form a unique constellation. It, in turn, helps Acadians identify themselves as such, even though today they also define themselves as francophones living in a particular province or community and, for some, as speakers of a prestigious, influential, international language.

Moreover, maritime Acadians live where their history unfolded, giving them a kind of rootedness, a direct link with their past, that most francophones elsewhere in Canada (Québec excluded) can never experience. For the latter are either migrants from Québec or immigrants from abroad, most of the memorable collective events of their past having taken place in another part of the world rather than where they presently live. The francophones of Ontario exemplify well this estrangement from the culture and history of their "mother country" – Québec – as do some of those who live in Newfoundland and Labrador. The francophones of Newfoundland's Port-au-Port Peninsula, by contrast, have a direct link with their past resembling that of their Acadian counterparts.

Part III
Minority Societies

Chapter 7
Francophone Societies: Newfoundland and Ontario

Why join Newfoundland (Terre-Neuve) and Ontario in the same section, when the first is clearly a small minority society and the second a large minority society with a couple of majority regions? In part this is a marriage of convenience: a chapter on Newfoundland alone would be small because of the comparatively sparse literature on its francophones. Additionally, however, when it comes to francophone history and contemporary lifestyle in minority circumstances, Newfoundland and Ontario provide some of the most vivid and informative contrasts available in Canada. For example, nearly all the francophone communities in Ontario are home to people whose ancestors in one way or another originated in Québec (Lavoie, 1994: 128), whereas the francophone communities on Newfoundland's Port-au-Port Peninsula – the most francophone area of that province – were settled mainly by immigrants from western France. In this chapter, however, it is not my intention just to compare these two provinces with each other, but also to effect from time to time comparisons with Acadia and especially with Québec. In doing this, I will discuss in the order set out in chapter 5 the same five areas of everyday life: geography, community structure, education, language, and culture. Newfoundland is considered first, then Ontario.

Newfoundland

Today, Newfoundland's francophones are concentrated in three regions: Saint John's, the Port-au-Port Peninsula, and the Labrador City area (see figure 7.1). Newfoundland's 2590 mother-tongue francophones comprise only about one-half percent of the province's general population, although 3.9 percent of that population (21 415) have a knowledge of French (Statistics Canada, 1998a). The greatest numerical and proportional concentration of mother-tongue francophones in Newfoundland is in the Port-au-Port area, where in Division 4, Subdivision E (an administrative unit), in which l'Anse à Canards (Black Duck Brook) and La Grand' Terre (Mainland) are located, they constitute 9.7 percent of the overall population. The cultural and demographic centre of the region, however, is situated in Cap Saint-Georges, where 23.1 percent of the population of 1019 is mother-tongue francophone (Statistics Canada, 1998b). This latter group, says Magord (1993: 76), has one of the lowest assimilation rates of all francophone groups outside Québec. Indeed, it has even experienced a modest raise in its numbers, while the sizes of many analogous groups elsewhere in Canada are declining. This trend is all the more remarkable given the rate of exogamous marriages for the whole of Newfoundland: calculated from 1996 census data, it is 78.7 percent, the highest in Canada.

Approximately half the francophones in Newfoundland live on the Port-au-Port. Most of the rest live in the Saint John's area, with a still smaller number living in or near Labrador City, where over recent decades, intermarriage and out-migration have reduced considerably their presence in this region. In 1996 they made up 4.4 percent of the population, a decline of 5.4 percent since 1991 (Charbonneau, 1992: 86).

Figure 7.1

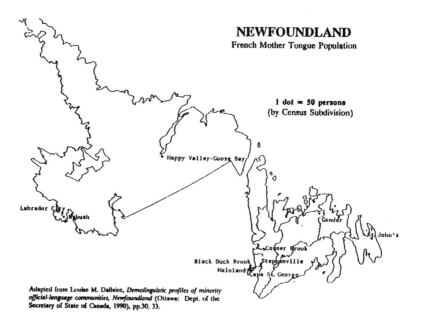

NEWFOUNDLAND
French Mother Tongue Population

1 dot = 50 persons
(by Census Subdivision)

Adapted from Louise M. Dallaire, *Demolinguistic profiles of minority official-language communities, Newfoundland* (Ottawa: Dept. of the Secretary of State of Canada, 1990), pp.30, 33.

French Labrador was peopled primarily by Quebeckers seeking work in the construction of Labrador City or in the exploitation of iron ore. The francophone population of Saint John's is of rather more varied background, coming from France, Québec, Saint-Pierre et Miquelon, and Acadia, primarily Nova Scotia (Charbonneau, 1992: 73). The section in chapter 2 on the origins of the francophones living on the Port-au-Port indicates that, in this regard, it differs immensely from the other two regions.

Community Structure

Like other francophone communities operating in minority circumstances, the main institutions on the Port-au-Port Peninsula are leisure, education, religion, and the family. As in Acadia, francophones in this region give substance to these institutions by establishing sizeable networks of francophone friends and relatives and by creating a number of organizations in the form of clubs, societies, associations, and informal small groups. Here, too, individuals use French in different ways within this structure.

The Church can be dealt with in a short paragraph, for it seems to have little or no relevance among contemporary Port-au-Port francophones. Magord (1995: 125) concluded from his research there that

> religion represents one of the rare dominant group structures to which Franco-Newfoundlanders have access. [Nevertheless] a growing number of the latter perceive it as an authoritarian mechanism of assimilation. Moreover, in arranging a unique gathering of anglophone and francophone groups, the church sometimes becomes, paradoxically, a setting for experiencing discrimination. (translation)

Indeed, one main reason the early settlers had for leaving France was to escape religious authority (Magord, 1993: 74). In my tour of the area I found a single Catholic chapel in La Grand'Terre, whose bilingual sign attests the mix of language groups observed by Magord. It is also noteworthy that Charbonneau (1992) mentions neither the Church nor its religion.

Magord maintains that the suspicion of religious authority among these francophones is but one facet of their collective rejection of all authority. Down through the years this stance has given rise to various informal structures within the family and the neighborhood characterized by solidarity, reciprocity, and conviviality.

Historically, these Franco-Newfoundlanders have tended to develop a strong sense of belonging first by working together and then by playing together, as done in evenings of singing, dancing, telling stories, and listening to music (usually their own folk music). To be sure, less of this happens today than earlier, given the breakdown of isolation of the Peninsula that began in the 1940s, but these activities nonetheless remain as possible casual and serious leisure outlets for those who find them interesting. In addition, the rich natural environment of the area invites free-time participation together in fishing, hunting, skiing, and hiking and camping. And some francophone youth from the Port-au-Port participate in the organization *Franco-Jeunes*, whose activities include competing in the francophone youth games held annually in Labrador and Acadia.

The provincial organization that speaks for all Newfoundland francophones – the Fédération des francophones de Terre-Neuve et du Labrador – is based in Saint John's, also the seat of the provincial government. Francophone parents have also established a province-wide organization. Moreover, Cap Saint-Georges, La Grand'Terre, and l'Anse-à-Canards each have a town association, which for the first two is their only formal francophone organization (Charbonneau, 1992: 70).

In 1989, La Grand' Terre opened its own school-community centre. A school-community centre is at once an organization and a building providing facilities for French primary and secondary education and a space for francophone social, cultural, and organizational needs. Besides the usual facilities for schooling at the two levels, most centres of this sort also contain an auditorium as well as office and meeting space for local clubs and associations. Some house a small library, an art gallery, or a day care centre. The idea is to create a geographically-based social and cultural rallying point for local francophones. An Acadian innovation initially launched in Fredericton, New Brunswick, in 1978, it was subsequently copied by several francophone communities in the Maritime Provinces and more recently by the one in Kingston, Ontario (Pitre, 1992: 20). Calgary opened the first such establishment in the West in 1997. Many of Canada's minority francophone communities have community centres or cultural centres without an adjoining school.

On the whole, francophone organizational life on the formal level is thin compared with that routinely found in much of Acadia. Organizational life on the informal level is another matter, however. Here complicated networks of friends and family have emerged, whose members spend their leisure together, and when needed, aid each other in times of sickness, accident, natural disaster, and similar situations (Magord, 1995: 94-95). The evenings at home mentioned earlier – those consisting of music, dancing, and story telling – also take place within this informal structure. And the serious leisure activities of hunting, fishing, skiing, and pursuing individual sports as part of the annual francophone games are all conducive to the development of interpersonal ties, thus contributing further to the informal organizational life of the French population of the Port-au-Port Peninsula.

In all this, francophone economic life has been reduced to near extinction, that sphere now being almost exclusively the province of the area's anglophones. The only exception to this generalization appears to be the operations of an economic development group that in 1994 prepared a five-year plan for promoting tourism on the Peninsula and in the adjacent Stephenville area. Indeed, a number of Port-au-Port francophones have had to move to Stephenville to find work, the fishery, their economic mainstay from the beginning, having now virtually collapsed.

Education and Language

Newfoundland has no francophone or bilingual colleges or universities. But after a protracted legal struggle, Franco-Newfoundlanders recently gained the right to manage their own education (*Infoaction*, 1997). The Government of Newfoundland, in February 1997, signed an agreement to this effect with the federal government. Before this, francophone schools were managed by what amounted to anglophone school boards. Today, francophones in Newfoundland have access to six French schools, four of them French sections in an English school. The other two are fully-French institutions operating in La Grand'Terre (in its school-community centre) and Cap Saint-Georges. In addition, French pre-school programs (*la prématernelle*) are available in these two Port-au-Port towns and in Labrador City (Canadian Heritage, 1994c).

As for the French used on the Port-au-Port Peninsula, Charbonneau (1992: 91) holds that it is one of the richest and most original forms found in North America. He quotes Gerald Thomas, linguist and folklorist at Memorial University of Newfoundland:

Their speech is not the speech of Paris, of Québec, or even of Acadia. It is a French that was shaped over nearly 150 years .... Given that it has its origins in Brittany, one finds, as much for the French language as for the language of Brittany, a vocabulary, pronunciation, syntax, and system of forms that owes much to the western provinces of France, in general. (translation)

In fact, French on the Port-au-Port Peninsula would have died out in the 1960s, another victim of modernization, were not some young members of the community determined to revitalize their linguistic and cultural heritage (Magord, 1993: 75). This resulted for a time in the curious situation in which these young adults could speak in French with their grandparents, but not with their own parents. French literacy programs were soon instituted in the area to help eliminate this untoward family division.

Culture

Although culture in the Port-au-Port area is mostly produced and consumed on the informal level, unlike in Acadia, for example, some formal events do occur nevertheless. The most celebrated of these is the music, dance, and song festival *Une longue veillée*; it is held annually each August in Cap Saint-Georges and involves local artists supplemented by a good number of artists from Acadia. In addition, each year contains a couple of local folk festivals, some theatre productions, and sporadic displays of locally-produced crafts and paintings. From this milieu the occasional individual star emerges, including most notably Émile Benoit, a fiddler and storyteller known well beyond his hometown of l'Anse-à-Canards. He has performed in France, Norway, Louisiana, and Great Britain, receiving in 1988 from the Société nationale des Acadiens the prestigious medal "Léger-Comeau" (Charbonneau, 1992: 95).

Every June 24th, while Québec and much of the rest of francophone Canada is celebrating the *Saint-Jean-Baptiste*, the Franco-Newfoundlanders of the Port-au-Port are busy celebrating *La Chandeleur*. And just what is this event?

Formerly, in the middle of winter in the different regions on the West Coast, family provisions would run low. The francophones therefore had to unite to deal with this problem. The spirit of solidarity was ever present . . . . For example, if one family lacked potatoes and another flour, a friendly exchange was organized between the two.

Furthermore, public collections were organized. Thus some people would pass from house to house collecting enough provisions to make a big meal. All the community was invited to sample the different foods. The people were most proud to participate in this act of sharing. This is why they would signal their devotion by attaching a ribbon on a long pole which was carried by the king, himself one of the collectors. This event, known as *"courir la Chandeleur,"* has become a francophone tradition. (translated from an article by Julie Olivier reprinted in Charbonneau, 1992: 71)

Today, local francophones annually re-enact *courir la Chandeleur* by walking from Cap Saint-Georges across the high hill behind the town to La Grand'Terre on the other side, where the event finishes in a rollicking evening of music and folk entertainment.

In the sphere of communications, Newfoundland's francophones have access to S.R.C. radio and television in Moncton and Montréal as well as a community radio station in Labrador and a community television station in la Grand'Terre. *La Gaboteur,* a monthly published in Stephenville, has been providing local francophone news since 1984, although it temporarily ceased publication in 1998, and since then, its sponsor has been searching for operating funds (Conseil de la vie française en Amérique, 1998: 4). The local history, *Contre vents et marées* (Charbonneau, 1992), like its equivalent found in so many other parity and minority francophone communities and regions in Canada, undoubtedly serves to enhance the senses of belonging and Frenchness so essential for the survival and development of Franco-Newfoundland. A community museum centred on local francophone heritage will soon open on the Port-au-Port; it will become another resource for reaching these two goals, while being a tourist attraction with potential for boosting the frail francophone economy.

Ontario

The historical development of French Ontario presented earlier bore on the four regions of heaviest francophone concentration in the province: Ottawa-Prescott-Russell, Windsor, Sudbury-North Bay, and Timmins-Kapuskasing-Hearst. To this list Toronto and Hamilton must now be added, which like other major Canadian cities have for many years been the destination of large numbers of francophones seeking employment or education, often both (see figure 7.2). Finally, three much smaller cities lying outside these regions warrant brief mention. Welland, a community on the Niagara Peninsula with a population of 48 100 in 1996, has attracted

Québec francophones since the 1920s to work in its various industries (Cardinal, Lapointe, and Thériault, 1988). They constituted 13.6
percent of the population in 1996. Tecumseh is a suburb of Windsor
whose population of 12 828 was 8.1 percent francophone in 1996.
Once a favorite route of the *voyageurs* and more recently a magnet
for francophone industrial labor, it was in the past a French town
(Jackson, 1994). Penetanguishene on Georgian Bay, population of
7290 in 1999, was in that year 18.7 percent francophone.

Figure 7.2

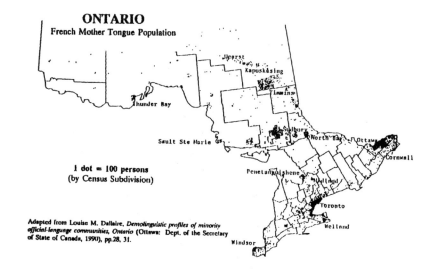

ONTARIO
French Mother Tongue Population

1 dot = 100 persons
(by Census Subdivision)

Adapted from Louise M. Dallaire, *Demolinguistic profiles of minority
official-language communities, Ontario* (Ottawa: Dept. of the Secretary
of State of Canada, 1990), pp.28, 31.

   In absolute figures, Ontario has the largest number of mother-
tongue francophones of any province outside Québec: 520 845, or 4.8
percent of the total population (Statistics, 1998a). Slightly over 12
percent of the population, or 1 281 835 people, have a knowledge of
French; they can hold an extended conversation in that language on
a variety of subjects. Table 7.1 contains the numbers and proportions
of mother-tongue francophones and speakers with a knowledge of
French living in the large cities and selected medium-sized cities in
Ontario's French regions.

Table 7.1 Mother-Tongue French and Knowledge of French in selected Ontario Cities

City (by CMA)	No. of mother-tongue francophones	Percent of total CMA population	No. who know French	Percent of total CMA population
Ottawa (Ontario part)	143 675	19.0	303 915	40.2
Toronto	62 850	1.5	342 995	8.1
Hamilton	10 590	1.7	42 205	6.8
Windsor	14 300	5.1	29 460	10.7
Sudbury	48 130	30.0	66 155	41.6

Source: Statistics Canada (1998a)

Note, however, that in comparison with the rest of Ottawa, the proportion of mother-tongue francophones is considerably higher in its enclave of Vanier: 54.5 percent, rising to over 60 percent when only anglophones and francophones are compared (Statistics Canada, 1998b).[1] Note also that first-language francophones in the small cities of Northern Ontario, especially Hearst, Kapuskasing, Timmins, and North Bay, constitute significantly larger proportions of the overall city population than they do in the medium- and large-sized cities described in Table 7.1. Hearst, for example, is 86 percent francophone; in Kapuskasing the ratio is over two-thirds.

Community Structure

The Ontario francophone communities exemplify well the general rule that holds in all Canadian francophone societies lying outside Québec: communities with the largest proportions of francophones are small in size and these proportions are lower in larger communities and lower still in very large communities. For example, in 1996, Hearst's population of 6049 was 86 percent mother-tongue francophone, compared first with neighboring Kapuskasing, a city of 10 036 population of which 67.3 percent was francophone, and then with Timmins, whose population was 47 499, with 39 percent of it being francophone. That same year in eastern Ontario, 79.1 percent of the 967 residents of Plantagenet were mother-tongue francophone, while nearby Alexandria – a town of 3531 – was 57.5 percent francophone, and Cornwall 50 kilometres away with a population of 47 403 was only 31.3 percent francophone. Finally, compare all these proportions with those of still larger cities: Ottawa (19.0%), Windsor (5.1%), and Toronto (1.5%). These figures are important because, as the proportion of French-speaking residents declines, so does the completeness of their institutions.

My drive through Hearst revealed a community almost as thoroughly French as Caraquet, New Brunswick, and similarly-sized communities in Québec. Bousquet (1992) writes that, especially in Prescott-Russel County near Alexandria, francophones dominate to the extent that local entrepreneurs can work in French and local anglophones assimilate to French at a rate of three percent. In this area, the one in Ontario with the greatest concentration of francophones, 17 of its 18 municipalities are officially bilingual (Bousquet, 1992). Apart from mentioning their existence, little more will be said about the structure of these communities since it is hardly typical of minority francophone life.

Therefore, given that most of Ontario's francophones live as a linguistic minority, it is important to examine the incomplete community structure that evolves in this situation. The provincial organization representing this minority to the outside world is the Association canadienne-française de l'Ontario (ACFO); its branches, themselves significant local rallying points, are found in 22 communities throughout the province. Specialized province-wide organizations also exist for francophones in each of the following groups: jurists, parents, teachers, youth, women, secondary-school students, and the elderly. Added to these are the scores of local clubs, among them 49 Richelieu Clubs of Ontario (Guindon and Poulin, 1996: 445), 20 cultural centres, many chapters of the Chevaliers de Colomb, numerous French parishes, and myriad small societies and associations centred on a variety of leisure interests, community services, and self-help concerns.

Depending on the size of the local francophone population, then, organizational life on the formal level in Ontario, even in minority circumstances, can be most involved. That many francophones live in one of the francophone regions no doubt augments the organizational side of their lives, for if the group or service they are interested in does not exist in their town, they may conveniently find it in the neighboring community. Moreover, the French school is becoming increasingly important as a main conduit for transmitting French language and culture to the community's next generation (Gérin-Lajoie, 1996). Turning to the informal level, there also exists in Ontario francophone life a vast organization of interpersonal relationships and social networks of friends and relatives. And here the scope of activities pursued in the informal sphere expands considerably, because Ontario francophones have more cities of all sizes available to them and hence more leisure activities to choose from than their counterparts in the rural areas and small towns of Atlantic Canada.

In fact, a highly satisfying linguistic lifestyle is available for many. Sociologically speaking, a lifestyle is a distinctive set of shared patterns of behavior organized around a set of coherent interests or social conditions or both. Participants explain and justify these patterns with a set of related values, attitudes, and orientations which, under certain conditions, become the basis for a separate, common identity.[2] Note that this definition refers exclusively to group lifestyles. This restriction is not to deny the existence of idiosyncratic, highly personal, lifestyles led by recluses, workaholics, people suffering from acute mental disorder, and other loners. Rather the restriction recognizes that, to this point, the study of lifestyles has concentrated almost entirely on shared patterns of tangible behavior, with the result that little information exists about individual lifestyles.

According to the foregoing definition, some lifestyles serve to identify their participants. In other words, the participants are members of a category of humankind who recognize themselves and, to some extent, are recognized by the larger community for the distinctive mode of life they lead. Prostitutes, beach habitués, travelling sales people, and the institutionalized elderly are identifiable in many ways, possibly the most visible being their peculiar lifestyles. The same can be said for the francophone enthusiasts pursuing many of the serious leisure activities.

Thus, a profound lifestyle awaits anyone who routinely pursues a serious leisure career in, say, amateur improvisational theater (*la Ligue d'improvisation*), volunteer work with *les Scouts et Guides*, the hobby of weaving, or that of back-country canoeing. And it is possible that this person also finds exciting, albeit clearly less profound, lifestyles in such casual leisure pastimes as socializing at home with francophone friends and attending French films at a local cinema. But many other forms of casual leisure, for example routine sun tanning or strolling in the park, are often not shared with others and therefore cannot be considered lifestyles according to the preceding definition. Moreover, in themselves, these activities are too superfi-

cial and unremarkable to serve as the basis for a recognizable mode
of living.

A central component of this linguistic lifestyle is the special
social world which begins to take shape when enthusiasts in a particular field pursue substantial shared interests over many years.
According to David Unruh (1979; 1980) every social world has its
characteristic groups, events, routines, practices, and organizations.
Each is held together, to an important degree, by semi-formal, or
mediated, communication. In other words, in the typical case, social
worlds are neither heavily bureaucratized nor substantially organized through intense face-to-face interaction. Rather, communication
is commonly mediated by newsletters, posted notices, telephone
messages, mass mailings, radio and television announcements, and
similar means.

Each social world is a diffuse, amorphous entity to be sure, but
nevertheless one of great importance in the impersonal, segmented
life of the modern urban community where formal work organizations are now becoming increasingly marginal in the everyday
affairs of many city people (Rifkin, 1995; Stebbins, 1998a: chap. 8)
and where francophones seek involvement with their linguistic *con-
frères*. Part of this importance comes from the freedom its participants have to enter it (given the right qualifications) and leave it.
Part comes from their voluntary identification with the social world
and its central activities – e.g., stamp collecting, amateur hockey,
volunteer president of the local branch of ACFO. Moreover, because
they are so diffuse, it is common for their members to be only partially involved in the full range of activities these formations have to
offer. After all, a social world may be local, regional, multi-regional,
national, even international.

So the more urbanized francophones find a great deal of casual
and serious leisure to chose from, and the range of choices expands
with the size of the city. But nowhere is choice unlimited. In fact, language can limit choice, when it is not already limited by taste, availability, and time and income. For instance, it was mentioned earlier
that only six of the 16 areas of volunteer activity are normally available to francophones who want to speak French while performing
the activity. In these days of government cutbacks, nearly all francophone organizational activity outside Québec is conducted by volunteers, some volunteering as casual leisure, some doing so as serious leisure. Most of this volunteering, however, is confined to the

fields of education, religion, recreation, civic affairs, human relationships, and the arts.

A discussion of structure in the Ontario francophone community would be seriously incomplete without mention of the cultural and community centres that are so common in the northern and eastern regions of the province. Diane Farmer's (1996: 82-90) unique study of these organizations reveals that although the first one was established in 1950 in Sudbury, most have come to life since 1970, doing so at a rate that amounts to a social movement. As of 1995-96 she counted 39 such centres, with 24 being members of the Assemblée des centres culturels de l'Ontario, whose mission is to strengthen the ties between the different centres and act as a advocate for them in the wider anglophone and francophone milieux.

Farmer concludes that these centres are first and foremost meeting places for local francophones. Many also serve as cultural and educational establishments, thereby helping to establish a sense of identity and belonging in their francophone patrons. In particular, a cultural or community centre is a resource offering, according to its budget, the following services: secretarial, printing, and meeting rooms and office space (for francophone organizations). Many contain a library, an arts and crafts boutique, perhaps even a cafe as well as a day care service and some space for displays and receptions. Additionally, some centres educate francophones and the general public about francophone history and tradition by offering plays, shows, concerts, festivals, and expositions related to the local or regional French community. And some offer adult and continuing education courses and workshops on a variety of subjects of interest to francophones, including sport, leisure cooking, arts and crafts, and even some academic subjects.

In his study of Alexandria, a parity community, Rayside (1991: 176-181) describes the francophone linguistic lifestyle at the balance point where the two language groups are most or less equal in size:

> Although French can routinely be heard in more shops and offices than ever in Alexandria and has even become dominant in a few, the working language in settings where francophones and anglophones come into contact is still invariably English. The service clubs, volunteer associations, and recreational groups, which claim to be open to both English and French, all operate almost exclusively in English. As a result, learning English has long been virtually obligatory for local francophones.

Today, Alexandria's anglophones and francophones engage in much the same kind of work and leisure, although they often do this in separate spheres. For only in these spheres are the former assured of routine expression in French. Rayfield reports that some church-related groups, some sports leagues, certain clubs, and certain leisure activities (e.g., snowmobiling) are clearly French. Some businesses are patronized chiefly by francophones, including one of the two supermarkets and, of course, the *caisse populaire*. Certain factories, depending especially on the language used by management, are dominantly French or English.

Finally, it is necessary to look briefly at francophone economic activity as an aspect of community structure. At the centre of the local economy are the *caisses populaires*, in particular, and the co-operative movement, in general. Both were major instruments of economic development in the twentieth century and both are likely to continue playing this role well into the future. Presently 57 *caisses* operate in French Ontario, and the Fédération des caisses populaires de l'Ontario has been an auxiliary member of Québec's Desjardins movement since 1989 (Guindon and Poulin, 1996: 28-29). Moreover, when a community has a sufficiently large proportion of francophones, a variety of French businesses are sure to spring up as well. This tendency justified founding in 1983 the Chambre économique de l'Ontario.

Education

Until recently in Ontario, management of French education was as complicated as the demographic distribution of francophones in the province and the two are closely related. A major part of the problem is reckoning with Ontario's 358 French elementary and secondary schools. In the 1980s four French-language school boards existed in Toronto, Ottawa-Carleton, Prescott, and Russell; they governed approximately a quarter of the francophone schools in the province. In sixty of the remaining school boards, French-language sections were established for the purpose of governing the francophone schools within. The other seven school boards provided no education in French. In 1996 Ducharme (1996: 22) reported four ongoing legal actions, each related at bottom to the failure to provide independent French-language school boards beyond those already established or to the failure to properly fund those already established. Here is another instance of the use of the courts by minority francophones to secure implementation of rights guaranteed them under the 1982 Charter. The legal action was successful. The Government of Ontario agreed early in 1997 to instituting seven new school boards, to be put in operation in 1998, thus giving francophones across the province control of their schools (*Le Franco*, 1997a: 2).

Franco-Ontarians also have a range of post-secondary educational opportunities, including an all-French agricultural college, two bilingual university colleges, four bilingual community colleges, and three technical colleges, of which one, la Cité collégial in Ottawa, is all-French. The two universities serving the province's francophones – Université d'Ottawa and Université Laurentienne (located in Sudbury) – are both bilingual. Francophones in Toronto have access to the bilingual Collège universitaire de Glendon, affiliated with York University, while those in the North who cannot arrange to go to Ottawa or Sudbury can attend the bilingual Collège universitaire de Hearst, an affiliate of Université Laurentienne.

Université d'Ottawa enrolled in 1997-98 over 25 000 full- and part-time students, making it the largest bilingual university in North America. Founded as a college in 1848 by the Oblate Fathers, it offers today a full range of undergraduate, masters, and doctoral programs in both languages. Although the figure was once higher, francophone students presently account for around 36 percent of the total number of students. Professors at the University must pass a rigorous test certifying their competence to teach in their second language.

Université Laurentienne is much smaller, enrolling 6137 full- and part-time students in 1997-98, of whom 16 to 17 percent are francophone. It is one of Canada's new universities, founded in 1960 by the Jesuits expressly to serve the linguistically mixed regions of north and north-central Ontario. Since professors are not required to be bilingual, francophone students find their choices limited to programs in commerce, management, the humanities, and the social sciences. The science programs are only available in English. The University offers selected masters and doctoral programs in addition to a wide range of undergraduate programs. Collège universitaire de Glendon enrolled 1977 full- and part-time students in 1996.

Language

Since French Ontario was figuratively described earlier by Louder, Trépanier, and Waddell (1996) as one of the bilingual foothills of purely-French "Mount" Québec, this is the appropriate place in this book to introduce the linguistic concept of diglossia. Diglossia is the systematic use by a community of two different languages or varieties or dialects of a language in different situations. Ferguson (1959) argued that, when people in the community use their two languages in all their social roles, when the two are universally applicable everywhere in their lives, these languages have a non-diglossic relationship. By contrast, when use of the two languages is confined to particular roles and the two cannot be effectively used in other roles normally enacted using the other language, the relationship between the two is diglossic.

Laponce (1996: 85-87) argues that, if French is to survive away from the centre – Québec – in such places as Ontario, and even more peripherally, in Newfoundland, the prairies, and British Columbia, then a diglossic relationship between it and English is the only realistic alternative. This relationship, says Laponce, should be intentionally striven for in the French schools and universities, where in the terminology of this book, students would be helped and encouraged to develop vocabulary consistent with the institutional incompleteness of their communities. They would learn the vocabulary needed to communicate with francophone friends and relatives in family (which includes all sorts of household matters), leisure, education, and according to personal interest, religion.

Cazabon (1996: 313), in writing strictly about education in Ontario, would likely find this strategy too restrictive, however, for he is convinced that as much work is available there in French as in English. It follows that students growing up as francophone in one of the francophone regions would do well to seek education in the former. Such advice could be extended to students in northern and eastern New Brunswick, but not to other francophone regions of Canada, unless of course, they would be prepared to move to a more strongly French area of the country to work in French. In this regard, Landry's (1997: 161-162) advice that, where French linguistic vitality is relatively weak, as it is outside Québec and parts of Ontario and New Brunswick, primary and secondary schools should adopt the "maximalist" solution to bilingual education. That is, to ensure that students acquire an additive bilingualism, all their educational material should be in French, save their English language classes.[3]

Culture

With 39 cultural and community centres in operation, the cultural life of Franco-Ontarians living in the areas of francophone concentration has, by this fact alone, the potential to be reasonably well developed. It is often in these establishments where Ontario's six professional francophone theatre companies perform and where people can enjoy the dramatic presentations of some 40 adult and student amateur groups. Ottawa has long been the centre of French-language theatre in Ontario. Fifty professional performers and 400 amateurs in the other stage arts combine with the thespians to offer Ontario's francophones close to 600 plays and concerts a year (Canadian Heritage, 1994d). Several major arts and heritage festivals, among them *Nuit sur l'étang* (Sudbury, founded in 1973) and *Festival franco-ontarien* (Ottawa, founded in 1972), enrich still further the French cultural life of this province while providing an important outlet for local francophone talent. The Alliance culturelle de l'Ontario speaks for this diverse collection of artists. Some of the folklore of Franco-Ontario is displayed at the Centre de folklore Franco-Ontarien in Sudbury. Ontario also has a vigorous francophone film industry centred in what is known today as Studio documentaire Ontario/Ouest of the National Film Board. Between 1975 and 1995 this organization, formerly titled the Centre Ontarois, produced 65 films (*Le Franco*, 1995: 15), most of them documentaries.

French Ontario boasts several established writers, among them Jean-Marc Dalpé, Patrice Desbiens, Hélène Brodeur, Gabrielle Poulin, François Paré, and Daniel Poliquin. Jean-Marc Dalpé, a poet and playwright, won the 1988 Governor General's Award in drama for his play *Le chien*, and François Paré won the 1993 non-fiction Award for his book *La littérature de l'exiguité*. Robert Paquette is a well-known singer, poet, and song writer, a combination referred to in Canadian francophone circles as a *chansonnier*. Patrice Desbiens, also a poet, was the subject of the Ontario-produced film "*Mon Pays*"; it was selected as the best documentary at the 1992 Montréal art film festival (*Le Franco*, 1995: 15). These writers are, however, primarily regional in their appeal, having for the most part not established themselves outside Ontario.

In the field of communications, four publishing houses operate in French Ontario. The oldest, founded in Sudbury in 1973, is les Éditions prise de parole. Les Éditions l'interligne began operations in Ottawa in 1981, taking over publication of the literary magazine *Liaison*, founded three years earlier. The next house appeared in Ottawa in 1982 under the name of les Éditions du Vermillon. Then in 1988 in Hearst, les Éditions du Nordir came into being; it publishes *Atmosphères*, a multidisciplinary magazine. Young Franco-Ontarians have their own periodical titled *Clik*.

French Ontario is also well provided with mass media publications, including the Ottawa daily, *Le Droit*, and 13 weeklies. Radio-Canada produces French radio and television programs in Ottawa and Sudbury. It is joined on the airwaves by Chaîne française de TVOntario, the only French-Canadian public education television network outside Québec, several stations from Québec, and in many communities, by TV5 as well. There are also a multitude of private and community radio stations.

And legends abound. The following one about using consecrated bread to find the body of a drowned person (Dupont, 1985: 33) is shared by many Ontario francophones:

> A river is treacherous during the spring when it is full. At Sturgeon Falls a youth drowned, and the river would not yield his body. The locals had been searching for seven days, when my father said to three men: "come with me, we'll find it." He took a loaf of consecrated bread, decorated it with candles, placed it in a canoe, and then released it into the eddy. The bread began turning and turning in the eddy; then quietly, the tongues of flame [on the candles] flickered and it went upstream against the current up to the bottom of the falls. There, the loaf started turning in circles, as though it were searching, then it stopped still. "Search here, you will find it." They weren't very confident, but it was not long [and] they hooked the body of the drowned youth with a gaff and he was raised up.
>
> This story, it's pure truth; consecrated bread can wander from one side of the river to the other and it does not lie. My ancestors, they were fishermen on the high seas, and after damages, they would have some drowned colleagues to find and if they did not have consecrated bread, they would place some candles on a loaf of sailor's bread. I knew of people who would stick instead some needles in the bread, or who would use cedar stakes which would remain erect next to the body of the drowned man. But there was nothing better for finding a drowned person than "habitant's bread," blessed by the curé just before serving it; some people from Détroit, Essex, tried this out in 1940. (translation)

Despite this wealth of cultural material, Bellavance (1994b: 13) writes that it is not widely consumed by Ontario francophones.

Citing a report on the matter, he says it is the popularity of American culture that induces Franco-Ontarians to ignore their own culture much of the time. Distribution is also a problem in a province with the geographic spread of Ontario; this situation forces many artists to continuously apply for travel subsidies to the more remote francophone communities.

Conclusions

To draw once again on the centre-periphery analogy, foothills French Ontario, like its counterpart in New Brunswick, stands out clearly against the islands of francophones in Newfoundland. Still, northern and eastern Ontario is not as monolithically francophone as northern and eastern New Brunswick. To be sure, a few small communities exist in the former where the proportions of francophones exceed 90 percent, but they are scattered, interspersed with communities, many of them small cities, containing significant numbers of anglophones. Moreover, these anglophones do not behave like a minority, if in fact they constitute one numerically. They often own businesses that francophones patronize, they join organizations in numbers sufficient to force the conversation into English, they have the advantage of being members of the North American majority.

Thus, because they, too, must contend from time to time with the larger anglophone milieu and the many ramifications of living there, Franco-Ontarians must face up to many of the same issues as minority Franco-Newfoundlanders and Acadians. These issues are in fact enduring features of minority, and to some extent parity, living in francophone Canada; they will be considered anew in chapter 10 in the discussion of francophone lifestyles in western Canada.

Chapter 8
Contemporary Issues in Newfoundland and Ontario

As before, the issues considered in this chapter bear in one way or another on the survival of French language and culture and the development of parity and minority societies. There is a uniformity about this across the country, excluding of course the majority societies where francophones dominate and French institutional completeness is the rule. But elsewhere, in all of Newfoundland and central, southern, and western Ontario, certain issues loom large, notably, imperceptibility, identity, exogamous marriages, universities, and language and assimilation. But if the issues are the same, they are not, however, manifested the same way from society to society or even within a particular society.

Imperceptibility

The French fact in St. John's, Newfoundland, as in all medium- and large-sized Canadian cities outside Québec, is virtually imperceptible. It would be literally invisible in these communities, were it not for bilingual signs on bilingual schools, all-French signs on a very small number of all-French schools, and where they exist, French signs on local francophone cultural and community centres. Francophone visibility was not quite this low, however, on the Port-au-Port Peninsula.

Signs on the highway leading to this geographic protrusion proudly announce – albeit in English – that this is Newfoundland's "French Shore," the "Country of our French Ancestors." French names like Benoît, Jesso, Simon, and Lainey appear on many a roadside mail box, but as every researcher in this field knows, the people named there could be so assimilated to English that for them their name is the sole remnant of their ethnic past. All commercial signs were in English the year I drove through the area.

Nonetheless, my single transaction, which I initiated in French at the general store in La Grand'Terre, was conducted in a mixture of French and English. The sign on the Catholic chapel in the same community is partially bilingual and its community-school centre is announced entirely in French. The town's welcome sign is equally bilingual, as are those of Cap Saint-Georges and l'Anse à Canards. The latter two also have cultural centres, both clearly identified in French, while Cap Saint-Georges is the home of a few public spaces and institutions, each with bilingual identification. These villages have no *caisse populaire*, no chapter of the Chevaliers de Colomb, no francophone clubs or day care centres. The very few stop signs on the Peninsula are in English, while no one has bothered to mark the roads in any language.

On the institutional support measure of ethno-linguistic vitality, then, the three most francophone communities of the Port-au-Port give the reasonably sharp-eyed visitor an impression of relatively low French visibility, approximately that of the French Shore in New Brunswick and of many communities on Prince Edward Island. Generally speaking, all these areas offer good examples of the scattered bilingualism so common in Atlantic Canada. Yet, Pointe-de-l'Église stands out in this comparison as noticeably more French than the other communities on either French Shore of the two provinces, as does Abram-Village in Prince Edward Island.

The entire range of French perceptibility from low to high is evident in Ontario, with cities like Sault Sainte-Marie, Thunder Bay, and Toronto (Maxwell, 1977; Savas, 1990) exemplifying the low end of the scale. Even though all three have significant francophone populations for cities (in 1996, 4.3 %, 2.5%, 1.5% respectively), the first two officially declared and then widely publicized in the early 1990s their status as unilingual anglophone communities, indicating thereby the low importance their officials assign to the francophones in their midst. By contrast, many francophone communities in northern and eastern Ontario can be described as having moderate French perceptibility.

The single most significant distinguishing feature separating this latter set of communities from those low on the dimension of perceptibility is the conspicuous presence of bilingual commercial signs. Other indicators of substantial francophone numbers such as bilingual street and stop signs, signs identifying francophone organizations, and bilingual signs on church property are also important in this regard, but because money can be made or lost when language groups feel included or excluded, commercial signs appear to be the most sensitive. Certainly this was my impression on visiting Timmins, Prescott, and Kapuskasing, each describable as a moderately perceptible francophone community. At the high end of this scale stand towns such as Hearst, Moonbeam, and Mattice-Val Côté;

running from 86 to 91 percent francophone, these towns are as thoroughly francophone in most respects as Caraquet and Edmunston in New Brunswick.

Identity

Juteau (1980) observed that, early in the history of French Ontario, personal identity was anchored in the local francophone community and its culture, a unique combination that fostered special relations with neighboring francophone communities and their cultures. To the extent a broader collective identity also existed, it was that of *"Canadien,"* a label shared at the time with Québec francophones as this term was defined earlier. Between 1840 and 1867, however, both the local and the collective identity increasingly gave way to that of French Canadian in contradistinction to that of English Canadian. Still later, as conflict over the right to educate their children in French gripped the region – a strictly provincial matter – the identity of Franco-Ontarian soon gained ascendancy (Cardinal, 1994: 75). The effect of this tension was to highlight the lack of adequate French education as a major problem and distinctive feature of life in French Ontario vis-à-vis life in French Québec.

More precisely, Farmer (1996: 45-48) traces the rise of the identity of Franco-Ontarian to the introduction in 1912 by the Ontario government of Regulation 17. Bowing to pressure from some anglophones, in particular the Orange movement, and the Irish Catholic Church, the provincial government decreed that from thereon English would be the language of instruction and communication in Ontario. French would be tolerated in the early years of primary school, but not after that. Ontario's francophones, being in no mood to accept this ukase, immediately set about militating for its repeal. In the process, they became conscious of their common destiny as a minority language group both in their province and in their Church. As it turns out, their collective efforts paid off, for Regulation 17 was repealed in 1927. The state and other supporters of the measure, it seems, had hoped it would speed assimilation of the Franco-Ontarians.

How badly this strategy fared is evident in the modern propensity of some Ontario francophones to identify themselves as Ontarois, their French *gentilé*, or name for the inhabitants of a place, community, region, or country. Moise (1998) found in a survey of Franco-Ontarians that many still identify with the oppressions their ancestors endured at the hands of Ontario's anglophones, who dominated the spheres of politics and education. Commendable acts of resistance were often recalled during the interviews that Moise conducted for his study.

Magord (1996: 147) describes the complicated identity situation facing the francophone residents of the Port-au-Port Peninsula. All see themselves as Franco-Newfoundlanders, but different age groups further qualify this categorization. Those over 60 years of age who lived with the "old French" identify themselves as French descendants from France, while those between 40 and 60, who were young adults in 1949 when Newfoundland joined Canada, prefer the label of "Canadian." Those between 20 and 40 are most likely to identify themselves as Franco-Newfoundlanders without further qualification. The youngest generation (below 20 years of age) is inclined to see itself as bilingual, supporting the francophone side of this identity through contact with France, Québec, and Acadia and through involvements related to their French education and to their ethnic culture and history.

It is evident from the foregoing discussion of linguistic identity that institutions and collective autonomy are far from complete in the francophone communities of Newfoundland and in those in many parts of Ontario. For this reason it becomes difficult to see how Franco-Newfoundlanders and many Franco-Ontarians can identify themselves exclusively in provincial terms. In fact, these francophones also identify with aspects of the very anglophone community that undermines the completeness and autonomy of their own group, because these aspects of their everyday existence are also attractive. To be sure, this observation rests on the assumption that linguistic minorities in this situation have a choice. That they can attempt to ensure their autonomy and institutional completeness or that they can abandon to some degree these goals in favor of developing certain ties with the larger anglophone community. True, especially at work and in the commercial world, the large majority of minority francophones must accept involvement with the anglophone world. But because they are nearly always bilingual, it is also true that they do often have choices in others areas of life (Cardinal, Lapointe, and Thériault, 1994). For example, when selecting a leisure activity, they can choose one that is anglophone or francophone or use whichever language they prefer in activities that are linguistically neutral (e.g., skiing, hiking, window shopping, watching a parade). In this regard, city folks enjoy a larger selection than their country and small town cousins.

Furthermore, if the urban francophones living in parity and minority circumstances cannot exclusively identify with their language community, it does not necessarily follow that their identity is "indecisive," as Thériault (1994) has argued. It is equally possible, at least for city dwellers, that their francophone identities emerge from the conditions they encounter in their everyday lives and from their desire to participate from time to time in the larger anglophone world. In fact, research evidence suggests that, far from being indecisive, they unambiguously identify themselves as bilingual and bicultural persons (Mackey, 1997: 24; Stebbins, 1994: chap. 8).

What conditions of urban life make it possible for francophones there to maintain a bilingual identity? One condition is the distinctive linguistic lifestyle they lead, as this idea was defined in the preceding chapter. Every status group has its special mode of living seen in the shared patterns of behavior that have taken shape with reference to common interests and activities. The lifestyle of urban francophones becomes increasingly bilingual to the extent that these patterns of behavior bring them in touch with both the francophone and the anglophone institutions in their city, exemplified by working in English and socializing with family in French.

A bilingual, French-English lifestyle can be experienced in Canadian cities because of the enormous variety of social worlds available to francophones there. In turn, the social worlds to which individual francophones belong are evident in their **mosaic of activities**, in their participation in certain events, activities, and organizations. According to this conception (Stebbins, 1997), each urban francophone has his or her unique mosaic. The mosaic of Jacques, for example, might be composed of francophone amateur acting (social world), volunteer work with anglophone children (social world), participation in a francophone social club (activity), and attendance at anglophone professional hockey games (events). The mosaic of Danielle might consist of volunteering at the French school of her children, singing in an anglophone community chorus, spending some of her leisure time with her French-speaking family (activities), and attending the annual local folk festival held in English (event).

The four concepts considered here – bilingual and bicultural identity, mosaic of activities, linguistic lifestyle, and social world – shed further light on the complex, albeit segmented, social life of francophones living as linguistic minorities in Canada's large cities. These concepts also help specify the nature and degree of institutional incompleteness and partial autonomy with which they must constantly live. Yet in this environment seemingly so inimical to their ethnic interests, many urban francophones have nevertheless managed to hack out a viable bilingual-bicultural existence, an achievement the Calgary study suggests they are most proud of (Stebbins, 1994: 103-104).

Exogamous Marriages

Comparing the two provinces, it is clear that exogamous marriage poses a greater problem in Newfoundland, with its rate in 1996 of 78.7 percent, than in Ontario, whose rate that year was 42.4 percent. The latter figure masks some significant rural-urban differences, however, for this rate in the Toronto and Hamilton areas, for example, was 78.2 percent (Statistics Canada, 1998). Many francophone leaders hold that the higher the rate of exogamy, the greater the risk of assimilation to English by the children produced in these mixed unions. That this rate has been rising for many years in many francophone areas outside Québec is commonly seen as grounds for still further alarm.

Yet the situation may not have as many deleterious effects on francophone community survival as some predict (e.g., Bernard, 1990; Castonguay, 1998). For instance, as we saw in chapter 6 in the discussion of mixed marriages in Acadia, research findings suggest that children in them are significantly more likely to learn French and learn about francophone culture if the union is type-1 (female francophone-male non-francophone), rather than type-2 (male francophone-female non-francophone). As for adult francophones, Heller and Lévy (1993), in their study of francophone women in mixed marriages living in Sudbury, Toronto, and Ottawa, found three conditions of special importance in determining whether they continue their existence on the "linguistic frontier" by trying to retain their fluency in French. One is the degree of separation of the local anglophone and francophone communities; the less the separation the greater the movement toward English. The second is the possibility of receiving a local education in French; the greater this possibility the less likely the movement toward English. The third condition is the value of French in the labor market; the higher its value the lower the propensity to rely on English.

This study underscores the fact that language used at home – the principal measure for those concerned about the rates of linguistic exogamy and assimilation – is by no means the only area of everyday life in Canada where French is learned and used. O'Keefe (1998:

34) has criticized the tendency to rely uniquely on home language data when discussing the effects of exogamous marriages:

> The so-called rate of assimilation . . . tends to underestimate the use of minority languages because the home language data reflect only the language most often spoken. Two or more languages may well co-exist within a home. In fact, this is more often the case in mixed families. Moreover, the language may be present in non-spoken areas (TV, radio, reading). . . . [Furthermore] home language data can tell us nothing about the fact that French may very well be used outside the home, for instance at work, in the school, with family or friends. In mixed families, it is not uncommon for children to be sent to a minority language school in order to reinforce their mastery of the French language. Under these circumstances, schools serve as a counterweight to the home language environment.

Generally speaking, then, it can be argued that leisure, educational, and possibly even work activities play a major role in helping develop and maintain a person's desire and capacity to use French in parity and minority circumstances.

Universities

One problem faced by Ontario francophone universities is finding ways to encourage French-speaking youth to attend university in the proportion observed among anglophone youth in the province. Educational authorities at l'Université d'Ottawa estimated in 1992 that this rate was 50 percent lower for francophone youth compared with anglophone youth (Lusignan, 1992: 4), although the rate varies according to speciality (e.g., higher in the arts, education, and social sciences, lower in medicine and engineering). In this regard, were it not for the great influx of students from Québec, the proportion of francophone students at this University would be even lower (Lusignan, 1998a: 22).

In some quarters it is believed that, when francophones constitute only a third or less of all students at a bilingual university, it becomes an effective instrument of assimilation to English. Moreover, it is argued that many francophone youth prefer a purely French educational environment. The solution proposed by the ACFO is to establish in Ontario an all-French university; according to a study it commissioned, such an institution could attract as many as 20 000 students (Lusignan, 1992: 4). But, on the one hand, the

President of the University of Ottawa remains unconvinced that enough francophone students would enrol in such an institution to justify obtaining all the complex equipment required by the many different arts and science programs. Offering bilingual programs, on the other hand, brings in anglophones and raises the number of students and income from tuition, all helping to pay for and thus justify these capital acquisitions. In an era of budget trimming in education, an all-French university is at this time little more than a pipe dream.

The cry for a francophone university is loud and clear among the French-speaking students and professors at Université Laurentienne, for here too, assimilation to English is a major problem (Meney, 1992: 4). Moreover, courses in French at this university, because they serve only 16 to 17 percent of all its students, are often offered at unpopular (i.e., night, early morning) or widely different times. As a consequence, francophone students face special difficulties in scheduling their courses. Besides this problem they must also deal with the issue of language quality in the bilingual courses, where many anglophones enrol bringing with them a weak mastery of French.

The problems of assimilation, quality of French, limited course offerings, and so on are by no means limited to Ontario, a situation that prompted the founding of the Regroupement des universités de la francophonie hors Québec (RUFHQ). This organization, which speaks for and serves 13 institutions, established in June, 1999, a nation-wide network of graduate and undergraduate courses available by means of the new technologies (e.g., Internet, videoconferencing). The services of RUFHQ are also available outside the walls of its constituent members to francophones in provinces like Newfoundland and British Columbia where French higher education is not directly available. This network not only provides a broader range of courses for post-secondary francophone students, it also helps delay contact in the educational sphere with anglophone culture. The likelihood of assimilation should therefore decline for students pursuing their studies in this purely or nearly pure francophone learning environment.

Presently, significant numbers of francophone students, frustrated with the lack of French-language courses in their field of interest, transfer to an anglophone university, abandoning the francophone or bilingual institution where they were previously enrolled (*Le Franco*, 1996: 3). Thus the dearth of sufficiently-broad course offerings in French at the university level has emerged as a contemporary Achilles heel of the quest for survival and development of francophone Canada's parity and minority communities. As a result, many potential future leaders of these communities are being both pulled and pushed toward the English side of Canadian academic life as they try to pursue a course of studies that their French or bilingual institution cannot adequately provide. Modern technology and the modern student's propensity to use it may, however, turn out to be in combination a true savior of francophone life in parity and minority circumstances.

Language

Heller (1994) writes that the 1970s in Ontario was a period of francophone middle-class political activism aimed at resisting anglophone domination in the spheres of language and education and improving the quality of French taught in the schools. The goal of this movement was to establish an all-French system of education using standard French as both the language of instruction and the language of the school environment. In this quest, they were opposed by the francophone working class of the province, who believed that, given the realities of the anglophone-dominated labor market, bilingual schools better served their interests. Notwithstanding this opposition, a network of schools offering instruction in French was established toward the end of this decade.

After this, the struggle became more focussed, revolving by and large around three desiderata: 1) creating a unilingual francophone school environment, 2) ensuring high quality French within it, and 3) arranging for access to francophone post-secondary education for youth and thus for occupational careers for them heretofore closed to people without such education. With respect to the first and second desiderata, Ontario's francophone middle class contended that English was heard much too often in the schools, both inside and outside the classroom, and further, that it was much too often heard in the French spoken by young people, a language vitiated by anglicisms. In other words, some students were speaking standard French, some were speaking vernacular French, usually French riddled with anglicisms, and some were speaking alternatively French and English.

Aided by linguistic research conducted in the 1980s, educators began working toward the first two desiderata in an attempt to broaden the vocabulary of the typical student to cover the usual situations he or she encounters in everyday life. Linguists discovered that a narrow French vocabulary is a principal reason for resorting to English; many students are ignorant of the French words and phrases needed to function in many of the situations they find themselves in outside the school environment. Additionally, linguistic research supports the recommendation that vernacular French also be taught. Vernacular communication is common among youth, and if they cannot talk in vernacular French, it is certainly possible that they might cease using French of any kind in their circles, trying instead to communicate with each other in vernacular English.

Heller (1994) concluded that, although Ontario's middle-class francophones have basically reached their goals, they could not have succeeded without their working-class counterparts, whose large numbers were crucial in helping justify a separate French educational system. Evidence exists of an interclass consensus on the desirability of this system, but the question of French unilingualism *vis-à-vis* French-English bilingualism in the schools remains contentious, a seemingly perennial threat to the solidarity of the Ontario society. As always, the possibility of assimilation to English and the anglophone world is the Sword of Damocles hanging over francophones living in parity and minority circumstances.

Assimilation

In chapter 6, I introduced the institutional component of the concept of "ethnolinguistic vitality" as a vehicle for discussing the degree of perceptibility of minority francophone communities. Now I should like to examine in its entirety the idea of vitality, with an eye to tempering the fear of and skepticism about assimilation that currently upsets many Canadian francophones (first- and second-language), some of whom are social scientists. I draw here on the overview provided by Michael O'Keefe (1998: 7-11), mainly of the linguistic work of Giles, Bourhis, and Taylor (1977) and Landry and Bourhis (1997).

The basic proposition in this theory, as adapted to francophone Canada, is that the degree of ethnolinguistic vitality of a parity or minority community is a strong indicator of the tendency of mother-tongue and second-language francophones to use French there. The theory further predicts, in this instance for anglophone majority societies such as Canada, that when ethnolinguistic vitality is low, the tendency to assimilate to English is high. Based on his review of the literature in this field, O'Keefe (1998: 10) identified seven "key factors" that influence the vitality of a given language:

ๅ Symbolic – Is the language an official language? Are there official activities that cannot be accomplished in this language? Are there areas where the language is prohibited?

ๅ Demographic – What are the numbers, proportion, fertility, etc. of the language community?

ๅ Institutional – Are services (governmental and other) available in this language? How complete a range of institutions are available to the language community? Does the linguistic community manage and control its own institutions?

ๅ Education – To what extent is access to quality education available in this language?

ๅ Status and Prestige – Is the language one that is viewed as prestigious, for instance, is it used internationally, in key national institutions, does it facilitate travel, open access to cultural materials/products, or is it spoken widely by the elite within a society?

ๅ Identity – The sense of community can be an important consideration. What is the value members attach to their identity as members of the linguistic community? How important is language to the personal identity?

ๅ Utility – What is the economic and social utility of the language? As utility is not only economic, non-economic motivations should be considered as well. Is access to modern communications media possible in the language? Does the language facilitate travel to desirable destinations and does it widen cultural horizons?

How are these seven factors manifested in French Ontario? Turning to the first, note that French is an official language in all federal installations in Ontario, even if the province is not itself officially bilingual. Nowhere in Ontario to my knowledge is French prohibited, while it would absolutely essential to hear it in, for example, the opening ceremonies of a new francophone school or public monument. Having dealt with the demographics of French Ontario in the preceding chapter, little more need be said except to note that they convey an optimistic picture in some localities, a pessimistic one in others. In a parallel sense, institutional completeness and hence institutional perceptibility are evident in communities like

162 of Minority Societies

Hearst and Timmins, while incompleteness is equally evident in the big cities of Toronto and Hamilton. Part of this completeness, present even in many communities where there is otherwise significantly less of it, is the widespread availability of primary and secondary French education. But it is also clear that university education is not as available as it should be; therefore it presently contributes less to linguistic vitality than it could were it to be expanded such as described earlier by using the new technologies. Finally, I have argued throughout that the institution of leisure plays an important role in sustaining the vitality of French in parity and minority circumstances.

Is French prestigious? French is without doubt one of the world's main languages, officially recognized in one way or another in 44 countries, including Canada. Thus knowing it clearly facilitates travel in these countries, as well as some others (e.g., even though neither of us knew the other's mother tongue, I once spent a delightful evening conversing with a Japanese person because we both knew French). Moreover, French is the language of the political and educational elite in, for example, several African countries. Lastly, it is the only language one can use to obtain cultural and commercial goods in many parts of the aforementioned 44 countries. Even in Québec, off the beaten anglophone tourist path, French is the only workable language for acquiring these goods. A visit to, say, the Saguenay-Lac Saint-Jean region attests this observation.

The struggle over language in the schools, recounted in the preceding section, is evidence of the value of French for the individual and collective identities of Ontario francophones. In fact, a main theme of this book is that being either a first- or second-language francophone is a personal identifier of considerable importance for most people possessing this linguistic capacity. Finally, turning to the last factor, French has significant utility in Ontario. For instance, it gives access to the range of cultural activities and products considered in chapter 7. Furthermore, it helps qualify its speakers for bilingual employment opportunities, and in northern and eastern Ontario, for unilingual francophone employment opportunities. Reading, listening, and speaking in French also open the door to a great range of cultural experiences not available in English (e.g., French books, plays, films, television, and conversations). If I may be permitted one more anecdote from my own travels: while dining in a Latin Quarter cafe in Paris, I learned a great deal about how some

Frenchmen view Canada. French was the only possible language of communication in this situation.

O'Keefe (1998: 53-54) believes, as do I, that assimilation and francophone community survival and development are not wholly antithetical processes. He goes on to observe that

> the challenge that assimilation represents to any minority community is real and probably permanent. Just as we speak of a sustainable rate of development, perhaps we should be asking ourselves what is the rate of assimilation compatible with a sustainable minority community. While community development is necessarily a work in progress, there are unmistakable signs of progress. . . . Many past analyses of Francophone communities outside Québec have looked only at the proportion these communities represent in the total population. . . . [This] is a very poor indicator of assimilation of Francophone communities. . . . Leading indicators of minority community vitality allow us to present a more complete portrait of the current health and future prospects of these communities.

O'Keefe concludes that the vitality of these communities cannot be fully measured using demographic data only, but must also be estimated in terms of the spirit, determination, and sense of identity present there.

Conclusions

Recalling once again the centre-periphery analogy, this chapter has provided a comparative tour of the francophone foothills to the immediate west of Québec and the francophone archipelago situated far east of that province. The contrasts are immense, even within Ontario, not to mention those between Ontario and the remote and isolated Port-au-Port Peninsula. The contents of this chapter nevertheless suggest that, for Newfoundland and Ontario, it is not as Arnopoulos (1982) once questioned in her book *Hors du Québec point de salut?* (Outside Québec No Hope?). Today it is evident that these francophone societies will not only survive but also develop, even if the kind and amount of development will vary significantly between them.

The same can be said for many of the communities making up the francophone societies in western Canada. To continue the analogy, the communities in this region tend to cluster, thereby forming a linguistic archipelago. Moreover, they, too, are by no means dead, even if they are more or less imperceptible to passers-by. The goal of the next two chapters will be to show just how lively these imperceptible islands of francophone communities really are in western Canada. It will become evident that, although many of the issues are the same as in other parts of the country where francophones live in parity or minority circumstances, the history and development of francophone communities in the West are not lacking in special features.

Chapter 9
Francophone Societies in Western Canada

Nowhere in Canada is the image of "small islands of French" more vividly sketched than on the Canadian prairies, where these clusters of communities stand out in relief against the many clusters of other ethnic communities who also helped settle the region. Here, beyond the mountain and foothills of French North America, lies a truly archipelago-like formation as seen in a distinctive geographic dispersion of a language (Louder and Waddell, 1983). Yet this tendency is not at all evident in British Columbia, even though it is also clearly evident in Atlantic Canada: in Newfoundland, in Labrador, and on the Port-au-Port Peninsula; in Nova Scotia along the French Shore and on Cape Breton island; and in Prince Edward Island in the Évangéline and Tignish areas. On the prairies the tendency is weakest in Manitoba and strongest in Saskatchewan and Alberta.

Geography

Saint-Boniface, where today approximately half the population is francophone, has always been the undisputed centre of French language and culture in Manitoba, and as noted earlier, is also generally regarded as the cradle of that language and culture for Western Canada.[1] Modern Saint-Boniface is one of many districts composing the city of Winnipeg, the latter being the home of over 32 000 first-language francophones as recorded by the 1996 census. They make up 4.9 percent of Winnipeg's population (Statistics Canada, 1998a), with nearly half of them living east of the Red River in Saint-Boniface (Hallion, 1997: 129) and many others living in neighboring Saint-Vital, also a district of the city. In Winnipeg itself, 11 per cent, or 72 710, of its residents have a knowledge of French. Manitoba is home to 50 565 mother-tongue francophones, or 4.5 percent of the population, a figure that grows to 9.5 percent of the population when the 104 635 second-language speakers are added.

Figure 9.1

MANITOBA
French Mother Tongue Population

1 dot = 50 persons
(by Census Subdivision)

Beausejour
St. Claude   Winnipeg St. Boniface
Notre Dame de Lourdes   Ste. Anne
La Broquerie
Pierre-Jolys

Adapted from Louise M. Dallaire, *Demolinguistic profiles of minority official-language communities, Manitoba* (Ottawa: Dept. of the Secretary of State of Canada, 1990), pp.29, 32.

Table 9.1 Francophone Composition of Selected Manitoba Communities

Community	Total Population	Percent francophone
Saint-Claude	609	65.7
Notre-Dame-de-Lourdes	620	77.4
Saint-Pierre-Jolys	925	67.6
Sainte-Anne	1511	52.3
Saint-Léon and Bruxelles (part of Lorne Municipality)	2167 (of Lorne)	29.5
La Broquerie	2493	32.5
Saint-Malo (part of Salaberry Municipality)	3067 (of Salaberry)	48.6
Sainte-Agathe and Saint-Adolphe (part of Ritchot Municipality)	5634 (of Ritchot)	29.1
Taché	8273	21.1

Source: Statistics Canada (1998b)

As figure 9.1 shows, the sole francophone island in Manitoba is bounded on the north by Winnipeg, generally radiating from there south and southwest to the border with the United States. Table 9.1 indicates that in 1996 a number of these communities, especially the smallest, contained significant francophone majorities.

Nowhere else in Western Canada is francophone life so centrally organized as in Manitoba and its *plaque tournante*, Saint-Boniface. Saskatchewan, in contrast especially with Manitoba and somewhat less with Alberta, has a comparatively dispersed population of francophones (Kaltz, 1997: 91), who reside in two main islands, one in the centre of the province, the other in its southern region. Each island falls within the ambit of an urban centre; it serves as the destination of many of the migrants leaving the area and has its own symbolic francophone community of the migrant variety. Saskatoon, the centre for the central island, had a population of 216 445 in 1996, with 1.9 percent, or 4210 people, being mother-tongue francophone and 6.7 percent, or 14 235 people having a knowledge of French and English. The centre for the south is Regina, a city of 191 480 inhabi-

Figure 9.2

SASKATCHEWAN
French Mother Tongue Population

1 dot = 50 persons
(by Census Subdivision)

Adapted from Louise M. Dallaire, *Demolinguistic profiles of minority official-language communities, Saskatchewan* (Ottawa: Dept. of the Secretary of State of Canada, 1990), pp.31, 34.

tants of whom 2825, or 1.5 percent, were francophone in 1996 and 5.6 percent, or 10760 people, knew both official languages. Saskatchewan's population of 976615 is 2.1 percent first-language francophone and 5.2 percent know both languages.

The populations and proportions of each that are mother-tongue francophone in the central and southern islands are presented in tables 9.2 and 9.3.

*Table 9.2 Francophone Composition of Selected
Central Saskatchewan Communities*

Community	Total Population	Percent francophone
Debden	423	42.6
Zenon Park	259	65.6
Saint-Denis (part of Grant No. 372 Municipality)	490 (of Grant)	36.7
Saint-Brieux	507	23.7
Batoche and Saint-Isidore de Bellevue (part of Saint-Louis No. 431 Municipality)	1227 (of Saint-Louis)	48.5
Prince Albert	34 777	4.2

Source: Statistics Canada (1998b)

*Table 9.3 Francophone Composition of Selected
Southern Saskatchewan Communities*

Community	Total population	Percent francophone
Willow Bunch	431	34.8
Bellegarde (part of Storthoaks No. 31 Municipality)	462 (of Storthoaks)	29.2
Ponteix	544	65.6
Gravelbourg	1211	55.0

Source: Statistics Canada (1998b)

Alberta presents still another profile of francophone islands. There are four, labelled here as eastern, central, northwestern, and southern (see figure 9.3). The province as a whole is home to 52375 mother-tongue francophones, or 1.9 percent of the population, a ratio that jumps to 6.8 when its 180125 second-language francophones are included. The eastern island is organized socially and

Figure 9.3

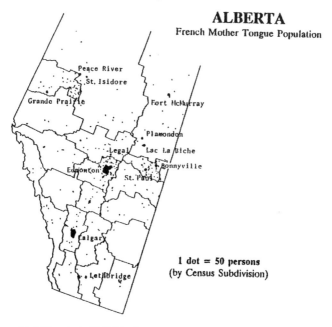

ALBERTA
French Mother Tongue Population

1 dot = 50 persons
(by Census Subdivision)

Adapted from Louise M. Dallaire, *Demolinguistic profiles of minority official-language communities, Alberta* (Ottawa: Dept. of the Secretary of State of Canada, 1990), pp.30, 33.

economically around the two largest cities in the area: Saint-Paul and Bonnyville. Its profile is presented in table 9.4. The Municipal District of Bonnyville encompasses several villages with significant proportions of francophones, as does the County of Saint-Paul.

Table 9.4 Francophone Composition of Selected Eastern Alberta Communities

Community	Total population	Percent francophone
Plamondon	256	31.3
Lac la Biche	2611	7.7
Grand Centre	4176	18.2
Saint-Paul	4861	18.2
Bonnyville and Medley (part of Municipal District No. 87)	17 352 (of MD 87)	10.5

Source: Statistics Canada (1998b)

The central Alberta island revolves around Edmonton as its social and economic hub, whose influence also radiates to the eastern and northwestern islands. Most communities in the central island house significant proportions of commuters who work in Edmonton (see table 9.5)

Table 9.5 Francophone Composition of
Selected Central Alberta Communities

Community	Total population	Percent francophone
Legal	1095	29.7
Beaumont	5810	8.8
Morinville	6226	8.0
Rivière qui Barre, Lamoureux, and Villeneuve (part of Municipal District of Sturgeon, No. 90)	15 945 (of Sturgeon)	4.6
Saint-Albert	46 888	3.6
Edmonton	862 595	2.5

Source: Statistics Canada (1998a; 1998b)

There are 64 295 first- and second-language francophones in Edmonton; they account for 7.5 percent of the city's population.

Viewed in terms of proportions, the northwestern island is decidedly the most francophone area of Alberta. As table 9.6 indicates, its two largest cities there are Grand Prairie and Peace River.

Table 9.6 Francophone Composition of
Selected Northwestern Alberta Communities

Community	Total population	Percent francophone
Donnelly	375	60.0
McLennan	867	26.5
Falher	1149	60.1
Tangent (part of Municipal District of Birch Hills No. 19)	1356 (of Birch Hills)	12.9
Saint-Isidore & Marie-Reine (part of Municipal District of East Peace No. 131)	2264 (of East Peace)	17.9

Jean Coté, Guy, and Dréau (part of Municipal District of Smoky River No. 130)	2491 (of Smoky River)	56.6
Peace River	6536	5.5
Grande Prairie	31 140	3.1

Source: Statistics Canada (1998b)

Marshall (1993) reports that nearly all the 250 residents of Saint-Isidore are French-speaking, even though they almost always have to use English when filling their routine needs elsewhere in the area.

The southern island is centred on Calgary, whose 14 241 mother-tongue francophones comprise 1.7 percent of that city's population. Its 60 430 residents who know French as either a first or a second language make up 7.4 percent of the population. The southern island also includes three of the four mountain national park communities of Alberta, which form minor francophone centres in their own right. French-speaking youth from eastern Canada help account for the relatively high ratios found in these places (see table 9.7). And it appears, for reasons yet to be discovered, that they prefer the Alberta mountains to those in British Columbia, for the proportions of francophones are unexceptional in the national park communities of the second.

Table 9.7 Francophone Composition of Alberta National Park Communities

Community	Total population	Percent francophone
Waterton	279	5.4
Lake Louise	1305	8.4
Jasper	4301	6.7
Banff	6098	6.4

Source: Statistics Canada (1998b)

In fact, the settlement patterns of francophones in British Columbia bear no resemblance to those in the other nine provinces. The primary difference is that 54.2 percent of them are concentrated in the Vancouver and Victoria areas, with the rest being scattered across the province in no discernible pattern. British Columbia has 60 675 mother-tongue francophones, or 1.6 percent of the population, a figure that jumps to 6.8 percent (250 365 people) when sec-

Figure 9.4

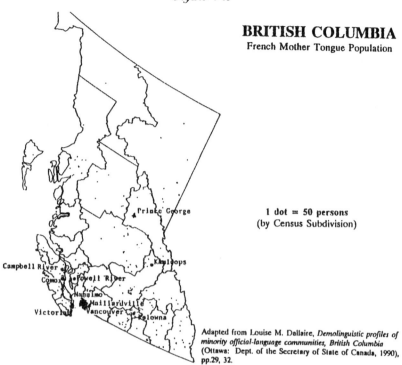

BRITISH COLUMBIA
French Mother Tongue Population

1 dot = 50 persons
(by Census Subdivision)

Adapted from Louise M. Dallaire, *Demolinguistic profiles of minority official-language communities, British Columbia* (Ottawa: Dept. of the Secretary of State of Canada, 1990), pp.29, 32.

ond-language speakers are counted (Statistics Canada, 1998a). The 27 250 first-language francophones in Vancouver account for 1.5 percent of that city's population, of which 7.4 percent (124 635 people) know both official languages. Considered just one of the many minority groups in town, they constitute a mobile segment of the population, for there is a marked tendency, even among teachers of French, to stay only a few years before moving elsewhere (Bélanger, 1992).These figures are somewhat higher in Victoria, where 5640 mother-tongue francophones constitute 1.9 percent of the city's population and 8.7 percent (26 050 people) know both languages. Even the former enclave of Maillardville has been decimated by assimilation to the point where the francophone population is but a tiny minority. Still, it is an active minority, for it is served by a French school and a scout and guides association. Moreover, in 1997 the Société Maillardville-Uni was to receive a measure of federal government support for constructing a community centre and holding its annual *Festival du bois* (Canadian Heritage, 1997: 37). Finally, it should be noted that francophones also help populate the North, although not in especially large proportions. The populations of

Yellowknife and Whitehorse, for example, are 4.1 and 3.7 percent mother-tongue francophone (Statistics Canada, 1998b).

Having now examined the proportions of first- and second-language francophones in every large city outside Québec, it is possible to compare these figures. The proportions and the ratios describing the gap between them are presented in table 9.8. The lower the ratio the greater the proportion of second-language francophones in the city's general population. In the migrant cities, mother-tongue francophones are in a minority situation vis-à-vis second-language francophones, whereas in the indigenous cities they are more or less in a parity situation.

Table 9.8 Ratios of First- and Second-Language Francophones in the Large Cities

Cities	% First-language francophones	% First- and Second-language francophones	Ratio of columns 2 and 3
Cities with migrant communities			
Toronto	1.5	8.1	.185
Hamilton	1.7	6.8	.250
Calgary	1.7	7.4	.230
Vancouver	1.5	7.4	.203
Cities with Indigenous communities			
Ottawa	19.0	40.2	.473
Winnipeg	4.9	11.0	.446
Edmonton	2.5	7.5	.333

The main conclusion, indeed possibly the only conclusion, to be drawn from this table is that mother-tongue francophones in the migrant communities are more likely than their linguistic cousins in the indigenous communities to rub elbows qua francophones with their second-language counterparts. This happens because, in the migrant communities, proportionately more second-language francophones are available to participate in francophone affairs, whether these be going to club meetings or festivals or patronizing services such as cinemas, book stores, and restaurants. In other words, in those communities second-language francophones add significantly to the number of French-speaking people needed to sustain collective life there. In this regard, these francophones are less important in the indigenous communities.

Community Structure

Like the Ontario francophone communities, those on the prairies tend to be consistent with the proposition that communities with the largest proportions of francophones are small in size and that these proportions are lower in larger communities and lower still in very large communities. Those in Saskatchewan present the largest number of exceptions to this rule, while those in Manitoba present the fewest. Along these lines, Denis (1993) has demonstrated that Saskatchewan communities with (1) a small number of francophone businesses also have (2) a small number of volunteer organizations and (3) a small number of sectors of social life in French. By contrast, communities strong on one of these three dimensions also tend to be strong on the other two. But these are all small towns. When Denis examined the province's medium-sized cities, he found the third dimension is strong, while the first two are weak.

Many other forms of community structure exist as well. One of these – the majority structure – is evident in those prairie communities whose francophone residents constitute 60 percent or more of the population; these include Saint-Claude, Notre-Dame-de-Lourdes, Saint-Pierre-Jolys, Zenon Park, Falher (officially bilingual), and the village of Saint-Isidore in Alberta. Each appears to enjoy a high degree of institutional completeness. I have personally visited nearly all those just mentioned (except Zenon Park), where I found French very much in evidence in the spheres of club life, religion, education, financial services (the *caisses populaires* are conspicuous), public services, and public communication (e.g., street signs, public notices). The commercial world is mixed French and English, however; signs here are sometimes in French, sometimes in English, sometimes bilingual and talk, where I could hear it, was in both languages and not infrequently switched to suit the needs of the interlocutors. In these places I got the impression that, without a working knowledge of French, it would be difficult to fully participate in community life. In short, the francophone lifestyle in these prairie towns appears to be much the same as in, among other places, the Municipal Districts of Clare and Argyle in Nova Scotia; Évangéline in Prince Edward Island; Dieppe and Shédiac in New Brunswick; and Kapuskasing, Plantagenet, and Alexandria in Ontario.

But as happens elsewhere in Canada, when villages and towns grow into small cities, the proportion of francophones falls below fifty percent and institutional completeness declines in parallel. Aunger (1993) describes the restricted institutional environment of present-day Saint-Paul, Alberta, a community that was once a francophone bastion in the region. His remarks square with what I observed in my visits to communities like La Broquerie, Sainte-Agathe, Willow Bunch, Legal, and McLennan. In the Saint-Paul of today, francophones are still active in such public institutions as the school board and town council, but they are less common there than anglophones. English speakers dominate the business sector of the community, even though a number of francophone employers exist and francophone customers patronize enterprises run by both language groups (except in banking where they prefer the local *caisse populaire*). Francophones also belong to an assortment of clubs and associations, and although these groups welcome members who speak both languages, English tends to dominate. Nonetheless, the town also has some exclusively francophone clubs.

In short, "contact with English speakers is more frequent in formal relations than in intimate relations; conversely, contact with other French speakers is more frequent in primary relationships than in secondary relationships" (Aunger, 1993: 74). Thus in Saint-Paul, the family has become the "bulwark" of the francophone community. By contrast, only 18.7 percent of Aunger's respondents reported that, when shopping, they dealt mostly with French-speaking clerks and merchants.

The number of institutions in which francophones can routinely participate in French is even more restricted in most of Canada's large and medium-sized cities. This generalization applies as much to Edmonton, Calgary, Vancouver, Hamilton, and Toronto as it does to Victoria, Halifax, Saskatoon, Regina, and similarly-sized communities. As already mentioned these institutions are leisure, religion, education, and the family. The francophone arts and cultural institutions constitute a sort of grey area in this respect, meeting some but not all the needs of local francophones. For the large majority of these people, it is impossible to work in French, and consumer activity carried out in French is sporadic, limited in the main to French bookstores and restaurants. True, a wide variety of services is available in *la belle langue* should people with corresponding needs want to take time to find them and, often, drive across town to use them. At work in all these cities are lawyers, insurance agents, real estate brokers, automobile mechanics, health professionals, travel advisors, funeral directors, and so on who can speak with their clients in French. But if the Calgary study (Stebbins, 1994) is representative, most francophones in these cities, being bilingual, prefer convenience to supporting their minority community in this way. Therefore they tend to use nearby, usually anglophone, services.

Still, each Western province has established at least one province-wide economic organization to serve francophone business people. But for reasons just given, entrepreneurs in the large and medium-sized cities must operate substantially in English, even though trying to expand their French-speaking clientele is considered a worthy goal. Manitoba is most developed in this regard, having at the provincial level a council on co-operation, a francophone chamber of commerce, and an economic development office.

Extrapolating again from the Calgary study, this situation gives rise to a distinctive, albeit restricted, linguistic lifestyle centred mainly on leisure (sometimes with family) and education (for those with school-age children). For some urban francophones religion, scientifically classified as a form of leisure (Bosserman and Gagan, 1972: 121-22), comprises another part of this lifestyle. Furthermore, as noted earlier, each person develops within these spheres his or her own mosaic of participation in the range of activities available in French.

This lifestyle is organized to a significant extent around various organizations: clubs, societies, and associations. The provincial organizations representing francophones in the West – Société franco-manitobaine, Association culturelle franco-canadienne de la Saskatchewan, Association canadienne-française de l'Alberta, and Fédération des francophones de la Colombie-Britannique – form through their local branches an important part of this organizational set, as do the various cultural and school-community centres. Apropos of the latter, Vancouver has had for years its Maison de la francophonie, and much more recently francophones in Calgary completed the Cité des rocheuses while those in Edmonton built their Cité francophone.

Related in complex ways to the centres and associations is an impressive collection of organizations set up for youth, sport, friendship, women, jurists, teachers, culture (e.g., music, theatre, dance), senior citizens, parents of school children, and certain special interests (e.g., history, immigrants, genealogy). The schools and churches also have a number of committees, each staffed by volunteers.

Finally, an ethnic (i.e., racial, national, religious) component is evident in some of the linguistic lifestyles in the modern city, for the *"nouveaux francophones"* – French-speaking immigrants and refugees from Europe, Africa, Asia, and the Middle East – tend to associate more frequently with each other than with native-born Canadian francophones, sometimes doing so within their own national organizations (Beaudoin, 1988; Savas, 1990: 30; Stebbins, 1994: 120).

Each person's mosaic of activities puts him or her in contact with one or more of these entities, but never with them all, since they are too many. Moreover, each participates in these activities along the lines of a finely-woven, albeit informal, network of friends, relatives, and acquaintances that likewise spans a part of the formal structure of organizations. No one can doubt that the urban francophone minority community has significant formal and informal structures and that both levels are vital for community maintenance and development.

Education

Although the manner in which it was done varies from province to province, all four Western provinces have now handed control of French language education to their francophone populations. This was no magnanimous gesture, however, for none of the four was inclined to correct their unconstitutional arrangements following proclamation in 1982 of the Charter of Rights and Freedoms, wherein the right to instruction in the minority language was firmly set out. Rather, francophones in all four provinces had to threaten legal action, and first in Alberta and then in Manitoba actually pursue it up to the Supreme Court of Canada, to goad provincial officials into providing education in French. In light of such resistance it is surprising that three of the four (British Columbia excepted) have now gone beyond the basic requirements laid down by the Supreme Court in 1990 in *Mahé*, the Alberta case. They have also established independent school boards run by their francophone constituents.

Despite these gains, French-language schools in Saskatchewan, with a handful of exceptions, have failed to attract sufficient proportions of eligible francophone students, throwing into question whether these schools are really needed (Kaltz, 1997: 93-94). The wide geographic dispersion of francophone communities in this province is said to be part of the problem, as is the high rate of assimilation to English.

Except for Newfoundland, the provinces east of Manitoba made arrangements for instruction in French either just before or just after proclamation of the Charter, thus doing so without legal pressure. The greater numbers and perceptibility of francophones in these areas were no doubt at the root of these changes. In the meantime, the older managerial models operating in the East are now being re-evaluated in light of the newer managerial arrangements established in the 1990s in the West. Ducharme (1996: 41) writes that:

accordingly, the changing nature of rights to instruction in the minority language has an impact on the school management models proposed. A management model that seemed appropriate when it was implemented may appear "outmoded" ten years later. This is particularly true in Ontario.

Consequently, francophone school management has recently come under attack in Ontario, with some complaints going as far as the United Nations Human Rights Committee. The changes in school management occasioned by this protracted contest of wills were described in chapter 7. Nevertheless, now that Newfoundland francophones have acquired their own school board, francophones in minority circumstances everywhere in Canada (except the three territories) now control French education in their province.

Turning next to francophone university education in the West, there are two unilingual establishments devoted to this mission, both formally linked with a larger anglophone university. The Collège universitaire de Saint-Boniface (CUSB) is an affiliate of the University of Manitoba, although it is situated at some distance on the other side of the Red River in the district of Saint-Boniface, where it began in 1818 as an independent Catholic college. The CUSB, one of the oldest university-level establishments in Canada, has been directed by a lay corporation since 1969. In 1996-1997 the Collège enrolled 750 regular students and 2532 students in continuing education. The regular students can pursue baccalaureate degrees in arts, science, and translation as well as baccalaureate and masters degrees in education. Both CUSB and the Faculté Saint-Jean in Edmonton, through their education programs, serve the voracious need in their respective provinces for teachers to work in the French-language and French-immersion programs.

The Faculté Saint-Jean (FSJ) has been one of the many faculties of the University of Alberta since 1978. It, too, is located "off-campus," six kilometres from the main University campus in Edmonton's district of Bonnie Doon on the site to which it was moved from Pincher Creek, Alberta, in 1911.[2] Until 1978 it was an independent Catholic institution. Its main mission as a teachers college has been recently expanded with baccalaureate programs in arts, science, French, and business administration (a bilingual program). It also offers a masters degree in education. Through the FSJ students can pursue at certain francophone universities in Québec and elsewhere in Canada degrees locally unavailable to them. In 1996, the Faculty enrolled 397 students.

Language

Apart from the several villages and small towns where French is a strong majority language, its ethnolinguistic vitality is a major concern in Western Canada, especially in the large cities. For outside these communities, first-language francophones cannot participate fully in the daily life of the larger community without knowing English, without being bilingual. From the standpoint of francophone community survival and development, the crucial condition is to ensure that the bilingualism achieved is additive rather than subtractive, that assimilation to English remains only partial. The evidence available on the matter (Stebbins, 1994; Bocquel, 1990), suggests that, as in parts of Ontario and Newfoundland, for example, a diglossic relationship develops between the two languages for the mother-tongue francophones who successfully resist complete assimilation.

I found in the Calgary Study (Stebbins, 1994) that a large number of that city's mother-tongue francophones are intensely proud of their French language and francophone culture. This would appear to be the foundation for what Bocquel (1990: 119) has dubbed the **normalitude** of French and English in the everyday lives of these French-speaking urban Canadians. In normalitude they sense they are no longer obligated to favor one language over the other. Bocquel explains that "it [normalitude] is simply having the freedom not to have to choose anymore between French and English, at which point they [francophones] have decided individually to preserve a francophone dimension of their identity" (translation). It is entirely natural for the vast majority of mother-tongue francophones in Calgary to use the two languages in their daily affairs, even while they are especially drawn toward, although not forced into, using French because of their strong attachment to it and an associated culture. Bocquel observed much the same attitude in Winnipeg. Moreover, there is reason to believe that normalitude is common throughout the West and in other areas of Canada where, among mother-tongue francophones, knowing English is absolutely essential for daily functioning, even though they are determined to retain their special linguistic identity and culture. Here diglossia is the only reasonable choice (Laponce, 1996: 85-87).

Culture[3]

Theatre is one of the most fully developed arts in the western francophone societies, and the jewel in its dramatic crown is Le Cercle Molière, a professional company based in Saint-Boniface. It has been functioning since 1925. Professional theatre is also available in Saskatchewan and Edmonton, with a semi-professional company performing regularly in Calgary. Additionally, numerous francophone writers are at work in the West, a number of whom are published by one of the two francophone houses in Winnipeg, Éditions du blé and Éditions des plaines or by the house in Regina, Éditions Louis Riel. Gabrielle Roy (1909-1983), one of Canada's most renowned novelists, who wrote in Québec and France, was nevertheless born and raised in Saint-Boniface. Many of Roy's works are based on her experiences in that community, where today her birthplace and childhood home – Gabrielle Roy House – is a popular museum. Other renowned francophone writers in the West include poet and novelist J.R.L. Léveillé and poet Paul Savoie, both natives of Manitoba. In 1996 Savoie received the *Prix du Consul Général de France* (Toronto) in recognition of his many works. Georges Bugnet (1879-1981), a writer of French birth who settled in Alberta, won several honors during his lifetime for his essays, poems, and novels. Two of the latter have been translated into English.

Francophone folkloric dance is also well represented in western Canada. A school for folk dance, music, and singing – l'Ensemble folklorique de la Rivière rouge – has been operating in Winnipeg for many years. Regular dance performances are presented by two groups in Saskatchewan, six in Alberta, and three in British Columbia. The *Gala Chant'Ouest*, inaugurated in 1989 under another name, is held annually in a selected community in the West; its object is to provide a showcase for and entertainment by regional francophone singing talent. Albertan Crystal Plamondon, a contemporary popular francophone folk and country singer, is well-known in Louisiana and throughout western Canada. Singer and composer Daniel Lavoie was raised in Manitoba, where he frequently returns from his present home in Montréal or his *pied-à-terre* in Paris. He won a number of international prizes in the 1980s and 1990s for his recordings of popular song, including the *Prix de la chanson française au Festival international d'été de Québec* (1992).

No survey of francophone culture in western Canada would be complete without mention of architect Douglas Cardinal, born in 1934 in Calgary. Saint Mary's church in Red Deer, Alberta, is considered his masterpiece, although he is also well known as architect for, among many other projects, the Edmonton Space Science Centre and the Musée canadien des civilisations in Hull, Québec. He was named to the Order of Canada in 1990.

Today the francophone performing arts in western Canada are most likely to be seen and heard in the cultural centres and school-community centres that have recently gained prominence in this region. As elsewhere in the country, these establishments also serve as museums, exposition halls, sites for talks and seminars, and the like, frequently organizing and presenting material of interest to local francophones. The performing arts have an additional outlet in the annual provincial festivals: *Festival du Voyageur* (Manitoba), *Fête Fransaskoise*, *Fête Franco-Albertaine*, and *Festival du bois* (British Columbia). The centres and the festivals complement the radio and television content broadcast by Société Radio-Canada, and in the large cities, by TV5. A few Québec television stations are available in Winnipeg. Finally, each province also publishes its own French-language weekly of long-standing.

In the West, as in other francophone societies in Canada, legends make up an important part of local francophone culture. Tatiana Arcand (1991: 138-139) recounts a Manitoba legend she says is particularly appropriate to the area:

> However, one of the most interesting forms of the manifestation of death is the one of fire, in particular the will-o'-the-wisp. These mysterious lights, according to certain people, can be explained scientifically: they would be fireflies, or alternatively the emanations of phosphorous of hydrogen which are given off by swamps and graves in cemeteries.

> But in the legend "The Headless Body," the inhabitants of Woodbridge [Manitoba] explain this phenomenon entirely differently. Here, this fire manifests itself in the form of small whitish lights shaped like balls, which shine along the railway. The people of this region see here the manifestation of the soul of a poor man whose head was severed by the wheels of a train. This soul, they say, returns to the place of

the fatal accident to try to find the lost head. Now it is believed that the head is a symbol of light and force. If the fire that enters the body allows a human to resume life, it is not surprising to find such a legend claiming that the person who has had a part of his body severed at the time of death, continues, in the form of fire, to search for his missing part. Such are the popular beliefs that give rise to this type of legend. [translation]

My reading of the legends circulating among western francophones suggests that most of these stories have roots in either Indian or Québécois culture, if not both.

Conclusion

In western Canadian francophone societies, with the partial exception of Saint-Boniface, survival has been an issue at least as salient as community development. Yet today, according to my observations around this region, most francophones speak optimistically and positively about development, pointing to the existence of their local French school system, the many community activities, and the favorable public reception of francophones (when compared with the past), to mention but a few such indicators. Talk of survival and possible disappearance down the road, although not explicitly forbidden, is nevertheless uncommon and certainly unwelcome.

But this outlook is relatively new, for in the past survival appears to have been the central worry, a sentiment that made development a peripheral interest (Allaire and Fedigan, 1991: 111). As further evidence of this earlier, more pessimistic attitude in the West, note that from 1928 to 1967 the monthly francophone newspaper serving Alberta, British Columbia, and the Northwest Territories had as its title *La Survivance* (survival) (Kermoal, 1998: 7-8). More optimistic titles became fashionable after 1967, as seen in *Le Franco* (Alberta) and *Le Soleil de Colombie* (British Columbia). Nevertheless, the concern about *la relève* still looms in much of the West like an oncoming prairie dust storm, a fear inflamed every five years by fresh census data on further assimilation and population decline among mother-tongue francophones. Will there be a future generation of francophones to replace the present generation of adults? Seen from another angle, the current liveliness of their communities contrasts, at times sharply, with the actual and projected decline as told by Statistics Canada figures and with the various problems they must tackle to prevent that decline and ensure further development.

Chapter 10
Contemporary Issues in Western Francophone Societies

Concerning the discussion in this chapter of the six contemporary issues selected for comparative examination in this book, it must be borne in mind that they are somewhat less problematic in Saint-Boniface than elsewhere in western Canada. Moreover, the issues have different faces in the large cities as opposed to the villages and small towns. Nevertheless, they constitute a familiar list of problems for many of Canada's parity and minority francophones, wherever they live, if not by now for readers of this book. For the final time, then, this chapter treats of the issues of imperceptibility, exogamous marriages, universities, language, and assimilation.

Imperceptibility

Following the approach used in earlier chapters, the question of perceptibility of local francophone communities is analyzed according to whether it is high, medium, or low. And as was found in other parts of Canada where francophones live in minority circumstances, in the West they experience highest perceptibility in the villages and small towns, medium perceptibility in the small cities, and ever lower perceptibility in the medium and large cities. As for the sample of towns mentioned in the previous chapter – Saint-Claude, Notre-Dame-de-Lourdes, Saint-Pierre-Jolys, Zenon Park, Falher, and the village of Saint-Isidore – all appear to enjoy a high degree of institutional completeness, and in harmony with this condition, all give off the usual indicators of Frenchness. As mentioned, I have personally visited these communities (except Zenon Park), where I found French much in evidence in the areas of club life, religion, and education as well as in financial services (especially the *caisses populaires*), public services, and public communication (e.g., street signs, public notices). Most of the commercial world, however, presents a mixture of French and English; signs here are sometimes in French, sometimes in English, sometimes in both languages and talk, where I could hear it, was in both languages, while it was common for speakers to shift languages to suit their own needs and those of their interlocutors.

Yet, in other prairie towns of similar size that I have also visited, perceptibility is much lower. I have in mind such places as La Broquerie, Sainte-Agathe, Willow Bunch, Legal, and McLennan. In Willow Bunch (34.8 % francophone), for example, the only visible signs of French are a bilingual town welcome sign, bilingual information about the local Catholic church, and the sign on the franco-phone cultural centre. Nevertheless, in the restaurant of the local hotel I heard four men at the next table talking animatedly in English about a wind storm that had blown through the night before and then, apparently because one of them slipped a French word into the conversation, heard the group switch abruptly to good quality French, remaining in that language for the next ten minutes (after which I left). In Ponteix (65.6% francophone), only the outdoor church information and the francophone cultural centre hinted at its predominantly French population. But a gas pump attendant held that "everyone in town speaks French." In short, low perceptibility is not an ineluctable sign of low linguistic vitality, even in small communities.

In the western cities, especially the largest, extremely low per-ceptibility is the norm, even though linguistic vitality is, in general, reasonably high. French would be literally invisible in such places, were it not for bilingual signs on the several bilingual schools, all-French signs on a very small number of all-French schools, and where they exist, the French signs marking the local francophone cultural or community centre. The urban French parishes, if the city has any, are also announced in French.

Edmonton is unique among the western cities (i.e., Winnipeg excluding Saint-Boniface, Regina, Saskatoon, Calgary, Edmonton, Vancouver, and Victoria), where in recent decades French visibility has grown considerably in the district of Bonnie Doon. The follow-ing institutions are now concentrated within approximately a six-block area: an all-French high school, a French Catholic church, a seniors' residence, a chapter of the Chevaliers de Colomb, a cultural centre and office building, and the Faculté Saint-Jean and its student residences. Located just a few blocks from this concentration is another francophone building that houses several other organiza-tional offices and a bistro. Census Tract 020, where all these institu-tions are located, was 11.7 percent mother-tongue francophone according to the 1991 Census (counting both single and multiple responses, Statistics Canada, 1993b). Just to the east, Census Tract 035 was 5.3 percent francophone, compared with 2.5 percent for the whole of Edmonton.

Identity

Research conducted in Manitoba and Alberta (Hallion, 1997; Stebbins, 1994) suggests that francophone linguistic identity in the Canadian West is as complex as anywhere in the country. It is anchored in two or three criteria: nationality, provincial residence, and linguistic capacity. Some francophones identify themselves as French-Canadian, while others identify themselves by their province, using such labels as Franco-Manitobain or Franco-Colombien (British Columbia). Some identify themselves both nationally and provincially. Whatever the combination, it is nearly always joined with the identifier of linguistic capacity, with being a speaker of French and with being bilingual in French and English. Because it is necessary to be able to speak English almost everywhere in the West, French-English bilingualism is seen to offer many advantages (Stebbins, 1994: chap. 8), while being paraded as a substantial achievement and for this reason a main source of personal pride.

But these francophones, who are assuredly not completely assimilated, have acquired a bilingualism that is clearly additive (Lambert, 1975). In this regard, they appear to rank their different everyday francophone and anglophone activities according to the emotional value of each. When compared with many of their anglophone activities (sometimes with the exception of work), most francophone activities have a strong emotional loading. It seems that these francophones value highly their language and culture as much for practical reasons as for reasons of preference and that they therefore resist total assimilation to the anglophone world, where they nevertheless participate extensively (see Lamy, 1978). Social psychologically-speaking, the bilingual-bicultural francophone identity ranks near the top of their "prominence hierarchy" (McCall and Simmons, 1978: 73-79), the classification of all a person's identities according to their general importance to him or her. I found in the study of the Franco-Calgarians, particularly among the younger generations, that their high esteem for French language and culture helped them implement linguistic "normalitude" (Bocquel, 1990: 119) in their everyday lives. On the most general plane, they felt little or no obligation to privilege one language over the other.

In particular situations, however, they do prefer French to English or vice versa, with preference being established according to the person's "salience hierarchy" (McCall and Simmons, 1978: 79-85). In a particular situation, the rank order of the more general prominence hierarchy may be temporarily altered to give expression to the identity or identities most important for the person at the moment, in that situation. This is in effect what Marchand (1998: 66) is referring to when she writes about the *"poly-identité"* of Manitoba's francophone youth. Depending on the social situation they happen to be in, these youth may identify themselves as Franco-Manitobains, West-Canadian francophones, francophones living outside Québec, French Canadians, North American francophones, or francophones of the Francophonie. They may further identify themselves, again according the needs of the situation, as bilingual or even as anglophone. Dallaire and Whitson (1998: 100) observed much the same in their study of Alberta francophone youth participating in the province's francophone games. But in Calgary, the importance of a bilingual identity was also evident among francophones of all adult ages (Stebbins, 1994: chap. 8).

In general, however, the foregoing observations hold best for youth. Older francophones in the West, particularly those already adult at the time of the Quiet Revolution, seem inclined to identify themselves more simply in national terms as French-Canadian as well as, in many instances, in provincial terms as Fransaskois, Franco-Albertain, and so on. The Calgary study shows that they, too, are also proud of their bilingual capacity. Meanwhile, francophone immigrants are likely to present still another profile of identities, emphasizing in certain situations their former national identity and, where appropriate, their racial distinctiveness. In short, research on francophone identity in the West, as well as that done elsewhere in Canada where francophones live in minority circumstances, harmonizes with Heller's (1996: 34-35) conclusion that their world is a world very much in transition, and this is why they are presently reshaping "the linguistic norms that symbolize and underlie francophone identity in Canada" (translation).

Exogamous Marriages

Looking west from Québec, it can be said that the greater the distance between it and a given province the higher the rate of exogamous marriages, as calculated provincially using 1996 census data (Statistics Canada, 1998a). Running parallel with this trend is another: the tendency in each province for its own rate to rise slightly with each decennial census. The rate of linguistic exogamy also increases with the rate of bilingualism as well as with living in a bilingual environment, for these conditions bring francophones and anglophones together more frequently than where the first are unilingual and live mainly in a unilingual environment.

♂	Ontario	42.7%
♂	Manitoba	53.2%
♂	Saskatchewan	71.4%
♂	Alberta	75.4%
♂	British Columbia	81.3%

The meaning of such figures was discussed in chapter 8 with reference to mixed marriages in Ontario and Newfoundland. What was said there about these unions, the risk of assimilation, and the role of leisure holds as well for the western provinces.

Although sending children to all-French schools or even to immersion schools can help offset the effects of the dominance of English in families founded by exogamous couples, special measures must still be followed at home if French is to be kept alive there. These, too, were spelled out earlier (chapter 6) and need not be treated again, except to note that they also apply with equal validity to the progeny of linguistically-exogamous marriages in the West.

Universities

Perhaps the greatest problem presently facing Canada's francophone universities operating in minority circumstances is the recent decline in their enrolments. An article on this problem disseminated by the news agency Association de la presse francophone (*Le Franco*, 1997: 9), although bearing primarily on the Université Sainte-Anne, Université de Moncton, Université d'Ottawa, and Collège universitaire de Saint-Boniface, nevertheless purports to speak with authority about the situation as it affects all francophone and bilingual institutions of higher learning in the country. The article says the decline has generally been viewed with alarm, as more than a mere temporary drop in registration. In the West, the Faculté Saint-Jean is also facing up to a reduction in the number of students.

The article presents the students' view of the cause of the problem: rising tuition rates. But spokespersons for the four universities named in the preceding paragraph are quoted as saying that other factors must also be considered. One is the students' perception that work requiring an advanced degree is now harder to find than in the past, especially in education, a bread-and-butter field at every francophone university and university-college in the country. But whatever the field, it is believed that many students are asking whether it is worth their time and money to obtain a university degree when, compared with the past, they have a significantly reduced chance of benefiting from it in the labor market. Data bearing on francophone and anglophone students released in 1998 by Statistics Canada indicate that, on average, students run up a $13 300 debt by the time they graduate with a bachelors degree. Twenty-two percent of these graduates had borrowed more than $20 000 to obtain this diploma (Marshall, 1998: B3). The problem, then, is whether students will be inclined to go this heavily into debt to acquire a degree whose payoff in terms of employment is much riskier than previously.

Apart from these issues, the CUSB and the FSJ, being unilingual francophone institutions, avoid some of the problems presently buffeting the bilingual establishments in Ontario. At one time, however, authorities at FSJ had to mount a campaign to discourage students from speaking English in the institution once outside the classroom (Chabot, 1992). My observations of activities in which I have been involved there over the past ten years suggest that the persuasive measures have paid off. They included posted notices, friendly reminders, and reasoned argument about the fragility of French in Edmonton and the need for all to work to preserve it wherever possible. These days I hear little or no English in the corridors of the Faculté Saint-Jean.

Language

From the evidence at hand on the western provinces, which has been mainly gathered in Manitoba and Saskatchewan, it is clear that, as in Ontario, many francophones speak a vernacular French that some confuse with standard French, often to their personal disadvantage. The linguistic situation is somewhat more complicated in Manitoba than in Saskatchewan. In the first, the current language base is an amalgam that emerged from three distinct strains: the French of people of European descent, mostly from France and Belgium; the French of the Métis; and the French of those who migrated directly or indirectly from Québec. Over the years these three groups have contributed to a common Franco-Manitobain vernacular French that contrasts in myriad ways with the standard French used in such formal settings as government and the schools (Marchand, 1997: 108). Even greater, of course, is its contrast with English in these settings, since French-speaking Manitobans, being mostly bilingual, also use that language with great frequency.

Vocabulary is one dimension along which contrast is most apparent, as seen for example in the numerous anglicisms in the vernacular language that are prudently avoided when standard French is employed. There are furthermore many regional words, expressions, and pronunciations that came to Manitoba with the francophone migrants along with their peculiar dialects or *patois* and that still have a place in the vernacular language of today. In a sense, then, Franco-Manitobans typically know two partially different French languages, and those who find themselves from time to time in one or more formal settings must learn which language to use and when.

But, as Hallion (1997: 134-135) found in her study of Franco-Manitobains, vernacular French serves as the language of emotion and the heart:

> Language of the family, transmitted principally at home, French is strongly tied to the emotionality of Franco-Manitobans. It is among them, for the most part, the "language of the inner circle," the "language of the heart." It serves to express the emotions and the sentiments: "When one is emotional or angry, you always turn to your language of . . . me, I am not capable of speaking in English, when things happen like that. I think in French, then it comes out in French" [interviewee]. It is also the language of communication in the family, the language of "respect": it is nearly always used with parents, always with grand-parents and often with brothers and sisters.[translation]

The emotional foundation of a language is laid at home in childhood during the routine activities that take place there. The Calgary study (Stebbins, 1994: 32) revealed that these activities are carried out, usually separately, by one or both parents with one or more of their children. The process begins with a set of activities in which one parent performs, as it were, to an audience of one or more of his or her children, typically by reading stories, telling tales, singing lullabies, and reciting nursery rhymes. These early experiences in French, sometimes expanded when the child recites a French prayer at bedtime, combine to form an initial, positive, three-way emotional bond linking the child with the language and the parent involved. At this point the child starts down the long road leading to mastery of his or her mother tongue, doing so in an atmosphere of love and warmth created by a mother or father who routinely provides nurturing through pleasurable and memorable experiences.

In one sense many francophone parents in Calgary said they had little choice but to conduct these activities in French, however eager they were to transmit their mother tongue to their children. When they were young their parents raised them in similar ways with stories, tales, and the like, which many years later are still known to them only in French. But even if they managed in their adult lives to learn English versions of some of these, the positive emotional loading acquired during the intimacy of their own childhood has permanently endowed the French versions with a most special appeal.

The tales, stories, and prayers are told and retold over the years as the child grows older, but the lullabies and nursery rhymes are soon replaced with activities in French that he or she initiates. The child's initiative is augmented by parental encouragement and sometimes parental insistence leading him or her, for example, to read in French, listen to recorded French songs, or watch children's programs on French television. In this manner, the language is learned, emotionally grounded, and internalized as the medium of immediate response to the social and physical environment in which the young person finds himself or herself at the moment.

Cox (1991) studied vernacular French in Saskatchewan, where he was able to demonstrate its existence among a sample of students ranging in age from 18 to 54. More precisely, he found a reasonably widespread understanding and usage of a number of words and expressions that seem to be limited to the Saskatchewan francophone scene. He concluded, much as was done earlier for Ontario, that it is foolish to deny students their linguistic heritage of vernacular French. In Ontario, a narrow vocabulary among students was discovered to be a main reason for resorting to English; French words and phrases were often not readily available to them for use in the diverse settings they enter outside the school and family environments. Cox's (1991: 105-106) findings suggest that it is as important to teach vernacular French in Saskatchewan as it is in Ontario. It is the language of youth, and if they are denied use of it, the possibility certainly exists that they could abandon entirely the use of French in peer circles, replacing it with English.

Assimilation

The parallel to this section in chapter 8, which bore on Ontario, was organized around two basic propositions. One, that the degree of ethnolinguistic vitality of a parity or minority francophone community is a strong indicator of the tendency for first- and second-language francophones to use French there. Two, that when ethnolinguistic vitality is low, the tendency to assimilate to English is high. Following O'Keefe (1999: 10), seven key factors known to influence the vitality of a given language were then presented and explored for their fit in Ontario: symbolic, demographic, institutional, education, status and prestige, identity, and utility. It also warrants repeating at this point that these factors give expression to the observation made earlier that a language can, and may well, be used in a number of ways (i.e., speaking, reading, listening, writing) in a number of settings (e.g., at home, work, leisure, church, school). Demographic variables, on which there has been a marked tendency in research and governmental circles to rely exclusively, in fact constitute only one of the seven factors in this list.

Following the same order of discussion for the francophone societies of western Canada as followed earlier for francophone Ontario, consider first the symbolic value of French in this region of the country. Thus, as elsewhere, French does appear in the West along with English in all official signs and publications of every federal government installation. Most of the time in the West this amounts to rather little visibility, however, limited as it is in the typical case to public information about a few buildings and offices. But the national parks constitute an interesting, if not glaring, exception, where a high proportion of non-commercial signs and announcements are bilingual and where bilingual personnel are available to serve both language groups. Moreover, particular measures have been enacted in recognition of the importance of francophones to an entire, dominantly anglophone community. For instance, the numerous historical sites in Saint-Boniface add up to a major tourist attraction in Winnipeg. Furthermore, not long ago, 91st Street in Edmonton was renamed rue Marie-Anne Gaboury in honor of the first white woman – of Québec origin – to come to Alberta. It is one of the main streets in the francophone part of Bonnie Doon. And Calgarians of both languages participated in a bilingual ceremony in June of 1996 inaugurating Rouleauville Square, a commemoration of Rouleauville, the city's only francophone community. It came and went during the 1890s.

An examination of the demographic data presented in the preceding chapter gives a varied but by now familiar linguistic profile freighted, as usual, with both optimism and pessimism. It is optimistic to the extent that a number of villages and small towns in the West are more or less retaining their high proportions of francophones, with some proportions even rising slightly. It is pessimistic to the extent that francophone proportions are very small in the large and medium-sized cities.

The issue of demographic profile leads to that of the demographics of linguistic assimilation; an issue saved for this chapter on the West, where according to quantitative measures, it is generally the most acute. A common operational definition of linguistic assimilation in a population is the percentage of people of a given mother tongue who have abandoned it and now speak another language, a process often measured by rates of home use of the languages in question (O'Keefe, 1998: 34). Adoption of another language in this way is referred to by Statistics Canada as **language transfer**, or **language shift**. When examining people who continue to speak their mother tongue at home, the process is one of retention; this is called **language continuity**. Table 10.1 shows the decline in French continuity since 1971 for all the provinces except Québec. An index figure of less than one means that French suffered more losses than gains in its exchanges with other languages, primarily English.

Table 10.1 Language Continuity Index – French

Province/Territory	1971	1981	1991	1996
Newfoundland	0.63	0.72	0.47	0.42
Prince Edward Island	0.60	0.64	0.53	0.53
Nova Scotia	0.69	0.69	0.59	0.57
New Brunswick	0.92	0.93	0.93	0.92
Ontario	0.73	0.72	0.63	0.61
Manitoba	0.65	0.60	0.49	0.47
Saskatchewan	0.50	0.41	0.33	0.29
Alberta	0.49	0.49	0.36	0.32
British Columbia	0.30	0.35	0.28	0.29
Yukon	0.30	0.45	0.43	0.46
Northwest Territories	0.50	0.51	0.47	0.43
Canada less Quebec	0.73	0.72	0.65	0.64

Source: O'Keefe (1998: 43)

As the number of families based on exogamous marriages increases, French linguistic continuity tends to drop. As noted previously, the rate of exogamy is high in western Canada. Moreover, everywhere outside Quebec the age groups 20 to 24 and 25 to 29 show the most marked decline in linguistic continuity as compared with all other age groups.

As for institutional completeness, its decline parallels the decline in proportions of francophones that occurs when community size increases. Nonetheless, it is safe to say that, in the West, more services are available in French in the big cities than in the small towns. In particular, more federal government as well as more commercial and professional services are available in the former. For instance, the francophone residents of Zenon Park, Saskatchewan – a town of 259 people – will likely have to drive as far as Saskatoon to find a francophone lawyer, psychiatrist, or bookseller. Of course, they would probably have to make the same trip should they want these services in English. But even if the needed services are offered in their own community, francophones may still ignore them. Thus Calgary has a good range of professional and commercial services, but, being highly dispersed geographically, few francophones reported using them (Stebbins, 1994: 82-83).

Where all minority francophone communities of every size are now complete, however, is in the realm of education. Judged by this factor linguistic vitality is high, although the current struggle for equivalence in facilities and funding suggests that it can rise still higher. The observations made in chapter 8 about the world-wide status and prestige of French also hold for the western Canadian francophone societies. These observations need not be repeated here. The same is true for the factors of personal and collective identity and the utility of knowing French. And the conclusion reached in chapter 8 about the ravages of assimilation holds for the present chapter as well: the vitality of these communities cannot be measured strictly in quantitative demographic terms. Rather any discussion of assimilation must also take account of the spirit, determination, and sense of identity found in such places. When this is done, it can be concluded that ethnolinguistic vitality is reasonably high in the West, and this notwithstanding the pessimistic demographic picture sketched earlier of low language continuity and high rates of assimilation and exogamous marriages.

Conclusion

The mother-tongue francophones of the western provinces, joined with those of Newfoundland, constitute the most enigmatic set of French-speaking Canadians in all the land. The demographic odds of their language and culture surviving are against them, a situation many have faced for most of this century. Moreover, although it has abated considerably, francophones in both regions once experienced significant hostility as exemplified by the derisive label of "jack o' tar," formerly used by some Newfoundland anglophones, and by the sporadic acts of hate aimed at francophones living in Calgary in the early- to mid-1980s (Stebbins, 1994: 106-107). And now, with seemingly endless reductions in federal funding for their local programs and organizations, minority francophones must surmount still other obstacles on the road to community survival and development (Stebbins, 1999).

Nevertheless, this book has taken throughout an optimistic stance on the questions of survival and development, while remarks made in the preceding section about reasonably high ethnolinguistic vitality in the West reflect my personal optimism with respect to those societies. Magord's (1993) observations of the French-speaking people of the Port-au-Port communicate a similar sanguine outlook in this regard. Our optimism is far more than wishful thinking, for it rests in good part on the present-day transition of the bases of francophone identity. As Heller was quoted as saying earlier: the linguistic norms that guide and symbolize francophone life in Canada are now being transformed. And remember, too, that especially the youth in the West have been observed to have multifaceted identities, one important component being the feeling of belonging to the world Francophonie. What, then, are the implications of the global francophone community for Canada's francophones living in minority circumstances?

Part IV
The Future

Chapter 11
Canada's Francophones in Global Perspective

Canadian francophones appear to be as caught up in the whirl-wind of globalizing trends blowing across the world these days as any demographic group in Canada, if not in the world. Whereas a single chapter is much too short to cover their involvement in all these trends, some trends do have special repercussions in the different francophone societies examined in the preceding chapters. Four of these are covered in this chapter: internationalization of francophone identity, internationalization of economic ties, increasing involvement in international francophone culture, and increasing involvement with francophone immigrants and refugees. Throughout this discussion the adjective "international" sometimes refers largely, if not exclusively, to North America, whereas at other times it denotes a truly world-wide perspective. Additionally, globalization seems to affect urban francophones more profoundly than it does their rural counterparts.

International Francophone Identity

Louder and Dupont (1997: 59-60) write that, as francophone Canadians' image of themselves as one of Canada's two founding groups fades in importance, a new international form of self-identification is moving up in their prominence hierarchy. Québec's preoccupation with the sovereignty question has, however, led to a peculiar juncture in this regard:

> Even if it remains the mother country of millions of North Americans and that it remains the principal francophone cultural home in North America, Québec, because of a lack of will or something else, has not really taken up the cause. Québec would truly like to do this, but it is far from being assured that the francophones outside its boundaries would follow it. This loss of direction means that the world Francophonie could acquire a much greater importance for francophones living in minority circumstances in Canada. (translation)

The Francophonie, an idea that originated in the African franco-phone states (Viaud, 1993: 64), is truly world-wide in the sense that every francophone culture is held to be distinctive and important, a particularly African perspective. In it, the cultures of such countries as France and Québec are regarded as no more important than the others. France, of course, is still very much the cultural and intellectual centre of this international formation and an inspiration to all countries who are part of it, but the significance of the cultures of the other countries is in no way diminished by its pre-eminence.

The Francophonie was defined in chapter 1 as the ensemble of governments, countries, and official instances having in common the use of the French language in their work and their exchanges with one another. It is now appropriate, however, to introduce a second definition more in line with the scope of the present chapter. Ager (1996: 1) says the Francophonie is also "an official organization of countries and regions whose leaders meet regularly to exchange views and consider joint policies and projects." Structurally, this entity is comprised of over six hundred international governmental and non-governmental organizations. The use of French is a main unifying force in the Francophonie, a formation Ager says is now providing an opportunity for a new international identity and a new means of global solidarity. Not counting internal jurisdictions such as Québec and New Brunswick, the Francophonie is constituted of 44 member and associate-member states located primarily in Europe, Africa, Asia, and North America.[1] Some are small – Seychelles had a population of 67 000 in 1994 – and some are relatively large – France had a population of 56 315 000 that same year (Ager, 1996: 95). Some contain substantial francophone minorities (e.g., Canada, Morocco, Mauritius), while in others francophones constitute a significant majority (e.g., France, Luxembourg, Monaco). Some number among the richest countries in the world, others are extremely poor. Thus the Francophonie is by no means a homogeneous bloc of nations, and as a result, they find plenty to disagree about.

Many issues such as democratization; environmental concerns; quality of French; and economic, cultural, and educational development are tackled at periodically-held summits to which the 44 nations are invited. Six more summits have occurred since the first one in France in 1986. Québec City was host to the second, held a year later, and Moncton hosted the seventh in 1999. One important product of the Québec meetings was the founding of the *Jeux de la*

Francophonie (the Francophone Games); its 2001 edition will take place in Ottawa-Hull. Another was that Québec became aware of the enormous economic benefits it could realize through the Francophonie. *La Belle Province* has played a major role there ever since, doing so to the extent that French Prime Minister Lionel Jospin recently cited Canada as the "beating heart" of the Francophonie (*Calgary Herald*, 1998: A7). Canada pays about 30 percent of the bills of the Francophonie, contributing in 1996-1997 approximately 61 million dollars to its various institutions (Aubry, 1997: A8).

Louder and Dupont (1997) point out that the Francophonie brings French-speaking Canadians, wherever they reside, into contact with other francophones who live in majority, parity, or minority circumstances in their own society. Furthermore, world-wide use of French helps validate its importance as a main world language. The Francophonie also opens up a variety of business and professional opportunities where speaking French is advantageous. It is even instructive, Louder and Dupont note, for Canada's minority francophones to know of and learn about their counterparts living elsewhere in the world, for the first come to realize that they and their problems are not always unique. In all this the phenomenal expansion of international electronic communication by way of electronic mail, fax messages, the world wide web (Cerulo, 1997: 397-399), and so on has greatly facilitated the mission of the Francophonie. Ager summarizes the essence of that mission:

> In general then, it seems that contemporary organised Francophonie has agreed that it is a voluntary community linked by a common wish to co-operate, and that its values involve dialogue, co-operation and partnership, particularly directed towards the development of less developed nations; (a somewhat recent discovery) respect for linguistic diversity, but well-established respect for cultural and religious diversity; and widespread acceptance of the correctness and universal applicability of the traditional declaration of the Rights of Man and of the fundamental liberties.(Ager, 1996: 60)

Lest it appear that all is unalloyed harmony in the modern Francophonie, Ager goes on to observe that some members remain suspicious of France's motives in this endeavor, a country they know for its colonialist tendencies and purist attitudes about the French language (on language, see for example Therrien, 1997: 24).

International Economic Ties

Ager (1996: 101-104) concludes from his review of the available evidence that external trade among the countries comprising the Francophonie is not for the most part with each other. And this despite the fact that two "franc zones" have been established, one in Africa, the other in the Pacific, where the local franc has a fixed parity with the French franc. In reality, most francophone countries trade with their neighbors, states usually dominated by other languages. Moreover, viewed against international investment practices in general, investments by francophone countries in other countries in the Francophonie are also unexceptional.

Nevertheless, instances of co-operation and partnership stand out in certain industries, between certain firms, and with respect to certain municipalities. The Mouvement Desjardins and Hydro-Québec are heavily involved at this level (for other examples, see Ager, 1996: 103). Moreover, 776 million dollars worth of partnerships and agreements were established in the wake of the second edition of the *Mondial de l'entreprenariat jeunesse* (world-wide conference on entrepreneurship for young people) held in 1998 in Ottawa (Lusignan, 1998: 2). Francophones from all parts of Canada attended the various talks and participated in the workshops. Ottawa also hosted the first edition, held two years earlier. Finally, many organizations in the Francophonie have an economic side to their operations, perhaps the most notable being the Forum francophone des affaires (francophone business forum). The Forum has as its purview the francophone countries in the southern hemisphere and the mobilization of savings, promotion of private enterprise, and restructuring and integration of regional economies there. The Forum held its meeting of 1996 in Saint-Georges de Beauce in Québec. In all this, plenty of scope exists for participation by Canadian francophone entrepreneurs, whether they live in a minority, parity, or majority society.

In comparison with those living outside Québec, francophones in Québec, as might be expected, have taken fullest advantage of economic opportunities available both inside and outside the Francophonie. As Thérien, Bélanger, and Gosselin (1993: 272) put it: "today, development of external trade permeates Québec's foreign policy in its entirety." The authors go on to observe that Québec has generally been more open than the rest of Canada to trade and foreign investment. For instance, given its close economic ties with the United States, Québec quickly became a leading champion of the

Free Trade Agreement with that country. Enterprising Quebeckers could thus become examples for parity- and minority-based francophones who would like to work within as well as outside the Francophonie.

Involvement in International Francophone Culture

Possibly still the most influential and certainly the oldest of the organizations making up the Francophonie is the Agence de coopération culturelle et technique (ACCT), founded in 1970 in Niamey, Nigeria. The meeting at which ACCT was established can also be qualified as the beginning of the modern Francophonie (Ager, 1996: 118). Nonetheless, ACCT was restructured and then renamed in 1997 Agence de la Francophonie, whose mission, among others, is to administer three programs of co-operation in education, development and solidarity, and culture and multimedia. In particular, the Agence operates programs in the live arts (including film), television, and publishing. These programs are specially designed to benefit francophone countries in the southern hemisphere, although countries in the northern hemisphere contribute significantly to making the programs possible. For example the Agence has recently instituted an information network for written press agencies in northern and southern countries; helped extend the network of local radio stations in these regions; and provided aid to radio, television, publishing, and the live arts within its jurisdiction.

Many a local cultural activity in the southern countries has benefited from support of this nature, which has also enabled artists from there and the northern countries to travel abroad to perform for francophones living in other parts of the world. Thus some of the international appearances of such Canadian performers as Céline Dion (Québec singer), Émile Benoit (Newfoundland singer and storyteller), and Édith Butler (New Brunswick singer and composer) have been directly or indirectly supported by the ACCT, Agence de la Francophonie, and still other organizations allied with the world francophone community. Those same organizations have also helped a sizeable number of foreign francophone artists perform in Canadian cities in nearly every province.

The Agence de la Francophonie also supports scholarly endeavors, with *Iapétus*, an interdisciplinary journal, being a recent example. The journal, whose first issue appeared in the fall of 1998, links the university communities of Africa and Québec through published book reviews, announcements of research projects, and scholarly papers in the fields of history, politics, literature, linguistics, and education. The title of the journal takes its name from the ancient sea that once linked Africa and North America.

The place of song in the Francophonie is special enough to warrant its own organization – the Conseil francophone de la chanson (CFC) founded in 1986. It has two principal objectives: to recognize and promote throughout the world francophone song and singers. In this regard, Céline Dion won in 1996 the *RFI-Conseil francophone de la chanson* trophy for her interpretation of Jean-Jacques Goldman's song *"Pour que tu m'aimes encore."* This prize is based on votes of listeners to hundreds of French-language radio stations around the world. That same year, CFC also co-ordinated the productions of several francophone artists who sang in Paris and Montréal as part of the program of the *Journée de la Francophonie* (Francophonie Day). Furthermore, it also arranged to televise the video recording made that day under the aegis of the Agence de la Francophonie (*l'Année Francophone Internationale, 1997*, 1997: 340).

The mounting concern for the future of the French language has permeated every part of the international francophone cultural scene. The main organizational outlet for this concern, within the framework of the Francophonie, is the Avenir de la langue française (ALF) (a group interested in the future of the French language). This organization is active on several fronts through its efforts to stimulate broader use of French, particularly in those sectors of life where a widespread tendency to use English prevails (e.g., commerce, science). The ALF holds that linguistic diversity is no impediment to the circulation of people, ideas, merchandise, or services. Rather the most pernicious obstacles to their movement are believed to be the twin trends of linguistic uniformity and hegemony of one language, almost always English. This situation has depressed French to the position of the world's second language (Massart-Piérard, 1993: 9). These conditions, it is further argued, limit growth of individuals, societies, and the knowledge-based economy (*l'économie de l'immatériel*), widely-acknowledged as the principal sector of employment in the future. The ALF is presently focussing its attention mainly on Europe, where the European Union is showing signs of being dominated more and more by English.

French Language

The Avenir de la langue française does not, however, try to resolve the conflicts presently besieging international French, conflicts that touch Canadian francophones as they do francophones living elsewhere in the world. Ager (1996: 51-55) discusses five "domains" of international use of French, showing in the process the seemingly unresolvable tensions that have come to haunt the language. Many Canadian francophones avoid some of these tensions, but must nonetheless put up with the others. It is important to review these tensions here, because French plays a pivotal role in the Francophonie; it is a main unifying force there.

One domain of international French is its status as a language of the elite. Although true for neither France nor Canada, for example, in many countries in Africa, Asia, and elsewhere, knowing French is a mark of prestige and an acquisition to be protected for the exclusive use of this special social class. With a mastery of French members of the elite can gain access to coveted high-level jobs and the honor, power, and influence accompanying such posts. As Bourdieu (1982) observes, these privileged people can control social life to the extent necessary to ensure perpetuation of their own class. When members of the Francophonie advocate mass public education in French, depending on the country being considered, they may be challenging the hegemonic privileges of its linguistic elite.

This elite benefits when French is the official language of their country. For in this domain the type of French used is administrative: a formal, written language, guided by numerous formulas of usage. As Ager (1996: 52) puts it, "administrative French is not an attractive nor an easy form to acquire." To be hired for a position whose qualifications include mastery of administrative French, the successful applicant must have a lengthy education and sufficient knowledge and acumen to pass written examinations demonstrating these achievements. In addition, a society with administrative machinery of this kind needs a steady supply of linguistically competent workers, presupposing thus an educational system, whether public or private, capable of meeting this requirement. But the quality of education has declined in some of the poorer countries in the Francophonie and with it the labor pool of workers schooled in administrative French.

The third domain is French as the language of education. As a language of education it may be required as a foreign language or, on a more demanding level, as a second language, albeit one learned and used from an early age onward. In the second situation, the age at which a child starts school is also the age at which he or she starts learning French, the language of education. In a number of countries in the Francophonie, including some in the North, French is a second language learned in precisely this manner. Unfortunately, in many of these countries – all of them in the South – mass education is in a dreadful state, and so it is likewise with the teaching of French on the popular level. In fact, these countries spend great sums of money on education, and they receive significant help from the First-World, in general, and from France, in particular, but mass education there remains submerged in a sea of problems:

> Most observers agree that the future prosperity of the former colonies must come about through education. But the dilemma is that if this education continues to be provided in French (or any other external language) it will continue to be ineffective, while if it is to be provided in national or local languages and thus be effective, that very process will spell the end of Francophonie as such and of a future for French (Ager, 1996: 53).

A special organization in the Francophonie known as the Conférence des ministres de l'éducation nationale has as one of its mandates to contribute to the elaboration and evaluation of educational policies of member states. The provinces of Québec, New Brunswick, Ontario, and Manitoba participate regularly in meetings of this group.

A fourth domain of French is its role as a vehicular language. A vehicular language is a practical language used in particular spheres of life such as commerce and science. It tends to be relatively free of cultural meanings, and because of its limited scope, relatively simple and easy to learn. As a vehicular language, however, French must compete with English, widely regarded by linguists as more suited to this domain. In other words, French, in contrast to English, has certain structural and lexical properties that render it less effective as a vehicular language. Since these properties are technical and hence beyond the scope of this book, interested readers can find a somewhat more detailed discussion of them in Ager (1996: 54-55).

The comparative unsuitability of French as a vehicular language adversely affects its role as a commercial language. This, the fifth domain, is especially evident in many African markets, which, however, are typically urban and therefore seldom patronized by rural people. But elsewhere French must compete in the marketplace with English, doing so as a vehicular language. In defending French, its proponents argue that it, too, is vehicular, since it carries French culture and values. What is more, they say these items have a place in such realms as commerce and science. And surely they do, but it is still true that, when communicated in vehicular French, they will have to be modified to accommodate the technical vocabulary of the sphere in question and the communication demands peculiar to it.

Canadian francophones are most directly involved in the commercial and vehicular language domains and their allied conflicts. But to the extent they are bilingual, they get the best of both worlds, being able to choose the more effective vehicular language for the occasion. And although French is an official language in Canada, the country has an efficacious, universal educational system that offers training to many of its people in the language of their choice more or less when and where they please. In good part for this reason, francophone and bilingual people in Canada fail to constitute an elite class in the ways francophones do in, for instance, certain African countries. In this regard, it was previously observed that French is used in Canada's francophone parity and minority societies in at least four institutional areas, and that here, too, participation is not restricted to a particular social stratum.

Francophone Immigrants and Refugees

For many French-speaking Canadians, international involvement in the Francophonie can occur without ever leaving home, especially if they reside in a large city. Hard to come by are precise figures on the number of first- and second-language francophone immigrants and refugees who arrive in Canada each year, the refugees having a special claim to permanent status in this country so they may escape physical danger or political persecution of their kind. Be that as it may, francophone foreigners are coming to Canada in significant numbers, making their presence felt across the land in all three types of francophone societies.

The large majority of these new arrivals head for Québec in general and Montréal in particular, where they face problems not always shared with the other two prominent categories of immigrant, the allophones and the anglophones. It was observed in chapter 4 that, today, the Québécois are for the most part eager to welcome francophones, and even allophones, from abroad, but since most people who migrate these days come from Third-World countries, their presence in Québec poses serious questions about how to integrate them into Québécois society, a First-World entity. Yet according to Langlois (1998: 18), in 1996 only 39 percent of the immigrants could speak French (i.e., had knowledge of French) in comparison with 33 percent who could speak English (and no French). (The remaining 28 percent were allophone.) Whatever their language, these immigrants are often racially, culturally, religiously, and even linguistically different from *pure laine* francophone Quebeckers. Also noted earlier was the dual problem of retaining the immigrants who do come to the province as well as those Quebeckers who yearn to move from it. In 1996, for example, 28 577 immigrants came to Québec, but after counting all who emigrated from Québec to foreign lands (whether immigrants returning home or Quebeckers leaving for another country), the province experienced a net gain through international migration of only 18 778 people.

No one seems to know exactly how many of the 9779 international migrants who left Québec in 1996 were francophones heading for another Canadian province. Nonetheless, some do precisely that, presumably following the historical pattern of Québec migration within Canada by moving mainly to Ontario, British Columbia, and Alberta in descending order of preference. In the meantime, some francophone immigrants to Canada go directly to one of the provinces outside Québec, possibly because they have heard about attractive employment opportunities in the area, have personal contacts there, or both. Unfortunately, detailed answers to this question are also lacking, chiefly because no statistical agency, provincial or federal, analyzes immigrants according to, what is for the study of Canada's francophone societies, four important criteria: French as first-language, French as second-language, country of origin, and destination within Canada (both initial and subsequent).

For example, in 1996 Alberta welcomed 88 immigrants who spoke French only, with 41 coming to Edmonton, 37 to Calgary, and 10 to other regions of the province.[2] But their countries (or provinces) of origin were not recorded. Considered annually, this constitutes but a very small percentage of all francophones in Edmonton and Calgary, even though their effect is cumulative and beginning to be felt. This is why two immigrant welcoming societies – one in Edmonton, one in Calgary – have been founded within the last ten years to help these newcomers integrate themselves into the local francophone and anglophone communities. Moreover, nonsectarian French schools opened their doors in 1996 in both cities. This was, in part, a response to the realization that some first-language francophones and many second-language francophones from abroad are not Christian and consequently fail to meet the criteria, should they even want to do so, for sending their children to French Catholic schools. What is unknown is how Canadian-born francophones in Calgary and Edmonton feel about these newcomers in their midst, most being racially and religiously different and most having a good command of the French language, though they often speak it with an unfamiliar accent.

In Ontario, Bellavance (1994a: 15) reports that certain observers see the ever-growing influx of foreign francophones to the province as a "lifesaver" for the French-language communities, particular those in the large cities. As in Québec, a significant decline in the francophone birth rate has occurred, resulting in the need to find other ways to maintain a viable proportion of francophones in the overall provincial population. Bellavance also finds that schools seem to be benefiting from the presence of foreign francophones in the population, since many of these newcomers want their children educated in French. He cites data from the Cité Collégiale in Ottawa indicating that around 30 percent of its students come from francophone immigrant families. Writing along these same lines, Denis Gratton (1994: 15) reports that, at one Ottawa French secondary school, immigrant students make up more than half the total number of students, and that their presence has improved the quality of classroom French used by Canadian-born Franco-Ontarians.

Although Ontario may be exceptional in this regard, further detailed analysis of this kind would require data about the effects of francophone immigrants on other minority francophone societies in Canada. Unfortunately, such data are unavailable. Table 11.1 does nevertheless show that, statistically, considerable variation occurred in 1996 among Canadian cities as to the proportion of francophone immigrants in their total populations, as measured by mother-tongue of respondent and counting both single and multiple census responses.

This table reveals several important patterns of francophone immigrant life in late twentieth century Canada. First, 82 percent of these immigrants live in the cities listed in this table; they are thus overwhelmingly an urban group. Second, 63.6 percent of all of Canada's francophone immigrants are found in Montréal and Québec City, especially the former. Third, a number of them – 16.8 percent – nonetheless prefer predominantly anglophone cities, where economic growth is presently the greatest and where the greatest demand for workers is therefore found, in this instance and in order of largest number, Toronto, Ottawa-Hull, Vancouver,

Calgary, and Edmonton. Fourth, the figures in Table 11.1 suggest that these francophones cut a rather large figure in the relatively small francophone communities of Saint John's and Victoria and a rather minor figure in the large city of Winnipeg. Just how well integrated these foreigners are depends, of course, on their length of residence in Canada. According to the 1996 census, slightly over 80 percent of all francophone immigrants had come to Canada before 1991.

Table 11.1 Proportion of Francophone Immigrants in Selected Canadian Cities

City	Number of Francophone immigrants	Percentage of total number of francophones
St. John's	135	19.7
Halifax	455	4.5
Québec City	7900	0.01
Montréal	106 185	4.9
Ottawa (Hull part)	3155	1.6
Ottawa (Ontario part)	6110	30.1
Toronto	13 305	27.2
Hamilton	800	8.3
Winnipeg	1030	3.3
Saskatoon	250	6.4
Calgary	1340	10.9
Edmonton	1195	6.0
Vancouver	4875	22.0
Victoria	635	12.7
Canada	179 370	2.7

Source: Statistics Canada (1998a)

Conclusion

It is evident that, from the standpoint of personal and social identity, economic opportunity, cultural expression, and cultural contacts with immigrants, the Francophonie is extremely valuable for Canadian francophones. A multitude of media and electronic links to all corners of the earth further enrich these possibilities, as does the general increase in international tourism. Apropos the latter, francophones can now travel more easily than ever from Canada to Belgium, France, and many other countries, visit there for short periods of time, and when touring for educational and cultural reasons, get to know some of their foreign linguistic counterparts just that much better. All this is part of the broader process of globalization, which generally appears to be a happy trend for the Francophonie. Latouche (1993: 52-53) observes for Québec that ethnic nationalism and the desire to settle historical scores with Canada's anglophones is passing, giving way to a new nationalism in a new global order founded on a pluralistic "civic" consciousness – being Québécois whether anglophone, allophone, or francophone. As Balthazar (1993: 15-17) puts it, rather than being ethnic, Québec's nationalism is now "territorial." From still another angle, the idea that Canada's francophones stand as one of the country's two founding groups is becoming increasingly irrelevant. In short, notwithstanding the thorny language problems considered in this chapter, the future of the Francophonie and the place of French-speaking Canadians within it has probably never been brighter.

All this is good news for the francophone societies examined in this book. Nonetheless, a strong Francophonie cannot alone guarantee their survival and development. At least as important are the everyday linguistic lifestyles led by the people who inhabit these societies. These lifestyles are constituted of their routine patterns of behavior that manifest and regularize their personal involvement with local happenings, some of which do not even unfold in French. International events, organizations, expressions of solidarity, and the like can assist local events and organizations and help buoy spirits and anchor identity, but they are no substitute for routine social interaction in French with friends and relatives, for groups that sponsor local festivals and activities, for organizations that speak for the local community, or for the physical presence of centres, schools, churches, and similar institutions. These must be established and maintained such that they can survive the usual storms of collective life, among the more violent being these days governmental budget cuts and shifting majority opinion about minority groups. Given the historical and contemporary backdrop painted in this chapter and those preceding it, what, then, does the future hold for Canada's francophone societies?

Chapter 12
Survival and Development of Francophone Canada

At the moment, many of Canada's francophone societies, as portrayed in this book, are surviving and doing so more than minimally. Québec and northern and eastern New Brunswick and Ontario obviously share the best prognosis in this regard, followed in moderately close succession first by Évangéline and then by the Clare-Argyle French shore and Saint-Boniface. The substantially francophone small towns and cities in Manitoba, Saskatchewan, and Alberta have the fourth best prognosis, and the francophone communities in the large cities appear not far behind in fifth place. Sixth, and still with a reasonable chance of surviving, is Newfoundland's Port-au-Port Peninsula (Magord, 1998). This is my outlook even if Québec separates (see also Cardinal, 1997: 63-65). But for the rest – Maillardville and the weakly francophone small towns and cities across the country – I am inclined, following Dean Louder (cited in Paquette, 1999:8), toward the attitude of *point de salut*.

The communities that are surviving on all six levels are also developing; they are doing more than maintaining the status quo. Rather they are pushing ahead by establishing new resources (i.e., new events, procedures, facilities, organizations), improving their educational basis, ensuring a certain measure of *la relève*, and working as much as possible toward self-sufficiency through volunteer work in every appropriate area. Development also depends on having accurate social scientific data with which to describe and measure what has been achieved and not achieved. Furthermore, development depends strongly on the personal growth of individual francophones in these communities (*l'épanouissement*), in particular on their capacity to speak French and on their ability to find a mosaic of work or leisure activities, or a mosaic of both, arranged in a linguistic lifestyle through which to express it and their identity as francophones or bilinguals. People who see themselves as francophone in whole or in part will strive in some way, often as volunteers, to help develop the community that they live in and that provides them with the opportunity to effect their personal growth. This chapter takes a close look at these conditions for personal and community development in an attempt to discover what must be done to ensure their realization.

Resources

Four resources for personal and community development are particularly important for Canada's francophone societies: ethnolinguistic vitality and bilingualism, economic development, expansion of the electronic media, and renewed interest in Québec in the minority francophone societies lying outside it. Together, these resources form a solid basis for the optimism just sketched.

Ethnolinguistic Vitality

The conclusion reached in chapters 8 and 10 that ethnolinguistic vitality is reasonably high in the francophone societies of Newfoundland, Ontario, and the western provinces points to a major resource for development. After all, French is the basis of these societies; it and francophone culture are first and foremost what their members are trying to protect and develop further. Nevertheless, some of the factors of ethnolinguistic vitality are, themselves, significantly affected by the desire of francophones to maintain and develop French in the local community. For example, French-speaking Canadians ordinarily initiate the process of acquiring the institutional services they want, and where necessary, follow through by lobbying for them or taking their case to court. The service in question might be a francophone school, choir, or cultural centre. Moreover, it is bilingual individuals who decide to publicly identify themselves as francophone or personally use their knowledge as a resource in getting work or touring a francophone part of the world. In short, expanding on the position taken earlier by Guindon and Dion and applying it now to the situation of francophones both inside and outside Québec, it can be said that, in an officially bilingual society like Canada, those who want French to survive there are going to have work at this project. Above all, this exhorts people to use the language wherever possible and appropriate, in conversation, economic transactions, and francophone and bilingual organizations. As the Epigraph indicates, francophones are known for such tenacity; for them *vouloir c'est pouvoir* (where there's a will there's a way).

Economic Development

Of the seven key factors of ethnolinguistic vitality, the one centred on utility leads most directly to the question of economic development as a resource. This resource takes two main forms: development of economic opportunities in French and the development of individuals who can take advantage of these opportunities. A number of pages have already been devoted to the first, where it was argued in the preceding chapter that the Francophonie offers the possibility of numerous business outlets and partnerships for Canadian francophones and in other chapters that local francophone-run businesses in the minority societies, though they must operate bilingually, can nevertheless profit further from patronage by a francophone clientele. The many francophone co-operatives and business organizations (e.g., clubs, councils, chambers of commerce) throughout minority francophone Canada attest the importance placed there on economic development. Indeed, Anne Cloutier (1998: 2) reports that this resource is viewed in many rural francophone areas of the country as the only road to cultural survival, for otherwise the youth of these areas will be forced to leave them to find work.

The second kind of economic development is much less often discussed, even though it is the more fundamental of the two being considered here. Cardinal (1997: 166) and Pendakur and Pendakur (1998) hold that this type of development rests on knowledge of languages as a form of human capital. The latter two argue that

> language knowledge can be viewed as a skill, and as such there should accrue economic benefits. At both a societal and individual level, the ability of citizens to speak more than one language may provide a competitive edge by allowing people to work in different sectors of the economy, and by increasing opportunities for international trade and tourism. (Pendakur and Pendakur, 1998: 90)

Their study revealed that this proposition tends to hold for Canada's two official languages, even though there is some variation in this respect among the three CMAs they studied: Montréal, Toronto, and Vancouver. Knowing a non-official language, however, proved only in rare instances to be advantageous in the labor market.

Indeed, belief in this proposition is in substantial part what many Canadians have been using in recent years to justify their support for the Official Languages policy. Churchill (1998: 74) has found that five considerations attract the most public attention in this debate: being bilingual is believed to lead to increases in:

- direct access to international markets;
- personal job mobility;
- major benefits for communities with a bilingual work force;
- contributions to tourism;
- export advantages.

Churchill (1998: 54) also concluded after reviewing a number of surveys that approximately 75 percent of Canadians say Canada should maintain its two official languages, while 25 percent of the population favors dropping them. Moreover, both official language groups tend to support federal official languages policies, governmental subsidies for a full range of services in both languages, and the right of official language minorities to be educated in their language. Odd as it may seem, however, most Canadians tend to underestimate the degree of public support just sketched here. Perhaps this misperception can be traced in part to publicity disseminated by the dissatisfied 25 percent, some being organized in pressure groups such as the Confederation of Regions Party in New Brunswick and the Association for the Preservation of English in Canada, whose scope is nation-wide.

Expanded Electronic Media

Since the first of April 1999 francophones everywhere in Canada outside Québec have had, in addition to the services of Société Radio-Canada (SRC), access to a second major French television network: TVA, a service provided by the Groupe TVA de Montréal (Lusignan, 1998c: 2). Coverage is intended to be truly coast to coast, as monitored and directed by an advisory committee of ten people chosen from different areas of the country. The fierce competition in Québec between SRC and TVA has now become nation-wide. Lusignan, writing before the implementation of pan-Canadian TVA, wondered how anglophones would react when the cable companies eliminated one American channel, a requirement the companies faced in making room for the new network. In the meantime, SRC is presently seeking permission to launch the Réseau de l'économie, or RDE, a network that will specialize in questions of consumption and the economy in Canada's francophone societies. These electronic initiatives constitute two more major signs of the importance that francophones assign to the economic resources that undergird their communities.

Québec's Interest in Minority Francophones

It was noted in the preceding chapter that, citing Louder and Dupont (1997), Québec's preoccupation with the sovereignty question has led to a peculiar juncture: even while it remains the mother country of millions of North Americans and the principal francophone cultural home in North America, Québec has not really taken up the cause of those living beyond its borders. Were it to change policy in this area, Québec could become a major element in the survival-development equation, the omnipresent *bête-noire* facing the parity and minority societies. In fact, signs of a genuine change in policy are in the air, despite arguments of some Québec nationalists that independence is the only way for Québec to escape the precarious situation in which many of these societies find themselves (Harvey, 1993: 52). They reason that, if these societies become stronger through help from Québec, this will be considered evidence that French language and culture can survive and develop within the federalist framework, making unnecessary any kind of political separation.

Two of the signs are symbolic. The first – Le Parc de l'Amérique Française, located within a couple of blocks of the parliament buildings in Québec City (corner of Claire Fontaine and blvd. René Lévesque) – was founded and commemorated in 1986 by René Lévesque, who felt a closer kinship with francophones living elsewhere in North America than many of his contemporaries. The park occupies an entire city block, and was built in honor of the North American descendants from the colonists who sailed to this continent from France. In addition to a great number of Québec flags, 12 other flags grace the park. They represent Acadia, Newfoundland, the provinces from Ontario westward, the two older territories, and the francophone areas of the United States as signified by the Acadian-Louisiana, French America, and French Midwest flags.

The other symbol of Québec's interest in North American francophonie is the Musée de l'Amérique Française; it is appropriately housed in the Séminaire de Québec, founded in 1663 and prominently situated within the walls of the old city. The Museum uses displays and artifacts in the fields of history, science, and the arts to highlight the cultural identity of North America's francophones. It offers not only a historical sense but also a contemporary sense of

French North America, as communicated through a series of short recorded interviews with selected francophones living in different parts of this continent.

In addition to these symbols, the Government of Québec has recently circulated a major policy statement clearly setting out its intention to establish ties with Canadian francophone communities beyond its borders, pledging to help them survive and develop. Louise Beaudoin, minister delegated to Canadian Intergovernmental Affairs, wrote in the Foreword of the 1995 policy statement that

> the Government of Québec recognizes that the francophone and Acadian communities outside Québec are very much alive and that they intend to prosper there where they find themselves. In the most general framework of its action within the international Francophonie, it is in the nature of things that Québec attach particular importance to ties with these communities. In this perspective, the present policy aims to establish a modern co-operation between them and Québec society by means of a common search for new and creative partnerships. (translation) (Government of Québec, 1995: 2)

In more detailed terms, this quotation signifies Québec's intention to contribute in various ways to projects favoring the use of French in areas recognized as essential according to the results of research on ethnolinguistic vitality, as well as according to the minority francophone communities themselves. In the main, these areas are culture, education, communications, and the economy. Sometimes this collaboration will take the form of helping to develop needed expertise, other times it will take the form of joint projects with certain minority communities and organizations (Government of Québec, 1995: 15-23). The same policy statement also described the establishment of appropriate organizational machinery (e.g., sessions of *concertation*, a triennial forum) and, within the Québec government, establishment of the Secrétariat aux affaires intergouvernementales canadiennes. Jacques Brassard (*Franc-Contact*, 1998: 5), a minister in the Government of Québec, observed of Canada's minority francophones: "doing nothing, ignoring them, ignoring their difficult situation, showing indifference with reference to them, is certainly not the route to survival" (translation).

At the 1997 Forum francophone de concertation, Lise Bissonnette (1997), *directrice* of *Le Devoir*, observed that the

Government of Québec can never become a substitute source of funding in the face of federal government monetary reductions to minority francophone organizations and projects. She believes nevertheless that plenty of scope exists for collaboration: "I hope that we will organize our common socio-cultural space, that it will become structured in such a way that new collaborations will take hold, whatever the political future of Québec" (translation) (Bissonnette, 1997: 11). Above all, she hopes these joint efforts will unfold outside the nationalist-federalist debate, well distanced from its political biases and machinations. The second Forum francophone will be held in March 2000, backed by a 20 percent increase in that part of the 1999-2000 Québec budget devoted to the Canadian francophonie (*Le Franco*, 1999: 2).

Education

The contemporary educational scene in the three types of francophone societies has been discussed at length throughout this book. But two new developments in this area, one real, the other possible, have yet to be fully considered. Both will help brighten the future of the parity and minority societies.

MicroRadio, a new Radio-Canada production centre, will soon start broadcasting educational radio programs for francophone children living outside Québec. This new service has been established in response to parents who maintain that, after educational television, educational radio interests their children the most (Lusignan, 1998d: 11). MicroRadio will also offer some programs on the World Wide Web.

Turning to the second development, which is presently only at the discussion stage, Gilbert (1999: 167-178) describes the need for establishing a University of the Francophonie (Université de la francophonie). Such an institution would be devoted to the scientific study of francophone Canada, a mission accomplished by its faculty and the graduate students who would attend it to receive training in the techniques of research. In practice, this university would operate as a nation-wide network of francophone universities, and so doing, could become an important new mechanism for generating solidarity both within and across Canada's francophone societies.

La Relève

From the present generation of francophone youth will come tomorrow's active core of adult francophones, the people who will see to the future survival and development of Canada's parity and minority societies. Notwithstanding the high rates of assimilation discussed in earlier chapters, some of today's francophone youth in these societies **are** retaining their language and culture. Evidence for this tendency is moderately favorable.

For example, Churchill (1998: 61) reports that the percentage of bilingual teenagers has grown in Canada from 17.7 in 1981 to 24.4 in 1996. In 1996 New Brunswick had the highest proportion of bilingual teenagers – 49.3 percent – while the Northwest Territories had the lowest – 7.8 percent. Favorable public opinion, parental support, and accessible all-French and French-immersion schools are among the antecedents explaining this trend. Yet chapter 10 described the decline that has occurred in language continuity (speaking one's mother tongue at home), and noted that everywhere outside Québec the age groups 20 to 24 and 25 to 29, *vis-à-vis* the other age categories, have shown the most marked movement in this direction. Of interest, however, is the fact that it is quite different for the 0 to 9 age group, where the tendency to use French as the home language rather than English has risen between 1971 and 1996 (O'Keefe, 1998: 43-44).

With respect to *la relève*, two other sets of figures add to this moderately favorable outlook. O'Keefe (1998: 46) reports that transmission of French to children in all-French families has risen slightly between 1971 and 1991, and risen dramatically for children in mixed families where the mother is francophone and the father is non-francophone. Table 12.1 shows the degree of change in this regard. Even while a good deal of progress remains to be made in mixed-language families, these recent trends are grounds for optimism.

Self-Sufficiency and the Volunteer

Chapter 6 explored the role of the key volunteer in Canada's minority francophone societies and provided a definition of this person as a knowledgeable, highly skilled, long-working devotee who contributes most substantially to the goals of community survival and development. The study of key volunteers in Calgary and Edmonton (Stebbins, 1998b) revealed a high degree of commitment

Table 12.1 Mother Tongue of Youth in French Mother Tongue and Mixed Language Families

	French in French mother-tongue families	French in mixed-language families
0-24 age group		
1991	92.2%	24.0%
1971	90.6%	10.6%
0-4 age group		
1991	95.3%	30.4%
1971	92.7%	13.4%

Source: adapted from O'Keefe (1998: 46-47, tables 8 and 9)

to the local francophone community. This was evident above all in their heavy load of volunteer activities, for which they typically shouldered extensive responsibilities. But it was equally evident in the large number of endogamous marriages, the Frenchness of their children, their preference for French schools, and their pro-federalist stance.

The work of volunteers, in general, and key volunteers, in particular, will be the saving grace of the parity and minority francophone societies as these societies limp through an era of reduced public and private support for their events, projects, and organizations. In other words, the road to reasonable self-sufficiency – total self-sufficiency being impossible – will be built and maintained by volunteers, aided where necessary by funds gathered for the most part from non-governmental sources such as lotteries, casinos, expositions, ticket sales to events, and dues and donations. Many a local minority francophone community is presently struggling to complete its journey to the promised land of reasonable self-sufficiency.

Although community survival and development are greatly aided in this process, it should be remembered that key volunteers also get something personal from their service to the collectivity. For they are motivated by both altruism and self-interest in their pursuit of volunteering as a special kind of leisure. In this regard, it was observed in the Calgary-Edmonton study that, of the ten rewards of serious leisure, four stood out as being especially salient for the volunteers of this study. Among these four, self-enrichment through the volunteer experience was by far the most powerful for the overall sample. It was at once a main personal reward and the reward most directly related to volunteering, for the personal benefits of altruism were particularly strongly felt here, or for a couple of key volunteers in the sector of religion, here they experienced the benefits of spirituality. Respondents in both cities ranked second the reward of group accomplishment and third the two rewards of self-enhancement and contribution to maintenance and development of the francophone community. In this way, the goals of finding substantial leisure and fostering collective survival and development are met through the same set of efforts put forth as a key volunteer. To the extent an entire community operates on this principle, it **will** reach a decent level of self-sufficiency, fostering along the way considerable personal growth of its volunteer members.

Conclusion

Few will doubt that this book, in general, and this final chapter, in particular, have painted the present and future of Canada's francophone societies in the rosy colors of optimism. Such a portrayal is easiest to accept for the majority societies forming the mountain and foothills of francophone Canada. For some observers, however, this picture becomes decidedly more incredible when the archipelago part of the centre-periphery metaphor is sketched in these same warm tones. For here they come face to face with the pessimistic stance of the demographers and other analysts of similar persuasion.

I have tried to show in various places in this book where the pessimists are on weak ground. This is primarily in the operationalization of key ideas such as home language and mother tongue and in the failure to recognize the many other ways of using the French language besides speaking it and the many other places to use it besides at home. Indeed, the general failure to acknowledge the importance of leisure in the daily lives and personal growth of parity and minority francophones and in the development of their communities stands as one of the most glaring deficiencies in the interdisciplinary field of North American francophone studies. But I believe enough evidence has been presented in this book to indicate clearly that parity and minority francophones spend significant amounts of their leisure time using French, that researchers in this field must redefine, or further define, what they mean in statistical terms by the concept of francophone, and that they must therefore hold in abeyance their pessimistic assessments until data gathered within the framework of the reconceptualized definitions have come in.

I would be surprised, given the contents of this book and the results of my own qualitative research, were the optimistic stance not substantially supported by the new data. But, then, these data, once gathered, should be allowed to speak for themselves. Moreover, acquiring such data could take some time, for operationalizing a new set of census definitions along the lines suggested earlier is no easy task, even though new operationalizations are now being considered. Additionally, I do recognize that, although it seems unlikely at present, a change in Canadian anglophone public sentiment in the direction of an extreme version of anglo-conformity and away from its present level of ethnic pluralism could quickly undermine some of the bases for the optimism expressed in this book. Nor is it impossible that some sort of internecine conflict might emerge that would destroy one of the majority or minority societies as an ensemble. This appears to be unlikely, however, since there have been any number of conflicts down through the years at all levels – local, regional, and national – which nevertheless always seemed to get resolved. After each period of conflict the community or society concerned moved on and not infrequently even profited from what had taken place (Cardinal, 1997: 109). Perhaps the greatest worry is that Canada's francophones, whether in Québec or outside it, might let down their guard, becoming complacent in their success and letting slide their use of French and their consumption of francophone culture. If Léon Dion (1993), in speaking for Québec, can warn that survival requires constant vigilance, this admonition must certainly be even more fitting for francophones living in parity and minority circumstances.

Meanwhile, let optimism be the watchword in research as it presently is at the grassroots level in all three types of societies, regardless of geographic location. Such an outlook is more likely to bear fruit, because researchers are more likely to devote their careers to studying a subject that promises to be around for awhile and francophones are more likely to devote themselves to working for their communities and establishing linguistic lifestyles within them if they believe those communities will persist. On this note, then, it would be good to let Arnold Toynbee have *le mot de la fin*, since it was his optimistic epigraph that opened this long discussion:

If the Great Powers stubbornly insist on clinging to the old concept of nationalism – which is out-dated now – peoples who have not found nationalism a happy experience may be the only ones who can give the world the fresh solution that it needs. I suspect that the coming people in the Americas may be the French Canadians.

Arnold Toynbee, *World Review* (March, 1948), p. 12

Notes

Chapter 1

1. George Hillary, Jr. (1955) analyzed no less than 94 sociological definitions of community.

2. Maillardville emerged between 1908 and 1910 as a community of francophone workers recruited from Québec and Saskatchewan to work in a saw mill on the Fraser River. Villeneuve (1983: 134) reports that Maillardville began an accelerated decline in the 1950s, reaching a point today where, according to impressionistic evidence, little activity takes place in French (Bélanger, 1992: 4; Société Radio-Canada, 1992). Still, such claims about the community's demise may be premature, given Tellier's (1993: 7) report that Maillardville's *caisse populaire*, the Village Credit Union, has just experienced a major expansion. Moreover, in 1997, the Société Maillardville-Uni received approval for a measure of federal government support to construct a community centre and finance its annual *Festival du bois* (Canadian Heritage, 1997: 37).

3. Relative to the size of the anglophone population, the proportion of francophones in Canada and in its major cities is declining, even though they are increasing in absolute numbers. Yet, for the study of lifestyles, for example, the absolute number is the more important figure, since it more directly bears on the question of the minimum number of people needed to sustain a francophone way of life in an anglophone milieu.

4. The Federal Government is not the only source of outside funding for projects leading to realization of the four goals, only the most generous. The Bureau of Québec also grants funds for francophone community projects implemented outside Québec, although the projects must be related in some way to it. And depending on the nature of the project, financial support may be obtained in the provinces from provincial or municipal agencies or from provincially-run lotteries. At one time the Catholic Church gave money for these purposes.

5. Given this complicated politico-linguistic status of Canadian francophones in their own country, it is arguable whether social scientific examination of them can be accurately classified under the heading of ethnic studies. For this same reason extending research findings in ethnic studies to the study of Franco-Canadians is fraught with difficulties.

Chapter 2

1. This section adheres to the sequence of Québec history followed by Françoise Tétu de Labsade (1990: chaps. 2 and 6).

2. Developing state-owned corporations was a main governmental strategy from 1960 to approximately 1985, the intent being to give Quebeckers some financial control of their own economy. Nevertheless, an economy sufficiently strong to endow Québec with significant economic self-sufficiency is not necessarily as strong an economy as desired. In 1998 Québec was still suffering with an unenviable credit rating, the product of unfavorable evaluations from such agencies as Moody's, Standard and Poor, and Dominion Bond Rating Service. To make matters worse, the big banks, using these evaluations to justify their actions, have been accused of moving cash out of Québec (*Calgary Herald*, 1998e: D3).

3. White-Indian half-breeds began appearing in North America shortly after the first explorers reached this continent, which indicates that the former are found everywhere on it. Because of their numbers and their critical role in helping to settle the West, the French-Indian Métis of the prairies are, however, the best-known of these mixed bloods.

4. If a private member's bill currently before Parliament gets passed, Riel will soon be exonerated of high treason and declared a Father of Confederation for his key role in negotiating Manitoba's entry into Confederation (Aubry, 1999: A6).

Chapter 3

1. I know of no equivalent procedure in English-speaking countries, and the word *la concertation* has no counterpart in the English language.

2. The Québec French linguistic scene is more complicated than this. Each of the six accents can actually be further analyzed into several sub-accents.

3. Since English-language comedy clubs also exist in Montréal, anglophones have their own comedy scene. Most francophone Quebeckers do not seem to patronize them, however, preferring instead to enjoy their comedy in French in the ways described in this paragraph, as well as through televised segments of the *Festival juste pour rire* and televised sketch and stand-up comedy programs.

Chapter 4

1. In the Manitoba legislature the motion for approving the Accord had to receive unanimous support. But Elijah Harper, member of the New Democratic Party and native Indian, repeatedly opposed it on grounds that it failed to sufficiently consider the constitutional situation of Native people.

2. Both ex-premier Jacques Parizeau and incumbent premier Lucien Bouchard have expressed their opinion that the question in the 1995 referendum was insufficiently clear and that the question in the next one should be unambiguous (*Calgary Herald*, 1998c).

Chapter 5

1. Reporting population data for political entities such as counties, municipalities, and municipal districts, as done here and, later, for the prairies, often obscures larger concentrations of francophones in one or more of their internal communities. Unfortunately, Statistics Canada census data are unavailable for the latter, which are always very small.

2. Because of the widespread tendency to see the idea of career as applying only to occupations, note that, in this definition, I use the term much more broadly. Broadly conceived, careers are available in all substantial, complicated roles, including especially those in work, leisure, deviance, politics, religion, and interpersonal relationships (for further discussion of this sociological use of career, see Stebbins, 1999: chapter 1).

3. Francophone day care facilities (*les garderies*) exist in every medium- and large-sized city in Canada. Formal education is not, however, one of their functions.

4. Information presented throughout this book on the history of Canada's francophone universities, their enrolments, and their objectives has been taken from the common website of two inter-

national organizations: the Association des Universités Partiellement ou Entièrement de Langue Française (AUPELF) and the Université des Réseaux d'Expression Française (UREF). The site's address is WWW.aupelf-uref.org (see the section on "*Établissements*").

5. As was done in chapter 1, the mother-tongue figures are a composite of Canadians who speak French only; French and English; French, English, and a third language; and French and another non-official language.

6. Most of the material for this paragraph and the following one was gathered from the provincial *Fact Sheets* published in 1994 by the Department of Canadian Heritage, Government of Canada.

Chapter 6

1. Single-parent francophone families exist just as single-parent anglophone families do. Such families are omitted from this analysis of exogamous families since very few of them were encountered in the Calgary study and, at least within the home, the question of the linguistic composition of the marriage is irrelevant.

2. All quotations I used this section come from interviews with the respondents in the Calgary study. Originally in French, these remarks were translated into English by the author.

3. It should be understood that volunteering in rural areas and small towns is substantially different from volunteering in the urban sub-communities. For example, there is generally more informal and less formal volunteering in the first when compared with the second, where the ratio of these two types is reversed. Formal volunteering, generally speaking, occurs in organizations, and the informal variety, which takes place outside them, is seen in the practice of helping among friends, neighbors, and relatives. Moreover, the range of volunteer opportunities appears to be much greater in the medium- and large-sized cities than in the towns and small cities. Additionally, it is possible that, when compared with city francophones, a significantly higher proportion of the rural and small town francophones have never moved from the locality of their birth. This creates in the rural communities a kind of stability unknown in their urban counterparts, where new arrivals

and departures are commonplace and the proportion of French-speaking people in the cities is generally much lower. At the same time, in the large cities, francophones are far more multi-dimensional. For example, they are more fragmented; considerable variation is evident according to age, occupation, religion, country of origin, leisure preferences, and possibly other dimensions along which groups and categories of people make their own claims and follow their own interests. Finally, urban francophones, when compared with their rural and small town brothers and sisters, carry out their activities in an atmosphere characterized by greater anonymity, impersonality, and tolerance of social differences.

Chapter 7

1. The anglophone-francophone comparison is justified in this instance by the presence of a large number of allophones in Vanier.

2. The following ideas of lifestyle and social world are more fully discussed in Stebbins (1998b).

3. This requires teaching English as a foreign language, as another subject, just as French and other foreign languages are taught in anglophone schools. Moreover, there is little worry in this approach that minority francophone students will fail to learn English. As Laponce (1966: 87) puts it: "but, no matter what is done, the assimilation pressure of English will remain so considerable that all other languages will continue to live under threat" (for an example, see Stebbins, 1994: 37-38).

Chapter 9

1. Taking as Saint-Boniface the three census tracts that border the Red River on its east side at The Forks (tracts 114, 116, and 117), I calculated the overall proportion of francophones for the three at 50.3 percent (Statistics Canada, 1993a).

2. The Collège Saint-Jean was founded in Pincher Creek in 1908.

3. The information on individual artists presented in this section, for the most part, was drawn from Morcos (1998).

1. Algeria, once highly French when a colony of France, has very few mother-tongue francophones today as an independent nation. Nonetheless, many second-language francophones can be found in the educated classes, who for all that are not inclined to urge their country to join the Francophonie.

2. These data are the product of a special analysis undertaken for the author by the Department of Advanced Education and Career Development, Government of Alberta, 1998.

References

Ager, Dennis. 1996. *Francophonie in the 1990s: Problems and opportunities.* Clevedon, Eng.: Multilingual Matters.

Allain, Greg, Isabelle McKee-Allain, and J.-Yvon Thériault. 1993. "La société acadienne: Lectures et conjonctures." In *l'Acadie des maritimes,* ed. Jean Daigle, 341-84. Moncton, NB: Chaire d'études acadiennes, Université Moncton.

Allaire, Gratien, and Laurence Fedigan. 1991. "Trois générations de Franco-Albertains: Recherche ethno-linguistique sur le changement linguistique et culturel." *Francophonies d'Amérique* 1:111-120.

Almgren, Gunnar. 1992. "Community." In *Encyclopedia of sociology,* Vol. 1. ed. Edgar F. Borgatta and Marie L. Borgatta, 244-50. New York, NY: Macmillan.

Anctil, Pierre. 1996. "La trajectoire interculturelle du Québec: La société distincte vue à travers le prisme de l'immigration." In *Langue, cultures et valeurs au Canada à l'aube du XXIe siècle,* ed. André Lapierre, Patricia Smart, and Pierre Savard, 133-54. Ottawa, ON: International Council of Canadian Studies.

Anderson, Alan B. 1985. "French settlement in Saskatchewan: Historical and demographic perspectives," Research Report No. 5. Saskatoon, SK: Research Unit for French-Canadian Studies, University of Saskatchewan.

L'Année francophone internationale 1997. Québec, QC: Université Laval.

Arcand, Tatiana. 1991. "Terre et Cythère: Perspectives universelles de légendes manitobaines." In *À la mesure du pays . . .,* ed. by Jean-Guy Quenneville, 133-46. Saint-Boniface, MB: Centre d'études franco-canadiennes de l'Ouest.

Arnopoulos, Sheila McLeod. 1982. *Hors du Québec point de salut?* Montreal, QC: Éditions Libre Expression.

Aubry, Jack. 1997. "'Francophonie' presence boosted." *Calgary Herald,* Tuesday, 18 November: A8.

Aubry, Jack. 1998. "Trudeau admitted Québec-strategy error." *Calgary Herald,* Sunday, 9 August: A16.

Aubry, Jack. 1999. "Metis leader on road to exoneration." *Calgary Herald,* Thursday, 14 January: A6.

Aunger, Edmund A. 1993. "The decline of a French-speaking enclave: A case study of social contact and language shift in Alberta." *Canadian Ethnic Studies/Études Ethniques au Canada* 25: 65-83.

Balthazar, Louis. 1993. "Faces of Québec nationalism." In *Québec: State and society,* 2nd ed, ed. by Alain-G. Gagnon, 2-17. Scarborough, ON: Nelson Canada.

Balthazar, Louis. 1997. "Québec and the ideal of federalism." *Québec society: Critical issues*, ed. Marcel Fournier, Michael Rosenberg, and Deena White, 45-60. Scarborough, ON: Prentice-Hall Canada.

Barla, Jean-Christophe. 1991. Entre le doute et l'espoir. *Le Franco* Dec. 6: 4.

Beaudoin, Réjean. 1988. "Les nouveaux francophones dans un milieu multiculturelle." In *Les outils de la francophonie*, ed. Monique Bournot-Trites, William Bruneau, and Robert Roy, 266-70. Saint-Boniface, MB: Centre d'Études franco-canadiennes de l'Ouest.

Beaulieu, Gérard. 1993. Les médias en Acadie. In *l'Acadie des maritimes*, ed. Jean Daigle, 505-542. Moncton, NB: Chaire d'études acadiennes, Université Moncton.

Behiels, Michael D. 1985. *Prelude to Quebec's Quiet Revolution*. Montreal, QC and Kingston, ON: McGill-Queen's University Press.

Bélanger, Daniel. 1992. "Les francophones de la Colombie-Britannique: Une communauté invisible et volatile." *Le Franco*, Friday, Mar. 20.

Bélanger, Michel. 1996-97. "Mon royaume pour . . . une chanson." *Infolangue* 1(winter):13-14, 17.

Bélanger, Yves. 1993. "Economic development: From family enterprise to big business." In *Québec: State and Society*, 2nd ed, ed. Alain-G. Gagnon, 390-406. Scarborough, ON: Nelson Canada.

Bélisle, Louis-A., 1969. *Petit dictionnaire canadien de la langue française*. Montréal, QC: Beauchemin.

Bellavance, Joël-Denis. 1994a. "Un nouveau visage: La francophonie ontarienne n'est plus la même." *Le Droit*, Wednesday, May 11:15

Bellavance, Joël-Denis. 1994b. "Vouée à l'adolescence: Les Franco-Ontariens laissent peu de place à leur culture." *Le Droit*, Tuesday, May 10:13.

Berger, Yves. 1997. "État d'urgence." *Infolangue* 1 (summer):7-8, 24.

Bergeron, Léandre. 1980. *Dictionnaire de la langue Québécoise*. Montréal, QC: VLB Éditeur.

Bernard, Roger. 1990. *Le choc des nombres. Dossier statistique sur la francophonie canadienne*. Ottawa, ON: Fédération des jeunes Canadiens français.

Bishop, Carol. 1988. "Les Ballets Jazz de Montréal." In *The Canadian Encyclopedia*, 2nd ed., vol. 1, 168. Edmonton, AB: Hurtig.

Bissonnette, Lise. 1997. "La francophonie canadienne et le Québec: Ruptures et retrouvailles." Talk presented at the Forum francophone de concertation 1997, 15 March, at Québec, QC.

Black, Jerome H., and David Hagen. 1993. Québec immigration politics and policy: Historical and contemporary perspectives. In *Québec: State and Society*, 2nd ed, ed. Alain-G. Gagnon, 280-303. Scarborough, ON: Nelson Canada.

Bocquel, Bernard. 1990. "Le français et les minorités francophones dans l'Ouest canadien." *Cahiers franco-canadiens de L'Ouest* 2:113-21.

Bosserman, Philip, and R. Gagan. 1972. Leisure behavior and voluntary action. In *Voluntary action research: 1972*, ed. David H. Smith. Lexington, MA: D.C. Heath.

Boudreau, Annette. 1995. "La langue française en Acadie du Nouveau-Brunswick, symbole d'appartenance, mais pas seulement . . ." In *Identité et cultures nationales: L'Amérique française en mutation*, ed. Simon Langlois, 135-52. Sainte-Foy, QC: Presses de l'Université Laval.

Boudreau, Raoul, and Marguerite Maillet. 1993. "Littérature Acadienne." *Acadie des maritimes: Etudes thématiques des débuts à nos jours*, ed. Jean Daigle, 707-50. Moncton, NB: Chaire d'études acadiennes, Université de Moncton.

Bourdieu, Pierre. 1982. *Ce que parler veut dire*. Paris, France: Fayard.

Bousquet, Robert. 1992. "Plus français qu'on l'imagine: Les francophones de l'Est ontarien." *Le Franco*, Friday, Jan. 24: 4.

Breton, Raymond. 1964. "Institutional completeness of ethnic communities and the personal relations of immigrants." *American Journal of Sociology* 70:193-205.

Breton, Raymond. 1994. "Modalités d'appartenance aux francophonies minoritaires. Essai de typologie." *Sociologie et Sociétés* 26:59-70.

Breton, Raymond, Wsevolod W. Isajiw, Warren E. Kalbach, and Jeffry G. Reitz. 1990. *Ethnic identity and equality*. Toronto, ON: University of Toronto Press.

Calgary Herald. 1998a. "Bouchard scores points on U.S. speaking tour." Saturday 23 May:A11.

Calgary Herald. 1998b. "Fifty per cent plus one not enough to separate, Quebecers say in poll." Sunday 30 August:A3.

Calgary Herald. 1998c. "Make wording of referendum clear: Parizeau." Friday 4 September:A19.

Calgary Herald. 1998d. "French PM cries `Vive le Canada.'" Thursday, 17 December: A7.

Calgary Herald. 1998e. "Banks deny siphoning cash out of Québec." Tuesday, 22 December:D3.

Calgary Herald. 1999. "Simple majority not enough to separate: Poll." Sunday, 31 October: A6.

Canadian Heritage. 1994a. Official languages New Brunswick fact sheet, Cat. No. S42-12/9-1994. Ottawa, ON: Minister of Supply and Services, Government of Canada.

Canadian Heritage. 1994b. Official languages Prince Edward Island fact sheet, Cat. No. S42-12/11-1994. Ottawa, ON: Minister of Supply and Services, Government of Canada.

Canadian Heritage. 1994c. Official languages Newfoundland fact sheet, Cat. No. S42-12/12-1994. Ottawa, ON: Minister of Supply and Services, Government of Canada.

Canadian Heritage. 1994d. Official languages Ontario fact sheet, Cat. No. S42-12/7-1994. Ottawa, ON: Minister of Supply and Services, Government of Canada.

Canadian Heritage. 1997. Action plan 1997-1999: Major objectives, Cat. No. CH10-1/98. Ottawa, ON: Minister of Public Works and Government Services Canada.

Cardinal, Linda. 1994. "Ruptures et fragmentation de l'identité francophone en milieu minoritaire: Un bilan critique." *Sociologie et Sociétés* 26:71-86.

Cardinal, Linda. 1997. *L'engagement de la pensée: Écrire en milieu minoritaire francophone au Canada.* Hearst, ON: Le Nordir.

Cardinal, Linda, Jean Lapointe, and J.-Yvon Thériault. 1988. *La minorité francophone de Welland et ses rapports avec les institutions.* Ottawa, ON: Rapport d'étude présenté au bureau du Commissaire aux langues officielles, Université d'Ottawa, Département de sociologie.

Cardinal, Linda, Jean Lapointe, and J.-Yvon Thériault. 1994. *État de la recherche sur les communautés francophones hors Québec 1980-1990.* Ottawa, ON: Centre de recherche en civilisation canadienne-française de l'Université d'Ottawa.

Castonguay, Charles. 1998. "Tendances et incidences de l'assimilation linguistique au Canada." *Études Canadiennes* 45: 65-82.

Cazabon, Benoît. 1996. "La pédagogie du français langue maternelle en Ontario: Moyen d'intervention sur la langue en milieu minoritaire." In *De la polyphonie à la symphonie: Méthodes, théories et faits de la recherche pluridisciplinaire sur le français au Canada*, ed. Jürgen Erfurt, 295-314. Leipzig, Germany: Leipziger Universitätsverlag.

Cerulo, Karen A. 1997. "Identity construction: New issues, new directions." In *Annual Review of Sociology*, vol. 23, ed. John Hagen and Karen S. Cook, 385-408. Palo Alta, CA: Annual Reviews Inc.

Chabot, Denis-Martin. 1992. "La langue d'instruction n'est pas celle des corridors." *Le Franco* May 1:4.

Le Chaînon. 1993. "Tous les marriages mixtes ne produisent pas les mêmes résultats." April 7.

Charbonneau, Paul M. 1992. *Contre vents et marées: L'histoire des francophones de Terre-Neuve et du Labrador.* Moncton, NB: Éditions d'Acadie.

Chiasson, Anselm Père. 1988. "Acadia." In *The Canadian Encyclopedia*, 2nd ed., vol. 1, 5-10. Edmonton, AB: Hurtig.

Churchill, Stacy. 1998. *Official Languages in Canada: Changing the Language Landscape.* Ottawa, ON: Government of Canada, Canadian Heritage.

Churchill, Stacy and Isabel Kaprielian-Churchill. 1991. *The Future of francophone and Acadian communities in a pluralistic society: Facing pluralism.* Ottawa, ON: Fédération des Communautés francophones et acadiennes du Canada.

Clarke, P.D. 1998. "Pêche et identité en Acadie: Nouveaux regards sur la culture et la ruralité en milieu maritime." *Recherches Sociographiques*, 39:59-102.

Cloutier, Anne. 1998. "Quand économie rime avec survie." *Le Franco*, Aug. 14 to 20: 2.

Cohen, Anthony P. 1985. *The symbolic construction of community*. London, Eng.: Tavistock.

Commissioner of Official Languages. 1989. *Annual Report 1989*. Ottawa, ON: Ministry of Supply and Services, Government of Canada.

Commissioner of Official Languages. 1994. *Annual report 1994*. Ottawa, ON: Ministry of Supply and Services, Government of Canada.

Conseil de la vie française en Amérique. 1998a. *Répertoire des Membres du Conseil de la Vie Française en Amérique*, 32nd ed. Québec, QC.

Conseil de la vie française en Amérique. 1998b. *Franco-Contact*, September.

Cormier, Yves. 1994. *L'Acadie d'aujourd'hui: Guide des provinces maritimes francophones*. Moncton, NB: Éditions d'Acadie.

Courtier, Bertin. 1992. "Astérix et les Gaulois." *Le Franco*, Friday, Jan. 10:4.

Cox, Terry. 1991. "Nos étudiants fransaskois et la `parlure fransaskoise' de Laurier Gareau." In *À la mesure du pays . . .*, ed. Jean-Guy Quenneville, 99-112. Saint-Boniface, MB: Centre d'études franco-canadiennes de l'Ouest.

Daigle, Jean. 1993. "L'Acadie de 1604 à 1763, synthèse historique." In *Acadie des Maritimes*, ed. Jean Daigle, 1-44. Moncton, NB: Université de Moncton, Chaire d'études acadiennes.

Dallaire, Christine, and David Whitson. 1998. "Growing up in *l'archipel*: Youth identities in the context of the Alberta Francophone Games." In *Canadian identity: Region/country/nation*, ed. Will Straw and J.-Yvon Thériault, 91-110. Montréal, QC: Association for Canadian Studies.

De Finney, James. 1996. "Mythes et symboles en Acadie." *Le congrès mondial acadien: L'Acadie en 2004 (Acts des conférences et des tables rondes)*, 227-9. Moncton, NB: Éditions d'Acadie.

Denis, Claude. 1996. "La patrie et son nom. Essai sur ce que veut le `Canada français.'" *Francophonies D'Amérique* 6:185-98.

Denis, Wilfred B. 1993. "La complétude institutionnelle et la vitalité des communautés fransaskoises en 1992." *Cahiers franco-canadiens de l'Ouest* 5:253-284.

Dion, Léon. 1987. *Québec 1945-2000: À la recherche du Québec*, vol.1. Québec, QC: Presses de l'Université Laval.

Dion, Léon. 1995. "La société québécoise." In *Horizon de la culture: Hommage à Fernand Dumont*, ed. Simon Langlois and Yves Martin. Sainte-Foy, QC: Presses de l'Université Laval.

Ducharme, Jean-Charles. 1996. *Status report: Minority-language educational rights*, Cat. No. CH14-5/1996. Ottawa, ON: Canadian Heritage, Government of Canada.

Dupont, Jean-Claude. 1994. *Légendes de l'Amérique française*, 9th ed. Sainte-Foy, QC: Éditions Dupont.

Durkheim, Emile. 1951. *Suicide*. New York, ON: Free Press.

The Economist. 1999. "The world language." 31 December.

Education Postsecondaire: Perspectives Francophones. 1998. Jan. 2:22-23.

Farmer, Diane. 1996. *Artisans de la modernité: Les centres culturels en Ontario français.* Ottawa, ON: Presses de l'Université d'Ottawa.

Ferguson, C. 1959. "Diglossia." *Word* 10:325-340.

Fischer, Lucy R., and Kay B. Schafer. 1993. *Older volunteers: A guide to research and practice.* Newbury Park, CA: Sage.

Fournier, Marcel, and M. Michael Rosenberg. 1997. School and the state in Quebec. In *Québec society: Critical issues,* ed. Marcel Fournier, Michael Rosenberg, and Deena White, 123-141. Scarborough, ON: Prentice-Hall Canada.

Franc-Contact. 1998. "Revue de presse," September: 5.

Gagnon, François-Marc. 1988. "Art." *The Canadian Encyclopedia,* 2nd ed., vol. 1, 121-23. Edmonton, AB: Hurtig.

Gérin-Lajoie, Diane. 1996. "L'école minoritaire de langue française et son rôle dans la communauté." *Alberta Journal of Educational Research* 42:267-279.

Gervais, Gaétan, 1993. "L'Ontario Français, 1821-1910." In *Les Franco-Ontariens,* ed. Cornelius J. Jaenen, 49-126. Ottawa, ON: Presses de l'Université d'Ottawa.

Gilbert, Anne. 1998. "A propos du concept d'Amérique française." *Recherches Sociographiques,* 34:103-120.

Gilbert, Anne. 1999. "Vers l'université de la francophonie." In *L'université et la francophonie,* ed. Marcel Martel, 167-178. Ottawa, ON: Centre de recherche en civilisation canadienne-française de l'Université d' Ottawa.

Giles, Howard, Richard Y. Bourhis, and Donald M. Taylor. 1977. Towards a theory of language in ethnic group relations. In *Language, ethnicity, and intergroup relations,* ed. Howard Giles, 307-348. London: Academic Press.

Goldenberg, Sheldon, and Valerie A. Haines. 1992. "Social networks and institutional completeness: From territory to ties." *Canadian Journal of Sociology* 17:301-12.

Gouvernment du Québec. 1995. *Politique du Québec à l'égard des communautés francophones et acadiennes du Canada.* Québec, QC.

Gratton, Denis. 1994. "Du renfort . . ." *Le Droit,* Wednesday, May 11:15.

Guindon, Hubert. 1988. *Québec society: Tradition, modernity, and nationhood.* Toronto, ON: University of Toronto Press.

Guindon, René, and Pierre Poulin. 1996. *Francophones in Canada: A community of interests,* Cat. No. CH3-2/1-1996. Ottawa, ON: Canadian Heritage, Government of Canada.

Hallion, Sandrine. 1997. "Le bilinguisme complexe des Franco-Manitobains." In *Canada et bilinguisme,* ed. Marta Dvorak, 129-38. Rennes, France: Presses universitaires de Rennes.

Harrison, Brian R. 1996. *Les jeunes et les minorités de langue officielle,* Cat. No. 91-545-XFP. Ottawa, ON: Statistics Canada, Government of Canada.

Harvey, Fernand. 1993. "Perceptions québécoises de la francophonie." In *La langue: Vecteur d'organisation internationale*, ed. Françoise Massart-Piérard, 47-56. Louvain-la-Neuve, Belgium: Academia-Erasme.

Hébert, Yvonne, and Robert A. Stebbins. 1993. "La francophonie de Calgary: Une étude démolinguistique." In *Une langue qui pense: La recherche en milieu minoritaire francophone au Canada*, ed. Linda Cardinal, 144-82. Ottawa, ON: Presses de l'Université d'Ottawa.

Heller, Monica. 1994. "La sociolinguistique et l'éducation franco-ontarienne." *Recherches Sociographiques*, 26:155-168.

Heller, Monica. 1996. "Langue et identité: L'analyse anthropologique du français canadien." In *De la polyphonie à la symphonie: Méthodes, théories et faits de la recherche pluridisciplinaire sur le français au Canada*, ed. Jürgen Erfurt, 19-36. Leipzig, Germany: Leipziger Universitätsverlag.

Heller, Monica, and Laurette Lévy. 1992. "Mixed marriages: Life on the linguistic frontier." *Multilingua* 11:11-43.

Heller, Monica, and Laurette Lévy. 1993. "Des femmes franco-ontariennes et situation de mariage mixte: Vivre sur une frontière linguistique." In *Un langue qui pense: La recherche en milieux minoritaire francophone au Canada*, ed. Linda Cardinal, 11-27. Ottawa, ON: Presses de l'Université d'Ottawa.

Hillary, George A. Jr. 1955. Definitions of community: Areas of agreement. *Rural Sociology* 20: 111-123.

Infoaction 1997. "An historic day for Newfoundland," July.

Jackson, John D. 1994. *Community and conflict: A study of French-English relations in Ontario*, rev. ed. Toronto, ON: Canadian Scholars Press.

Jaenen, Cornelius J. 1993. "L'ancien régime au pays d'en haut, 1611-1821." In *Les Franco-Ontariens*, ed. Cornelius J. Jaenen, 9-48. Ottawa, ON: Presses de l'Université d'Ottawa.

Joy, Richard J. 1992. *Canada's official languages: The progess of bilingualism.* Toronto, ON: University of Toronto Press.

Juteau, Danielle. 1980. "Français d'Amérique, Canadiens, Canadiens-Français, Franco-Ontariens, Ontarois: Que sommes-nous?" *Pluriel*, 24:21-42.

Kaltz, Barbara. 1997. "La fransaskoisie: Un état des lieux de la francophonie en Saskatchewan." In *Canada et bilinguisme*, ed. Marta Dvorak, 91-100. Rennes, France: Presses universitaires de Rennes.

Kermoal, Nathalie. 1998. "De *la Survivance* au *Franco*." *Le Franco* Nov. 20-28:8-9.

Lachappelle, Guy, Gérald Bernier, Daniel Salée, and Luc Bernier. 1993. *The Québec democracy: Structures, processes & policies.* Toronto, ON: McGraw-Hill Ryerson.

Laforest, Jacinthe. 1991. "Les Acadiens de l'Ile veulent garder maman et papa." *Le Franco*, Friday, Dec. 13:4.

Lambert, Wallace E. 1975. "Culture and language as factors in learning and education." In *Education of immigrant students*, ed. Aaron Wolfgang. Toronto, ON: Ontario Institute for Studies in Education.

Lamy, Paul. 1978. "Bilingualism and identity." In *Shaping identity in Canadian society*, ed. Jack Haas and William Shaffir, 133-40. Scarborough, ON: Prentice-Hall of Canada.

Landry, Rodrigue. 1997. "Education bilingue en situation minoritaire: Pour une identité culturelle." In *Canada et bilinguisme*, ed. Marta Dvorak, 151-66. Rennes, France: Presses universitaires de Rennes.

Landry, Rodrigue, and Richard Y. Bourhis. 1997. "Linguistic landscape and ethnolinguistic vitality: An empirical study." *Journal of Language and Social Psychology* 16:23-49.

Langlois, Simon. 1998. "Tendances de la société québécoise." In Québec 1998, ed. Roch Côté, 3-48. Montréal, QC: Fides/Le Devoir.

Laponce, Jean A. 1996. "Minority languages in Canada: Their fate and survival strategies." In *Language, culture, and values in Canada at the dawn of the 21st century*, ed. André Lapierre, Patricia Smart, and Pierre Savard, 75-88. Ottawa, ON: Carleton University Press and International Council for Canadian Studies.

Latouche, Daniel. 1988. "Québec." In *The Canadian Encyclopedia*, 2nd ed., vol. 3, 1793-1802. Edmonton, AB: Hurtig.

Latouche, Daniel. 1993. "'Québec, see under Canada': Québec nationalism in the new global age." In *Québec: State and society*, 2nd ed., ed. Alain-G. Gagnon, 40-63. Scarborough, ON: Nelson Canada.

Lavallée, Alain and Carole Lafond. 1998. "Les festivals au Québec: Entre économie et identié. Le cas d'un festival mondial de folklore." *Loisir et Société/Society and Leisure* 21:213-44.

Lavoie, Thomas. 1994. "Les régions linguistique au Québec et au Canada français." In *La région culturelle: Problématique interdisciplinaire*, ed. Fernand Harvey, 123-38. Québec, QC: Institut québécois de recherche sur la culture.

Le Franco. 1995. "1975-1995: 20 ans de cinéma en Ontario français." Sept. 16-22.

Le Franco. 1996. "Un réseau national d'éducation universitaire en français," Dec. 20-26.

Le Franco. 1997a. "Les Franco-Ontariens obtiennent la gestion scolaire," Jan. 17-23:2.

Le Franco. 1997b. "On manque d'emplois intéressants," Feb. 21-27.

Le Franco. 1997c. "Après la gestion scolaire . . . l'équivalence," Apr. 4-10:2.

Le Franco. 1999. "Le Québec intensifie son appui aux communautés francophones et acadiennes du Canada," Apr. 2-8: 2.

Lépine, Sylvie. 1992. "Un coup de jeunesse pour la plus ancienne université francophone." *Le Franco*, Friday, March 27:4.

Louder, Dean R. 1996. "Francophones aux Etats-Unis, 1990." In *L'ouest français et la francophonie nord-américaine*, ed. Georges Cesbron, 413-14. Angers, France: Presses de l'Université d'Angers.

Louder, Dean R., and Louis Dupont. 1997. "Nouvelle sphère de sens et champ identitaire francophone et acadien." In *La francophonie sur les marges*, ed.

Carol J. Harvey and Alan MacDonell, 53-66. Saint-Boniface, MB: CEFCO and Presses Universitaires de Saint-Boniface.

Louder, Dean R., Cécyle Trépanier, and Eric Waddell. 1994. "La francophonie nord-américaine. Mise en place et processus de diffusion géohistorique." In *Langue, espace, société: Les variétés du français en Amérique du Nord*, ed. Claude Poirier, 185-202. Sainte-Foy, QC: Presses de l'Université Laval.

Louder, Dean R., and Eric Waddell, eds. 1983. *Du Continent Perdu à l'Archipel Retrouvé: Le Québec et l'Amérique Française.* Sainte-Foy, QC: Presses de l'Université Laval.

Lusignan, Yves. 1992. "La mal-aimée des universités bilingues veut protéger ses acquis." *Le Franco* Apr. 10.

Lusignan, Yves. 1998a. "Le rêve fou des universités francophones." *Education Post-secondaire: Perspectives francophones* 2 (Jan.):22-23.

Lusignan, Yves. 1998b. "La jeunesse francophone mondiale brasse des affaires." *Le Franco* Oct. 2-8.

Lusignan, Yves. 1998c. "TVA sera accessible partout au pays." *Le Franco* Nov. 6-12:2.

Lusignan, Yves. 1998d. "Place à la radio éducative." *Le Franco* Sept. 4-10:11.

MacEwan, Grant. 1984. *French in the West/Les franco-canadians dans l'ouest.* Saint-Boniface, MB: Éditions des Plaines.

Mackey, William F. 1997. "Les dimensions du bilinguisme canadien." In *Canada et bilinguisme*, ed. Marta Dvorak, 19-32. Rennes, France: Presses Universitaires de Rennes.

Magord, André. 1993. "Vie et survie d'une minorité francophone hors Québec: Les Franco-Terre-Neuviens." *Études Canadiennes/Canadian Studies*, 34:67-78.

Magord, André. 1995. *Une minorité francophone hors Québec: Les Franco-Terreneuviens.* Tübingen, Germany: Max Niemeyer.

Magord, André. 1996. "Les 'vieux français' du nouveau monde. Présence française en identité culturelle chez les francophones de Terre-Neuve." In *L'ouest français et la francophonie nord-américaine*, ed. Georges Cesbron, 143-48. Angers, France: Presses de l'Université d'Angers.

Magord, André. 1998. "L'avenir de la langue française à Terre-Neuve." *Études Canadiennes* 45: 139-152.

Marchand, Anne-Sophie. 1998. "L'identitié franco-manitobaine: De l'indentité métisse au métissage des identités." In *Identité canadienne: Région/pays/nation*, ed. Will Straw and J.-Yvon Thériault, 57-72. Montréal, QC: Association for Canadian Studies.

Marshall, Andy. 1998. "Student debt loads rising across country." *Calgary Herald*, Wednesday 9 December:B3.

Marshall, Elizabeth. 1993. "Saint Isidore, Alberta: The little village that could." *Language and Society* 43 (Summer):12-13.

Martel, Marcel. 1997. *Le deuil d'un pays imaginé: Rêves, luttes et déroute du canada français.* Ottawa, ON: Presses de l'Université d'Ottawa.

Martel, Pierre, and Hélène Cajolet-Laganière. 1995. "Oui . . . au français québé-cois standard." *Interface* 16 (5):14-25.

Massart-Piérard, Françoise. 1993. "La langue, vecteur d'organisation interna-tionale: Perceptions et enjeux de la Francophonie." In *La langue: Vecteur d'organisation internationale,* ed. Françoise Massart-Piérard, 9-10. Louvain-la-Neuve, Belgium: Academia-Erasme.

Maxwell, Thomas. 1977. *The invisible French.* Waterloo, ON.: Wilfred Laurier University Press.

McCall, George J., and J.L. Simmons. 1978. *Identities and interactions: An exami-nation of human associations in everyday life.* New York, NY: Free Press.

Meney, Florence. 1992. "Des programmes en français, une université bilingue." *Le Franco,* Apr. 17.

Moise, Claudine. 1998. "L'histoire franco-canadienne ou les discours de la légitimité." *Études Canadiennes/CanadianStudies* 44:89-114.

Morcos, Gamila. 1998. *Dictionnaire des artistes et des auteurs francophones ed l'ouest canadien.* Edmonton, AB and Québec, QC: Faculté Saint-Jean and Presses de l'Université Laval.

O'Keefe, Michael. 1998. *Francophone Minorities: Assimilation and Community Vitality.* Ottawa, ON: Government of Canada, Canadian Heritage.

O'Neil, Peter. 1997. "Group seeking new blueprint for Canada-Québec partner-ship." *Calgary Herald,* Friday 14 March:A17.

Orientation Committee. 1992. *Project 2000: For a francophone space, final report.* Ottawa, ON: Fédération des communautés francophones et acadiennes du Canada.

Ouellet, Fernand. 1993. "L'évolution de la présence francophone en Ontario: Une perspective économique et sociale." In *Les Franco-Ontariens,* ed. Cornelius J. Jaenen, 127-200. Ottawa, ON: Presses de l'Université d'Ottawa.

Panet-Raymond, Jean. 1998. "Marrying social and economic development in Quebec." *Perception* 22 (June): 3

Paquette, Roméo. 1997. "La Fragilité des Minorités Linguistiques." *Franc-Contact (Bulletin d'information et de liaison de la vie française en Amérique)* Apr. 5:3 and 8.

Paquette, Roméo. 1999. "La nouvelle donne de la francophonie nord-améri-caine." *Franc-Contact (Bulletin d'information du Conseil de la vie française en Amérique)* 7 summer: 8.

Paulette, Claude. 1997. *Le fleurdelisé.* Sainte-Foy, QC: Publications du Québec.

Pendakur, Krishna, and Ravi Pendakur. 1998. "Speak and ye shall receive: Language knowledge as human capital." In *Economic approaches to language and bilingualism,* Cat. No. CH3-2-7/1998E, ed. Albert Breton, 89-120. Ottawa, ON: Canadian Heritage, Government of Canada.

Péronnet, Louise. 1993. "La situation du français en Acadie; L'éclairage de la lin-guistique." In *L'Acadie des Maritimes,* ed. Jean Daigle, 467-504. Moncton, NB: Chaire d'études acadiennes, Université de Moncton.

Péronnet, Louise. 1996. "Qu'est-ce qui distingue le parler français acadien des autres parlers français (de France, du Québec)?" *Le congrès mondial acadien: L'Acadie en 2004 (Actes des conférences et des tables rondes)*, 197-205. Moncton, NB: Éditions d'Acadie.

Pinard, Maurice, Robert Bernier, and Vincent Lemieux. 1997. *Un Combat Inachevé*. Sainte-Foy, QC: Presses de l'Université du Québec.

Pitre, Martin. 1992. "Une innovation acadienne dans la quincaillerie des outils de développement." *Le Devoir*, Saturday, June 13, *Cahier spécial/ "Francophonie canadienne."*

Pitt, Janet E.M. 1988. "Port-au-Port Peninsula." In *The Canadian Encyclopedia*, 2nd ed., Vol. 3, 1724. Edmonton, AB: Hurtig.

Plouffe, Hélène. 1988. "Butler, Édith." In *The Canadian Encyclopedia*, 2nd ed., Vol. 1, 307. Edmonton, AB: Hurtig.

Poirier, Marc. 1992. "La situation économique est un obstacle à l'accessibilité." *Le Franco*, Friday, April 3:4

Pronovost, Gilles. 1997. *Loisir et société: Traité de sociologie empirique*, 2nd ed. Sainte-Foy, QC: Presses de l'Université du Québec.

Putnam, Robert D. 1995. "Bowling alone: America's declining social capital." *Journal of Democracy* 6:65-78.

Rayside, David M. 1991. *A small town in modern times: Alexandria, Ontario*. Montréal, QC, and Kingston, ON: McGill-Queen's University Press.

Rifkin, Jeremy. 1995. *The End of Work*. New York, NY: G.P. Putnam's Sons.

Roy, Muriel K. 1993. "Démographie et démolinguistique en Acadie, 1871-1991." In *L'Acadie des maritimes: Études thématiques des débuts à nos jours*, ed. Jean Daigle, 141-206. Moncton, NB: Chaire d'études acadiennes, Université de Moncton.

Saint-Pierre, Annette. 1994. *Le Manitoba: Au coeur de l'Amérique*. Saint-Boniface, MB: Éditions des Plaines.

Savas, Daniel. 1990. "La francophonie en ville: Vivre comme francophone en milieu urbain." *Rapport final présenté à la Fédération des francophones hors Québec.*

Savas, Daniel. 1991. "Institutions francophones et vitalité communautaire: Motivations symboliques et fonctionnelles du choix de réseau institutionnel." In *À la mesure du pays. . .* ed. Jean-Guy Quenneville, 67-86. Saint-Boniface, MB: Centre d'Études franco-canadiennes de l'Ouest.

Resnick, Philip. 1991. *Toward a Canada-Québec union*. Montréal, QC, and Kingston, ON: McGill-Queen's University Press.

Roby, Yves. 1988. Alphonse Desjardins. In *The canadian encyclopedia*, 2nd ed., vol. 1, 588. Edmonton, AB: Hurtig.

Smith, David H. 1997. "The rest of the nonprofit sector: Grassroots associations as the dark matter ignored in prevailing `flat earth' maps of the sector." *Nonprofit and Voluntary Sector Quarterly* 26:114-31.

Smith, Donald. 1990. "Pour l'établissement d'une norme québécoise dans l'enseignement du français." In *Langue et identité: Les français et les francophones d'Amérique du Nord*, ed. Noël Corbett, 47-52. Sainte-Foy, QC: Presses de l'Université Laval.

Société Radio-Canada. 1992. *Les beaux dimanches*, Sunday, Dec. 29.

Statistics Canada. 1992. *Mother tongue: The nation*, Cat. No. 93-313. Ottawa, ON: Supply and Services Canada, Government of Canada.

Statistics Canada. 1993a. *Profile of Census Tracts in Winnipeg - Part A*, Cat. No. 95-360. Ottawa, ON: Minister of Science, Industry, and Technology, Government of Canada.

Statistics Canada. 1993b. *Profile of Census Tracts in Edmonton - Part A*, Cat. No. 95-385. Ottawa, ON: Minister of Science, Industry, and Technology, Government of Canada.

Statistics Canada. 1998a. *Nation Series Edition 3*, Cat. No. 93F0020XCB96003. Ottawa, ON: Minister of Industry, Government of Canada.

Statistics Canada. 1998b. *Statistical Profile of Canadian Communities*, HTTP://www.Statcan.ca. Ottawa, ON: Minister of Industry, Government of Canada.

Stebbins, Robert A. 1990. *The laugh-makers: Stand-up comedy as art, business, and life-style*. Montréal, QC, and Kingston, ON: McGill-Queen's University Press.

Stebbins, Robert A. 1992. *Amateurs, professionals, and serious leisure*. Montréal, QC, and Kingston, ON: McGill-Queen's University Press.

Stebbins, Robert A. 1994. *The Franco-Calgarians: French language, leisure, and linguistic life-style in an anglophone city*. Toronto, ON: University of Toronto Press.

Stebbins, Robert A. 1997. "La sociologie des francophones hors Québec: De nouveau concepts pour l'analyse du milieu urbain." *La francophonie sur les marges*, ed. Carol J. Harvey and Alan MacDonell, 67-77. Winnipeg, MB: Presses universitaires de Saint-Boniface.

Stebbins, Robert A. 1998a. *After work: The search for an optimal leisure lifestyle*. Calgary, AB: Detselig.

Stebbins, Robert A. 1998b. *The urban francophone volunteer: Searching for personal meaning and community growth in a linguistic minority*, Vol. 3, No. 2 (New Scholars-New Visions in Canadian Studies quarterly monographs series). Seattle, WA: University of Washington, Canadian Studies Centre.

Stebbins, Robert A. 1999. *Serious leisure: New directions in theory and research*. Manuscript submitted for publication

Tellier, Sylvain. 1993. "British Columbia's francophones." *Language and Society* 44 (Fall):6-8.

Tétu de Labsade, Françoise. 1990. *Le Québec: Un Pays, Une Culture*. Montréal, QC: Boréal/Seuil.

Thériault, J.-Yvon. 1994. "Entre la nation et l'ethnie: Sociologie, société et communautés minoritaires francophones." *Sociologie et sociétés* 26:15-32.

Thériault, Léon. 1993a. "L'Acadie de 1763 à 1990, synthèse historique." In *Acadie des Maritimes*, ed. Jean Daigle, 45-92. Moncton, NB: Université de Moncton, Chaire d'études acadiennes.

———. 1993b. "L'acadianisation des structures ecclésiastiques aux Maritimes, 1758-1953." In *Acadie des Maritimes*, ed. Jean Daigle, 431-66. Moncton, NB: Université de Moncton, Chaire d'études acadiennes.

Thérien, Jean-Philippe, Louis Bélanger, and Guy Gosselin. 1993. "Québec: An expanding foreign policy." In *Québec: State and society*, 2nd ed., ed. Alain-G. Gagnon, 259-78. Scarborough, ON: Nelson Canada.

Therrien, Denyse. 1997. "État d'urgence: Entretien avec Yves Berger." *Infolangue* 1(summer):7-8, 24.

Trépanier, Cécyle. 1996. "Le mythe de `l'Acadie des Maritimes.'" *Géographie et Cultures* 17:55-74.

Turcotte, Pierre. 1993. "Mixed language couples and their children." *Canadian Social Trends*, catalogue No. 11-008E. 29 (Summer):15-17.

Unruh, David R. 1979. "Characteristics and types of participation in social worlds." *Symbolic Interaction* 2:115-30.

Unruh, David R. 1980. "The nature of social worlds." *Pacific Sociological Review* 23:271-96.

Véronneau, Pierre. 1988. "Film in Québec." In *The Canadian Encylopedia*, 2nd ed., vol. 2, 767-69. Edmonton, AB: Hurtig.

Viaud, Pierre. 1993. "La francophonie en Afrique." In *La langue: Vecteur d'organisation internationale*, ed. Françoise Massart-Piérard, 57-67. Louvain-la-Neuve, Belgium: Academia-Erasme.

Villeneuve, Paul-Y. 1983. "Maillardville: À l'ouest rien de nouveau." In *Du continent perdu à l'archipel retrouvé: Le Québec et L'Amérique française*, ed. Dean R. Louder and Eric Waddell, 129-35. Québec, QC: Presses de l'Université Laval.

Waddell, Eric. 1994. "Un continent-Québec et une poussière d'îles. Asymétrie et éclatement au sein de la francophonie nord-Américaine." In *Langue, espace, société: Les variétés du français du Nord*, ed. Claude Poirier, 203-26. Québec, QC: Presses de l'Université Laval.

Whitaker, Reginald. 1984. "The Québec cauldron." In *Québec: State and society*, 2nd ed., ed. Alain-G. Gagnon, 18-39. Scarborough, ON: Nelson Canada.

White, Deena. 1997. Quebec state and society. In *Québec society: Critical issues*, ed. Marcel Fournier, Michael Rosenberg, and Deena White, 17-44. Scarborough, ON: Prentice-Hall Canada.

Index

Acadia 25, 95-129
    community structure of 99-108
    culture in 109-112
    economic basis of 104
    education in 105-107, 123-124, 126-127
    festivals in 111
    flag of 46
    folklore of 110-111
    French in 108-109, 192
    history of 42-46
    issues in 113-128
    music of 110
    national holiday of 46
    origin of name of 43
    periodicals (newspapers, magazines, etc.) in 111
    provinces in 43, 95
    radio in 111
    slogan of 46
    survival and development of 211-222
    television in 111-112
    writers in 109-110
Acadian Peninsula 95-96
Acadians 33, 44-46
    and family 100, 117-119
    association of 46
    geographic distribution of 95-99
Ager, Dennis, 198, 199, 200, 201, 203, 204
Alberta (francophone part) 168-171, 175, 177, 180, 182, 185, 186, 192, 206-207, 211
    see also Western provinces
Alexandria, Ontario 143-144

Allain, Greg 116
Allaire, Gratien 182
allophones 91
    as anti-separatist 22, 83-84
    defined 22
Almgren, Gunnar 26
Anctil, Pierre 83
Anderson, Alan B. 53
anglophones xiii-xiv,
    as charter group 23-24
    defined 20-21
    in Québec 39
    proportion of in Canada 29
Arcand, Tatiana 181-182
archipelago (*l'archipel*) model 55, 120, 145, 149, 163, 220
architecture 76-77, 181
Arnopoulos, Sheila M. 61, 163
art. *See* painting and painters
arts. *See* culture; individual arts
assimilation 28, 48, 51, 80, 124-125, 153, 157, 158, 160-163, 177, 182, 185, 187, 191-193, 218, 219
    see also bilingualism, additive; bilingualism, subtractive; exogamy
Association de la presse francophone (APF) 28
associations. *See* organizational life
Aubry, Jack 87, 224
Aunger, Edmund A. 175

Balthazar, Louis 85, 209
Barla, Jean-Christophe 47
Beaudoin, Louise, 216

Beaudoin, Réjean 30, 177
Beaulieu, Gérard 45
Behiels, Michael D. 40
Bélanger, Daniel 172, 223
Bélanger, Louis 200
Bélanger, Michel 73
Bélanger, Yves 41
Bélisle, Louis-A. 70
Bellavance, Joël-Denis 207
Berger,Yves 81
Bergeron, Léandre 70
Bernard, Roger 156
Bernier, Gérald 61, 85, 88, 89
Bernier, Luc 61, 85, 88, 89
Bernier, Robert 22
bilingualism (bilingual) 91
    additive 81, 89, 146, 185
    advantages of 205, 213-214
    definition of 21, 80
    in a parity community 143-144
    in cities 176
    in education 146, 159-160
    in majority communities 174
    in universities 107, 123, 157-159
    in Western provinces 179-180, 187
    normalitude and 179, 185
    official 140, 212, 213, 214
    rates of in Acadia and Canada 125, 218
    scattered 114-115, 152
    subtractive 80-81, 124
    see also exogamy; assimilation
bilinguals 33
    in Ontario 154
    in Québec 22, 80, 89
    interprovincial migration of 33
    proportion in Canada 21-22
Bissonnette, Lise 216-217

Black, Jerome H. 83
Bloc Québécois 85
Bocquel, Bernard 34, 179, 185
Bosserman, Phillip 176
Bouchard, Lucien 86, 225
Boudreau, Annette 127
Bourassa, Robert 85
Bourdieu, Pierre 203
Bourhis, Richard Y. 113, 160
Bousquet, Robert 140
Brassard, Jacques 216
Breton, Raymond 26
British Columbia (francophone part) 25, 54, 171-172, 177, 180, 182, 192, 206
    see also Western provinces
British North America Act 39
Bureau of Québec 223

caisse populaire (credit union) 64, 104, 144, 174
    as indicator of ethnolinguistic vitality 115, 183
Cajolet-Laganière, Hélène 71
Calgary 24, 27, 53-54, 87, 117-119, 120-122, 171, 173, 179, 180, 185-186, 189-190, 191, 193, 194, 206-207, 208, 218-220
Calgary Declaration 87
canadiens 38, 153
Cardinal, Linda 138, 153, 154, 211, 213, 221
Cartier, Jacques 37, 43
Castonguay, Charles 156
Catholic Church 38, 39-41, 223
    anglophone establishment in Québec and 40
    as indicator of ethnolinguistic vitality 115, 184
    colonization programs of 49-50, 53
    education and 45, 64-65, 106, 145, 178-179

in Acadia 45, 46, 100
in Newfoundland 133
in Ontario 48, 51, 140, 153
in the western provinces 52-
53, 178-179
Mouvement Desjardins and
64
Catholicism 25, 39
institutional incompleteness
and 89, 99
Cazabon, Benoît 146
CEGEPs 66-67
center-periphery model 54-55,
149, 163, 220
Cerulo, Karen A. 34, 199
Chabot, Denis-Martin 188
de Champlain, Samuel 37, 43
Charbonneau, Paul M. 132-133,
134, 135, 136-137
Charlottetown Accord 85, 225
charter groups 23-24, 42-43, 197
Charter of Rights and Freedoms
30-31, 105-106, 177
Charter of the French Language
(Bill 101) 70
Chiasson, Anselm Père 45
Churchill, Stacey 21, 29, 117, 213-
214, 218
Clarke, P.D. 116
Cloutier, Anne 213
clubs. See organizational life
Cohen, Anthony P. 26-27
Collège d'enseignement général et
professionnel (CEGEP) 66-67
Collège Saint-Joseph 45, 46
Collège universitaire de Saint-
Boniface 178, 187, 188
community and cultural centres
103, 134, 143, 146-147, 176,
181
concertation 62-63, 224
between Québec and minori-

ty francophone communities
216
Confederation 39
Conseil de la vie Française en
Amérique (CVFA) 28
Constitution
Act (of 1982) 42, 84
Charter of Rights and
Freedoms and 30-31
conferences on 42, 85, 87
Cormier, Yves 111
Cox, Terry 190
Cross, James 61-62
cultural centres. See community
and cultural centres
Culture
Francophonie and 201-102
in Acadia 104, 109-112
in Newfoundland 136-137
in Ontario 146-149, 162
in Québec 71-77
in Western provinces 180-182

Daigle, Jean 43
Dallaire, Christine 186
dance 73, 136, 180
Desjardins, Alphonse 64
Denis, Claude 33
Denis, Wilfred B. 174
Dion, Léon 71, 79, 90, 212, 221
distinct/unique society 77, 87
diglossia 146
Ducharme, Jean-Charles 144, 178
Dupont, Jean-Claude 110, 148
Dupont, Louis 25, 197, 199, 215
Durkheim, Emile 79

economic basis of minority societies. See minority societies
and communities, economic
basis of
économie sociale (nonprofit sector
in Québec) 63-64

Edmonton 25, 27, 53, 120-122, 170, 173, 180, 184-185, 188, 191, 206-207, 208, 218-220

education, francophone
    bilingual education and 146, 159-160
    day care (*les garderies*) and 225
    definition of 105
    ethnolinguistic vitality and 161
    in Acadia 105-107, 123-124, 126-127
    in Newfoundland 135
    in Ontario 144-145, 157-159, 178
    in Québec 64-67
    in Western provinces 177-179, 193
    institutional incompleteness and 89, 99, 157, 193
    international 203-204
    issues in 105, 135, 144-145, 159-160, 177, 178
    learning English and 227
    rights of official language minorities and 31, 105-106, 177
    survival and development of parity and minority communities and 217

English (language)
    as official 30-31, 105-106

Évangéline (district in P.E.I.) 98-99, 115, 211

Evangeline (poem) 45, 110, 127

exogamy (linguistic) 156-157
    defined 100
    in Acadia 100, 117-119
    in Newfoundland 156
    in Ontario156, 187
    in Western Canada 117-119, 186-187
    single-parent families and 226
    types of 117, 118, 156

Faculté Saint-Jean 178-179, 187, 188, 227

Falardeau, Jean-Charles 39-40

family
    in Newfoundand 134-135
    in Ontario 140-141
    in Western provinces, 189-190
    institutional incompleteness and 89, 99, 134-135
    See also assimilation; exogamy

Farmer, Diane 143, 153

fédéralistes 62

Fédération des communautés Francophones et Acadiennes du Canada (FCFAC) 28

Fedigan, Laurence 182

festivals 111, 136-137, 148, 172, 181, 223, 225

film 71-72, 147

de Finney, James 110

Fischer, Lucy R. 122

Forum francophone 216-217

Fournier, Marcel 65

francophile
    definition of 21

francophone
    census criteria of 20. *See also* francophone, definitions of
    communities and *l'espace francophone* 26-29
    communities, religious dimension of 25
    communities, types of 24-26
    culture 71-77. *See also* individual societies
    definitions of 20-21, 29-30, 32, 108, 125-126, 157, 220, 221, 226

indigenous communities 27, 173-174

migrant communities 27, 173

organizations. *See* organizational life

societies 19, 22-24. *See also* majority societies, minority societies, parity societies

symbolic communities 26-27

francophones

as charter group 23-24, 34, 37-41, 42-43

as volunteers 101-103, 120-122. *See also* volunteers and volunteering

history of in Canada 37-55

in Acadia 108-109

in national parks (Alberta) 171

in Québec 39. *See also* Quebeckers

migration of. *See* migration of francophones

mother-tongue (first-language) 21, 24, 25, 108, 165, 167-168, 170, 171-172, 173, 226

proportions of in Canada, provinces, territories 25-26, 29-30, 67, 97-99, 109, 125, 131-133, 137-140, 149, 152, 165-174, 223, 225

rural 24-25, 40, 44-45, 49-50, 53, 166, 168, 170-171, 226-227

second-language 21, 25-26, 29-30, 108, 138-139, 165, 167-168, 170, 171-172, 173

urban 24-25, 30, 33, 40, 53-54, 139-140, 142, 155-156, 173-174, 175-177, 207-208, 226-227. *See also* individual cities

see also majority societies, minority societies, parity societies

F(f)rancophonie 27-29, 92-93, 112, 197, 198-205

culture and 201-202

definitions of 27-28

economic ties within 200-201

future of 197-222

perceptibility of 27, 112, 113-115, 127, 151-153, 183-185

French Canadian 31-35, 91-92

definition of 32

French (language) 20-21

administrative 203

anglicisms in 68-70, 81, 109, 159, 160, 189

archaic words in 68

as commercial language 204-205

as official 30-31, 70, 161

as vehicular language 204, 205

Charter for the 70

chiac and 126

continuity 192-193, 218

dialects in 189

diglossia and 146, 179

future of 202

in Acadia 108-109, 124-127, 192

in British Columbia 146, 192

in Newfoundland 135-136, 146, 192

in Ontario 145-146, 159-160, 190, 192

in Québec 67-71

in Western provinces 146, 179-180, 188-191, 192

joual and 70

linguistic accents in 68, 224

prestige of 162, 203, 205, 228

protective legislation for 70-71, 87

quality of 68-70, 81, 109, 123, 126-127, 158, 159, 207

Sign Law (Bill 178) and 71,

80
standard 109, 126, 159
standard Québec 71, 188-189
status of 124, 161, 228. *See
also* French, prestige of
tensions surrounding 203-
205
threats to 79-81
transfer (shift) 192
vernacular terms and expressions in 68, 109, 126, 159, 160,
188-189, 190
French Shore (Nova Scotia) 97,
115, 152, 211
Front Libération du Québec 61-
62
Gagan, R. 176
Gagnon, François-Marc 75-76
Gérin-Lajoie, Diane 140
Gervais, Gaétan 48-49, 50
Gilbert, Anne 54, 55, 217
Giles, Howard 113, 160
goals, francophone community
32, 223
globalization and global order
xiii-xiv, 92-93, 194-209
Goldenberg, Sheldon 26
Gosselin, Guy 200
Grand Dérangement (Acadian
exportation) 44, 45, 110-111,
127
Gratton, Denis 207
Guindon, Hubert 71, 79, 80, 212
Guindon, René 103, 104, 140, 144

habitants 38
Hagen, David 83
Haines, Valerie A. 26
Halifax 25, 27, 97, 208
Hallion, Sandrine 165, 185, 189
Hamilton 25, 27, 137, 139, 173,
208
Harper, Elijah 225

Harrison, Brian R. 125
Harvey, Fernand 215
Hébert, Yvonne 99
Heller, Monica 118, 156, 159-160,
186, 194
Hillary, George Jr. 223

identity (francophone) 32-35
and ancestral ties 34-35
bilingual 155-156, 180
ethnolinguistic vitality and
161, 163
in Acadia 115-117, 127
in Newfoundland (Port-au-
Port Peninsula) 48, 154
in Ontario 153-156, 162
in Québec 90-93
in Western provinces 180,
185-186
types of 90-91
immigrants (and refugees) 83-84,
127-128, 177, 186, 205-208
to cities 207-208
immigration 82-83
indépendantistes 61
institutional (in)completeness 19,
24, 99, 140, 142-143, 154, 155-
156, 157, 175
ethnolinguistic vitality and
161, 162, 183-185, 193
Isajiw, Wsevolod W., 26

Jackson, John D. 138
Jaenen, Cornelius J. 48
joual 70
Joy, Richard J. 22
Juteau, Danielle 153

Kalbach, Warren E. 26
Kaltz, Barbara 167, 177
Kaprielian-Churchill, Isabel 117
Kermoal, Nathalie 182

Labelle, Antoine curé 49-50, 53
Lachapelle, Guy 61, 85, 88, 89
Lafond, Carole 75
Lambert, Wallace E. 79-80
Lamy, Paul 185
Landry, Rodrigue 146, 160
Langlois, Simon 81, 82, 83, 205-206
Lapointe, Jean 138, 154
Laponce, Jean A. 146, 180, 227
Laporte, Pierre 62
Latouche, Daniel 72, 209
Lavallée, Alain 75
Lavoie, Thomas 131
legends and stories 110-111, 148, 181-182, 190
leisure 100-101, 144,
    careers in 225
    institutional incompleteness and 89, 99, 141, 142, 157, 220
    lifestyles and 141-142, 154, 155, 211
    types of 101-103
Lesage, Jean 40-41
Lemieux, Vincent 22
Lépine, Sylvie 123
Lévesque, René 42, 70, 84
Lévy, Laurette 118, 156
lifestyle, linguistic 30, 89, 141-144, 155-156, 176-177, 179-180, 227
    dcfinition of 141
    importance in community survival and development 209, 211, 221
    in exogamous marriages 117-119
    mosaic of activities and 155, 177, 211
    social world and 142, 155, 227
Louder, Dean 25, 35, 54, 55, 67, 120, 145, 197, 199, 211, 215

Lusignan, Yves 159, 200, 214, 217

MacEwan, Grant 52, 53
Mackey, William F. 155
Magord, André, 47-48, 132, 133-135, 136, 194, 211
Maillardville 54, 172, 211, 223
majority communities 95-99, 137-139, 174
majority societies 57-128,
    as nations 92
    definition of 22
Manitoba (francophone part) 85, 165-167, 176, 177, 181-182, 186, 188, 189, 192, 211, 225
    see also Western provinces
Marchand, Anne-Sophie 186, 189
Marshall, Elizabeth 171, 188
Martel, Marcel 28
Martel, Pierre 71
Massart-Piérard, Françoise 202
Maxwell, Thomas R. 152
McCall, George J. 90, 185, 186
McKee-Allain, Isabelle 116
Meech Lake Accord 85
Meney, Florence 158
Métis 51-53, 188, 224
    definitions of 51-53
    Northwest Rebellion and 53
    Riel, Louis and 53
migration of francophones
    regional/intracontinental 33, 40, 49, 51, 55, 83, 127-128, 137-138, 188, 206
    rural to urban 55, 69
minority societies and communities 32
    as ethnic groups 23-24, 26, 33, 34, 224
    as exemplified by Saint-Paul, Alberta 175
    as minority groups 23-24
    as nation 33

conflict in 159-160, 221
definition of 23
development of 182, 209
economic basis of 104, 135,
137, 144, 175, 176, 199, 213-
214. *See also* individual societies
employment in French in
104-105
financial support (public) of
32, 223
Francophonie and 199
goals of 32, 223
in Acadia 43, 57-128
in Newfoundland 47-48, 131-
137, 151-152, 154, 156, 163
in Ontario137-149, 152-154,
156, 157-163
in Western provinces 165-194
optimistic/pessimistic view
of survival of 194, 211, 212-
217, 218, 220-222
personal growth in 211, 212-
217
la relève in 103, 182, 211, 218
self-sufficiency 218-220
survival and development of
182, 194, 209, 211-222
universities in 107, 123-14,
157-159, 178, 187-188, 225-
226. *See also* individual universities
see also education, francophone; francophones; volunteers and volunteering
Moise, Claudine 153-154
Moncton 96-97, 111
Montréal 40, 60, 71-77, 79-80, 111,
137, 202, 205, 207, 208, 213,
225
Morcos, Gamila 227
Mouvement Desjardins 64, 144,
200

Musée de l'Amérique Française
93, 215-216
music and musicians 110, 136

New Brunswick. *See* Acadia
Newfoundland (francophone
part) 47-48, 131-137, 194
community structure of 133-
135
culture in 136-137
economic basis of 135, 137
education in 106, 135
French in 135-136, 146, 192
identity in 154, 194
issues in 151-164
newspapers in 137
perceptibility of francophone
communities in 151-152
Port-au-Port Peninsula of 47-
48, 131-132, 133-137, 151-152
radio in 137
survival and development of
211-222
television in 137
Northwest Rebellion 52
Nova Scotia. *See* Acadia

October Crisis 61-62
Official Languages Acts 31-32,
48, 55, 105
O'Keefe, Michael 30, 115, 125,
156-157, 160-161, 163, 191,
192, 218
O'Neil, Peter, 87
Ontario (francophone part) 25,
48-51, 137-149,
community structure of 139-
144
culture in 146-149, 162
economic basis of 146, 162
education in 144-145, 153
festivals in 147
French in 145-146, 159-160,

190, 192
history of 48-51
identity in 162
issues in 151-164
migrants to 206
occupations of francophones
in 50-51
perceptibility of francophone
communities in 152-153
periodicals (newspapers,
magazines,etc.) in 148
publishing houses in 147
radio in 148
survival and development of
211-222
television in 148
theatre in 147
writers and writing in 147
organizational life (formal/infor-
mal)
as indicator of ethnolinguistic vitality 114
in Acadia 103-104
informal 134-135, 140-141,
175, 177
in Newfoundland 134
in Ontario 140
in Western provinces 174-177
of Acadians outside Acadia
116
provincial organizations and
103, 134, 140, 176
Ottawa and Hull, 25, 27, 48-49,
50-51, 139, 140, 144, 145, 147,
148, 156, 173, 199, 200, 207,
208
Ouellet, Fernand 51

painting and painters 75-76, 136
Panet-Raymond, Jean 63
Papineau, Louis-Joseph 39
Paquette, Roméo 122, 211
Parc de l'Amérique Française 93,
215

Parent Commission 66
parity societies and communities
32
as exemplified by
Alexandria, Ontario 143-144
conflict in 159-160, 221
definition of 22-23
Francophonie and 199
goals of 32
in Acadia 43, 97
personal growth in 211, 212-
217
self-sufficiency and 218-220
survival and development of
211-222
see also education, francophone; francophones; volunteers and volunteering
Parizeau, Jacques 86, 225
Parti-Québécois 42, 61, 62, 70, 80,
84, 85, 86
Paulette, Claude 92
Pendakur, Krishna 213
Pendakur, Ravi 213
perceptibility of francophone
communities 27, 112, 113-
115, 127, 151-153, 181-185
periodicals. See periodicals
(newspapers, magazines) in
individual francophone societies
Péronnet, Louise 109, 124-127
Pinard, Maurice 22
Pitre, Martin 134
Plouffe, Hélène 110
Poirier, Marc 123
Poulin, Pierre 103, 104, 140, 144
Prince Edward Island. See
Acadia
Pronovost, Gilles 68
publishers 147-148, 180
Putnam, Robert D. 122

Québec 19-20, 35, 59-94
    allophones in 22, 205, 206
    as distinct/unique society 77,
    87
    bilingualism in 89, 91
    birth rates in 70, 81-82, 83
    caisse populaire (credit union)
    in 64
    concertation in 62-63
    contemporary issues in 79-94
    culture in 71-77. *See also*
    Québec culture
    economic basis of 41-42, 87-
    90, 224
    économie sociale (nonprofit
    sector) in 63-64
    education in 64-67
    flag 92
    francophones outside
    Québec and 28, 93-94, 182,
    197, 215-217, 223
    Francophonie and 198-199,
    200, 201
    French language in 67-71, 89,
    162
    geographic distinctiveness of
    59-60
    government of 60-61, 88-89
    history of 37-42
    immigrants, effects in 83-84
    immigration to 82-83, 205-
    206
    migration from 206
    nationalism 209
    referendums on sovereignty
    and 84, 86, 91, 225
    regions of 60
    Riel, Louis and 52
    separatist movement in 61-
    62, 87, 197, 215, 217
    survival of 211
    trade union movement in 62-
    63

Québec City 37, 60, 75, 77, 92, 93-
    94, 207, 208
Québec culture 71-77, 182
    architecture 76-77
    circus 74
    comedy 74-75, 225
    dance 73
    film (French-language) in 71-
    72
    jazz 74
    painting 75-76
    song 73-74
Quebeckers (*Québécois*) 33, 35, 77,
    80, 84, 88, 89, 90-92, 93-94,
    205-206, 225
Québécois see Quebeckers
Quiet Revolution 40-42, 60-64,
    71-77, 82, 89-90, 91, 186

radio 111, 137, 148, 181, 202, 214-
    215,
    as MicroRadio 217
Rayside, David M. 143-144
referendums on sovereignty and
    84, 86, 91
Regina 167-168, 180
Regroupement des universités de
    la francophonie hors Québec
    (RUFHQ) 158
Reitz, Jeffry G. 26
religion. *See* Catholic church;
    Catholicism
Resnick, Philip 87
resources for personal and com-
    munity development 212-217
Richelieu International 103, 140
Riel, Louis 52, 224
Rifkin, Jeremy 142
Roby, Yves, 64
Rosenberg, M. Michael, 65

Saint-Boniface 27, 52-53, 55, 165,
    167, 180, 191, 211, 227

Saint-John's 131, 132, 133, 208
Saint-Pierre, Annette 52, 53
Salée, Daniel 61, 85, 88, 89
Saskatchewan (francophone part) 167-168, 174, 180, 190, 192, 193, 211
    see also Western provinces
Saskatoon 167, 208
Savas, Daniel 24, 32, 152, 177
Schaffer, Kay B. 122
school-community centres 134, 176, 181
séparatistes 61-62, 87
Sign Law 71, 80
Simmons, J.L. 90, 185, 186
Smith, David H. 120-121
Smith, Donald 70
song and singers 73, 110, 136, 180, 201, 202
sovereignty-association 42, 62, 84-87, 197
souverainistes 62
Stebbins, Robert A. 24, 29, 32, 33, 54, 74, 99, 101-103, 117, 120-122, 142, 155, 156, 176, 177, 179, 186, 189-190, 193, 194, 218-220, 225, 227
stories. *See* legends and stories
Sudbury 139, 143, 147, 148, 156

Taché, Alexandre Mgr. 53
Taylor, Donald M. 113, 160
television 111-112, 137, 148, 181, 214-215
Tellier, Sylvain 223
Tétu de Labsade, Françoise 59-60, 64, 65, 67, 71, 72, 73, 224
theatre 147, 180
Thériault, J.-Yvon 33, 115, 116, 138, 154, 155
Thériault, Léon 45, 46, 116
Thérien, Jean-Philippe 200

Therrien, Denyse 81, 199
Thomas, Gerald 135-136
Toronto 25, 27, 137, 139, 140, 144, 145, 152, 156, 173, 207, 208, 213
Toynbee, Arnold iii, 221-222
Treaty of Paris 38
Trépanier, Cécyle 35, 54, 116, 145
Trudeau, Pierre E. 85, 87
Turcotte, Pierre 117

Université de la francophonie 217
Université de Moncton 45, 107, 124, 187
Université d'Ottawa 49, 145, 157-158, 187
Université du Québec 66
Université Laurentienne 145, 158
Université Sainte-Anne 107, 123, 187
universities. *See* minority societies, universities
Unruh, David R. 142

Vancouver 25, 27, 171-172, 173, 207, 208, 213
Véronneau, Pierre 71-72
Viau, Pierre 197
Victoria 172, 208
Villeneuve, Paul-Y. 54, 223
vitality, ethnolinguistic 113-114, 124, 146, 160-163, 216
    indicators of 114, 152, 161, 191-193
    in Ontario 161-162
    in Western provinces 191-193
    working to achieve it 212
volunteers and volunteering 101-103, 120-122, 142-143, 176, 211, 219
    formal *vis-à-vis* informal 226-227

key volunteers and 120-121,
218-220
rewards of 219-220
rural *vis-à-vis* urban 226-227
self-sufficiency and 218-220

Waddell, Eric 35, 54, 55, 120, 145
Western provinces (francophone
part) 25, 51-54, 165-194
architecture in 181
community structure of 174-
177
culture in 180-182
dance in 180
economic basis of 174, 175,
176
education in 177-179, 187-188
festivals in 172, 181
French in 179-180, 192
history of francophones in
51-54
issues in 183-194
periodicals (newspapers) in
182
publishing houses in 180
radio in 181
song in 180-181
survival and development in
211-222
television in 181
writers in 180
see also individual provinces
Whitaker, Reginald 61
White, Deena 63
Whitson, David 186
Winnipeg 25, 27, 165, 167, 173,
179, 180, 181, 191, 208
work. *See* minority societies and
communities, economic basis
of
writers and writing 109-110, 147

Printed in July 2000 by

ON DEMAND PRINTING INC.

in Longueuil, Quebec